The Recovery of the
Historical Paul

The Recovery of the Historical Paul

BY

ROBERT MARTYR HAWKINS

D.D., Ph.D. (*Edin.*)

Professor of New Testament Language and Literature
VANDERBILT UNIVERSITY
NASHVILLE, TENNESSEE

NASHVILLE, TENNESSEE
VANDERBILT UNIVERSITY PRESS
1943

PRINTED IN THE UNITED STATES OF AMERICA
BY THE BAIRD-WARD PRESS, NASHVILLE, TENNESSEE

TO MY WIFE
REUBEN CLARKE HAWKINS

who has been to me
sun by day and
stars by night.

ACKNOWLEDGMENT

By gracious permission of the International Council of Religious Education, owner of the copyright, the author has at times quoted from the American Standard Revised Version of the Holy Bible, and has at other times made use of its phraseology.

Table of Contents

CHAPTER I
THE RECOVERY OF THE HISTORICAL PAUL.............................. 1- 20

CHAPTER II
THE EPISTLE TO PHILEMON................................... 21- 24

CHAPTER III
THE EPISTLE TO THE GALATIANS.......................... 25- 60

CHAPTER IV
THE EPISTLE TO THE ROMANS.............................. 61-151

CHAPTER V
THE FIRST EPISTLE TO THE CORINTHIANS...............................152-201

CHAPTER VI
THE SECOND EPISTLE TO THE CORINTHIANS...........................202-232

CHAPTER VII
THE FIRST EPISTLE TO THE THESSALONIANS.......................233-244

CHAPTER VIII
THE EPISTLE TO THE PHILIPPIANS...............................245-261

CHAPTER IX
THE SECOND EPISTLE TO THE THESSALONIANS......................262-269

CHAPTER X
THE EPISTLE TO THE COLOSSIANS..............................270-279

CHAPTER XI
THE EPISTLE TO THE EPHESIANS..............................280-289

APPENDIX
AN ANALYSIS OF THE PAULINE EPISTLES..............................290-291

Chapter I

THE RECOVERY OF THE HISTORICAL PAUL

THE phrase, "the recovery of the historical Paul," is suggested by that of "the recovery of the historical Jesus" which has dominated much of New Testament study in recent years. The simple comparison of the intricate web of theological dogmas which has been woven around the Christ in the creeds of the church with the records of his life and teachings in the gospels must bring the realization of the vast distance the church has traveled from the Jesus of history to the Christ of theology.

Basing its endeavor upon the just insight that its very belief in the truth and adequacy of the Christian religion must force the church to drink from the original springs of its truth and power, scholarship has striven to base its conception of Jesus upon its primary sources, the gospels. The problem of the recovery of the historical Jesus has often been stated in these terms; it is merely a question of a return to the Jesus of the gospels.

But any intelligent and adequate study of the gospels themselves must reveal how great an oversimplification such a formulation of our problem must prove to be. For it is at once realized how far the gospels are from being in agreement in their presentation of Jesus. The first difficulty encountered may well be the discovery of the great difference between the Jesus of the Synoptic Gospels, and the Jesus of the Gospel of John. This difficulty is often solved by taking the attitude that this obvious difference is that between a factual and an interpretative presentation of Jesus. This overlooks the fact that the difference is not merely one of interpretation; John modifies drastically even such factual matters as the locale of the ministry of Jesus, and the length of his activity. But even so, there has been a pronounced tendency to adopt the position that we may learn of Jesus as he actually was from the Synoptic Gospels.

But even this solution of our problem proves also to be an oversimplification. For the Synoptic Gospels are not to be distinguished from the Gospel of John by the mere recognition that they are factual, while it is interpretative. The Synoptics are themselves interpretations of Jesus. Each one looks at Jesus from its own point of view, and presents him in terms of its own values. It should be obvious that before we can hope to get back to the Jesus of history we must evaluate the accounts of him presented in the individual gospels and choose between them.

This choice has seemingly been facilitated by the discovery that the Gospel of Mark is our fundamental gospel. It is upon the basis of the Gospel of Mark that the framework of both Matthew and Luke has been constructed. In fact, almost the whole of the Gospel of Mark has been substantially reproduced in these later works. Because of this, many scholars have felt justified in concluding that in Mark we have a factual record of the life of Jesus, and that the Jesus of Mark is the Jesus of history.

It must be realized that the exaltation of Mark over Matthew and Luke must result, at least to some extent, in the disparagement of these later gospels. Mark cannot be a better, a more dependable source, than either Matthew or Luke, unless each of these be a less dependable source than Mark. For while each of them seems to have employed Mark as the fundamental document upon the basis of which his own account is constructed, each has made more or less change in the material taken over from the older document.

This is strikingly true in regard to the Gospel of Luke.

While the difference between Mark and Luke may not properly be discussed here, it must be pointed out that it is so great that there has been a widespread conviction among scholars that Luke must have had some "special source" upon which he relied even more than he did upon the Gospel of Mark. While it is by no means necessary to concur in this opinion, the number of scholars to which it has appealed, and the earnestness with which it is insisted upon, may be taken as indications of the seriousness of the differences between Mark and Luke.

The difficulty of recovering the Jesus of history from the gospels does not consist merely in the differences in viewpoint and valuation which are found in the individual synoptic gospels. It cannot be entirely resolved by the expedient of recognizing the priority and superiority of Mark, and by adopting the Jesus of Mark as the Jesus of history. For it is being increasingly realized that the Gospel of Mark itself does not stand at the beginning of a process, but well along toward its close. It is not a simple, firsthand, factual account of the life of Jesus. It is itself an interpretation of Jesus; by many it is insisted that it is equally as interpretative as John.

Regarded as sources for our knowledge of the life of Christ, the gospels suffer under two great disabilities. The first is that they are not contemporary documents; at least a generation elapsed between the events they record, and their record of them. The second is that they make no attempt to view Jesus objectively, and to give a bare factual account of his life. They are records, rather, of the reactions of a later day to Jesus; they are appreciations of him; they are statements of what he meant to the experience of his followers; they are records of faith rather than of fact. This is precisely what makes them of such incalculable value for religion. For religion differs from history in that it is not based upon facts, but rather upon the reaction to facts in the experience of religious subjects.

Scholars have sought to obviate these disabilities by endeavoring to penetrate even behind the gospels to more primitive and more adequate sources for our knowledge of the life of Jesus. This endeavor has taken the form, first, of an effort to analyze the gospels themselves into earlier sources from which they have been constructed. The result has been the clear realization that Matthew and Luke rest upon Mark, and perhaps upon a document made up principally of the sayings of Jesus. Other sources there may have been, but their identity has not been agreed upon.

But even the segregation of what ultimate sources may be discovered, or inferred, has not been deemed adequate. For even the most ultimate sources recoverable by literary analysis prove to be made up of smaller units, seemingly complete within themselves. There has, accordingly, been a second line of investigation, breaking the tradition up into its smallest recoverable units, and studying these to discover from them the facts and viewpoints obtaining in the time when the tradition was crystallizing. It is thought by many that in this way we may penetrate far behind the gospels into a more formative period in the belief of the church than is represented in the gospels themselves. But even so it does not seem that we have been able to get behind the period in which the church was adding its faith in Christ to its record of the facts of the life of Jesus. It was in fact its very faith in Christ which caused it to have any interest whatever in the facts of his life.

Two further difficulties must be taken into account in any

attempt to recover the historical Jesus from our gospels. The first is that the faith of the primitive disciples in Jesus was by no means uniform. This has given us such different estimates of him as the strong apocalyptic coloring of portions of Matthew and the determined anti-apocalypticism of the Fourth Gospel. The second is that there is a demonstrable development in our tradition even in its written stages, allowing us to infer at least as great a development in an earlier and more fluid oral stage of transmission.

And so the judgment must be recorded that in the present state of our knowledge, and it does not seem that any circumstances can be foreseen which will cause any radical alteration, the Jesus of history cannot be recovered with any degree of certainty. The recovery of the historical Jesus must be reduced to those inferences which may legitimately be drawn from the valuations recorded by those who looked upon him with the eyes of love and hope. That even love and hope did not avail for a complete understanding of him may be gathered by the frequency with which he addressed to those closest to him the plaintive query, "What, do ye not yet understand?"

The recovery of the historical Jesus is at best problematical. The adequacy with which our inferences drawn from the valuations placed upon him by his early followers, and recorded in the gospels, suffice for an objective account of the actual facts of his life will be differently estimated. They will seem most adequate to those who share in the love and hope with which his first followers looked upon him.

But the recovery of the historical Paul must surely rest upon a much firmer basis than the recovery of the historical Jesus. For while for our understanding of Jesus we must rely upon the testimonies of others, which were recorded in their present form many years after his death, and in which we can discern marked development, we have many letters written by the hand of Paul himself.

Our knowledge of the life of Paul has seemed the surest of all the results of New Testament study. For there has come down to us a book, the Acts of the Apostles, the larger part of which is given over to the account of his life and labors, together with a large body of documents which have been transmitted to us as letters which he wrote to his churches in the course of his missionary efforts. The result of the study of these twin pillars upon which our knowledge may rest has been a "standard" interpretation of the life and work of Paul. While it must be said that it could be wished that a larger degree of agreement might result from the definiteness of our source materials, there is a conception, at least of his life, which has been accorded widespread acceptance, which is true in lesser degree of his thought.

This "standard" interpretation of the life and work of Paul which is apparently held with such assurance by scholars is built up on the basis of the account of his life given us in the Acts of the Apostles, supposedly written by Luke, the author of the third gospel, supplemented, where may be, with details taken from Paul's own letters. It is the thesis of this study that this "standard" interpretation of the life and work of Paul must be insistently challenged because of the progress that has been made in our knowledge of one of the twin pillars upon which our ideas of Paul rest, and because of progress which may be made in our knowledge of the other.

The only account of the life and work of Paul which has come down to us in the New Testament is that contained in the Acts of the Apostles. This is supposed to be written by

Luke, who was a companion of Paul. Hence it is thought to be a firsthand account, written by one who was a participant in much of which he relates, and who had the best of opportunities to ascertain the truth of the rest. This should, therefore, be taken as the foundation upon which our interpretation of Paul must be built.

It is interesting to note how frequently this conception is being challenged. On the other hand, it is being insisted that the relation between the book of Acts and the Pauline epistles must be reversed. They, rather than it, must be taken as our primary sources; they must be the foundation upon which our knowledge of Paul must be built; they must be supplemented, where may be, with data from Acts, rather than vice versa.

It must never be forgotten that the author of the book of Acts is almost universally considered to have been also the author of the third gospel, that "according to Luke." Now we have seen that the third gospel differs so markedly in many important particulars from the first and second that many scholars have held that "Luke" has followed some "special source"; others have held that he has merely made many drastic alterations of the materials which lay before him. However that may be, we can have no assurance whatever that if we had other lives of the Apostle Paul, they would agree any more closely with "Luke's" than the other gospels agree with his "Life of Christ." Any study that may be made of "Luke's" use of his sources, especially his treatment of the Gospel of Mark, will show how drastically he has altered them.

"Luke's" account of the life of Paul has held the field; there is no other to challenge it. There has been much debate as to his trustworthiness as a historian. But from any careful study of his book itself, especially as an authority for the life of Paul, it is hard to see how it has commanded as much credence as it has. Right on the surface is the situation in regard to the conversion of Paul. Three accounts of this crucial experience in the life of his hero are given; they differ in significant details. Either "Luke" did not know the facts in regard to this turning point in the life of Paul, or he cannot be relied upon to give a clear and consistent account of things he did know. That this inconsistency is due to lack of knowledge would appear from the fact that he tells practically nothing of the incidents of Paul's labors even in those fields where his ministry stretched beyond weeks into months. For "Luke," and for those of us who depend upon him, Paul's longest and most fruitful pastorates are almost entirely blank.

Any estimate as to "Luke's" value as a historian must take into account the tendencies that are clearly discoverable in his writings. Chief among these is his predisposition in favor of Jerusalem, and of certain Jewish values in religion. While he is not as drastic as John in reallocating the center of gravity of the ministry of Jesus in Jerusalem rather than in Galilee, he has suppressed all mention of the appearances of the risen Jesus in Galilee. He has done this by substituting for Mark's (xvi: 7), "But go, tell his disciples and Peter, He goeth before you into Galilee: there shall ye see him as he said unto you," the quite different, (Lk. xxiv:6), "Remember how he spake unto you when he was yet in Galilee."

It must be carefully noted that there is in the Third Gospel not only this drastic suppression of the tradition of the Galilean appearance of the risen Jesus, but also the definite statement that he ascended into heaven, "that very day," i.e., the day of the resurrection. Scholars must decide whether the occurrence of a period of forty days between the resurrection and the ascension in the opening chapters of Acts is evidence that the two books were not written by the same author, or whether our most trusted historian is capable of representing the ascension in the gospel as occurring immediately, and in the Acts as only after forty days.

In connection with "Luke's" apparent prejudice in favor of Jerusalem, and other Jewish features of religion, there must be pointed out his exaltation of the apostles as a definite "college," having supreme and universal jurisdiction in the infant church, even to the point of sending delegations to inquire into the progress of missions, and to bring all spheres of expanding Christianity under their central authority.

But whatever may be thought of "Luke's" value as a church historian, he must be peremptorily challenged as an authority for the life of Paul. For here we have a second body of testimony in the letters that have come down to us from Paul's own hand. While the orbit of our two authorities is often seemingly distinct, there are many places where they approach each other closely enough to be compared. Such comparison has revealed that often it is most difficult to reconcile their accounts; at times it seems impossible to reduce them to agreement. It should go without saying that Paul's own letters must in every case be given the precedence over any other account.

"Luke's" general prejudice in favor of certain Jewish values in religion seems to have colored his account of Paul's method and message. For in the book of Acts we are told that Paul consistently went first to the synagogue in any community, and turned in despair to the gentiles only when the Jews had driven him out and it had become evident that they would not receive him. We search Paul's own letters in vain for any indication that this was his customary procedure.

Coupled with this is "Luke's" account of Paul's preaching. From this it would seem that he customarily laid the foundation for the Christian gospel in a long and tedious recital of the details of Israel's history, and based his exposition of the salvation in Christ upon the predictions of Scripture. To judge from Paul's own description of his preaching, as consisting in the proclamation in the demonstration and power of the Holy Spirit of the crucified Christ, "Luke's" conception of his message is as great a misapprehension as his idea of his method. It cannot increase our confidence in the accuracy of the account of Paul's preaching to observe how closely it is approximated by the type of preaching ascribed to Stephen. Perhaps all of "Luke's" preachers would have preached alike!

The same predisposition in favor of Judaism may be seen in the fact that in the last chapters of Acts Paul is represented as in full sympathy with Judaism; he is advised by James to purify himself with four brethren who had taken a vow, paying the charges for them, that all might see that "thou thyself walkest orderly, keeping the law" (Acts xxi: 24). This Paul did, (vs. 26). It passes the bounds of credence that he who had so strenuously contended with Cephas at Antioch that the ceremonial requirements of the law must no longer be observed, but that all must trust in Christ alone for salvation, (Gal. ii: 11-21), and with the Galatians that it must be Christ or circumcision, (Gal. v: 2-6), could thus have consciencelessly abandoned his Galatian gospel in favor of the observance of the law. The report of any such conduct upon his part would have wrecked his entire campaign in Galatia.

The most glaring contradiction between the account of Paul as given in Acts and his own report of an identical situation is to be found in the irreconcilable conflict between the second chapter of Galatians and the fifteenth chapter of Acts. The essence of the conflict is found in the circumstance that while Paul categorically states that he made no concessions whatever, and that the authorities in Jerusalem laid nothing upon him save that he remember the poor, Acts just as categorically states that a compromise was reached, in which the requirement was laid upon Paul that he enforce upon his converts abstinence from certain things offensive to Jews, from fornication, from things strangled, from blood, and from things sacrificed to idols. Both the absolute contradiction between the two statements, and the Jewish prejudice underlying the account in Acts, are clearly evident. Either "Luke" or Paul is wrong.

While it has been pointed out that our "standard" interpretation of the life and work of Paul has rested upon the account given in the book of Acts, it must now be said that the trend of scholarship is consistently in the direction of recognizing that the letters of Paul must be the primary source of our knowledge of him, and that the account in the book of Acts must be regarded as secondary. If the two sources were in even essential agreement, this distinction would have but little meaning. It is their divergence which gives it its importance.

This study has no disposition to argue at great length the case for or against "Luke." Reference may be made to standard introductions to the New Testament, or commentaries upon the Third Gospel and the book of Acts. In most of them the relevant evidence may be found, although there is not always sufficient penetration or courage to reach or to record what seems the inescapable verdict. But there is an increasing recognition that the sources to which "Luke" had access were at times rather scanty, at other times somewhat untrustworthy; that he himself does not seem to have had close enough acquaintance with the facts to reach independent judgments; that he seems to have confused duplicate accounts of the same "missionary journey," making two out of what was in reality one; and that his work is marked by readily discoverable tendencies which must be discounted.

The result of all this is that this source of our knowledge of Paul, upon which we formerly relied so implicitly, is now subject to considerable suspicion, and that any understanding of Paul, based primarily upon it, must be regarded as most uncertain.

Our attention is to be focused almost exclusively upon that other twin pillar of our knowledge of the work and thought of Paul, those writings which have come down to us from his pen, or under his name. It is our contention that in this sphere also the time has come when the generally accepted idea of Paul's life and work must be insistently challenged.

Anyone who is even moderately familiar with the course of New Testament scholarship will at once realize how greatly the field of "Pauline" literature has been narrowed. Fourteen letters were formerly ascribed to him. They were: Romans, I and II Corinthians, Galatians, Ephesians, Philippians, Colossians, I and II Thessalonians, I and II Timothy, Titus, Philemon, and Hebrews. Of these, four are almost unanimously denied to Paul. The clearest case is that of Hebrews; every consideration, whether of style, vocabulary, religious point of view, or even the uncertainty of traditional testimony as to its genuineness, must alike testify to the impossibility of its having been written by Paul.

It is true that if we reject the Pauline authorship we may be left in ignorance as to the name of its author; but it should be evident that failure to ascribe it with confidence to another hand does not compel us to admit that it was written by Paul. No verdict of scholarship can be more certain than that denying Hebrews to Paul.

The case in regard to the Pastorals (I and II Timothy and Titus), is scarcely less clear; scholarship is almost as unanimous as in the case of Hebrews in ascribing them to some author other than Paul. This is because they evidently reflect a time much later than that of the apostle; the church organization is much more developed, with bishops, elders, deacons, and even widows enrolled upon relief; doctrine appears equally developed; it has crystallized into an orthodoxy; particular care is to be given to scrutinizing the channels through which it is received, and to seeing that it is transmitted without any variation. Stress is placed upon the content of the creed; heretics are denounced without refutation; confession is of great value. Added to the historical discrepancies is the very great difference in vocabulary, and especially in syntactic usage, which is usually deemed sufficient to clinch the adverse verdict generally passed upon their authenticity. The doggedness with which the church has clung to the tradition of their Pauline authorship can scarcely increase our confidence in the value of its ascription of other materials to Paul.

More recent, and less general, is the challenge to the authenticity of the Epistle to the Ephesians. Reference to current work upon this epistle should make any lengthy discussion of its genuineness unnecessary. It, too, differs vastly from materials recognized as genuinely Pauline in style and diction. The structure of its sentences differs from those of

Paul's about as a lake differs from a mountain torrent. Many of its viewpoints can be demonstrated to be in basic contradiction to those of Paul. The very close connection between Ephesians and Colossians has long been recognized. The greatly developed Christology and Ecclesiology of these epistles must provoke our earnest challenge; they are far more Johannine than Pauline.

Difficulties have also long been acknowledged in connection with the genuineness of II Thessalonians. Many scholars have thought it differs too little from I Thessalonians to be independent of it, although they have not always been in agreement as to how the two are related. The chief difference is the communication of some most dubious apocalyptic materials. It has often been thought that it is much more anxious to insist that it is a genuine Pauline epistle, than any such epistle need to be. For these reasons many scholars have been inclined to reject it as Pauline.

Should one concur in these adverse verdicts, and from most, if not all of them, there seems no escape, there are left but seven epistles upon which one may base his knowledge of Paul without the danger of encountering a severe challenge. There are left Philemon, Galatians, Romans, I and II Corinthians, I Thessalonians, and Philippians. From these, if from any sources, we must derive our knowledge of Paul.

If the objection should be raised that this is too drastic a limitation of the sources of our knowledge of Paul, the answer must be given that it is, on the contrary, not drastic enough. Study of even these epistles, which are taken to be upon the whole genuine products of the apostle's pen, must raise the question whether they lie before us as he wrote them, or whether they do not in their present form incorporate many modifications from later or different points of view.

Some light may be thrown upon the problem by an assessment usually made of the Pastoral Epistles that they are based upon genuine fragments of letters written by Paul, but that these original Pauline materials have been drastically modified by a later writer, who still wrote under the name of Paul. The only alternative to this assessment would seem to be that even the portions usually thought to be genuine Pauline fragments are not themselves genuine; they, too, have been written by some Paulinist from genuine Pauline materials, or in imitation of them. If either of these assessments of the nature of the Pastoral Epistles be thought to be true, what assurance can we have that the same type of modification has not also been suffered by materials in other letters? It would seem that the phenomena presented to us by the Pastorals must raise the presumption of the possibility that other materials transmitted under the name of Paul have been equally worked over. The question should at least be investigated upon its merits in connection with each epistle.

It is the contention of this study that the acceptance as genuine of all the materials which have come down to us in even those epistles which are upon the whole believed to have been written by Paul is the exhibition of naïveté which cannot be justified by a thorough study of the phenomena, and that any acceptable solution of the Pauline problem is upon that basis impossible. For, to accept as genuine everything that stands in the present form of even the "major" epistles must lead to diametrically opposing conceptions not only in regard to such fundamental problems as Paul's basic understanding of the Christian gospel, but also in regard to such seemingly minor problems as the place of women in the life and ministry of the Pauline church, the relations which should obtain in Christian marriage, and the permissibility of eating things sacrificed to idols. Even after all the manipulations possible to the imagination of the most determined harmonistic exegesis have been exhausted, we are still left face to face with stark contradictions in matters both great and small.

But from this seemingly intolerable situation there is to be found simple and sure relief. For it must be noted that the problem of the recovery of the historical Paul is essentially different from that of the recovery of the historical Jesus. For while Jesus is supposed to have written nothing, and we are dependent for our knowledge of him upon a tradition which can be shown to have been colored by the valuations of the early church, and to have developed during the course of its transmission, in the case of Paul we have a considerable body of his own writings. To them we can, and must, apply all the criteria of both historical and literary criticism. If from such a bulk of first-hand documents the historical Paul cannot be recovered with a reasonable degree of certainty, it would seem that scholarship must admit either the inadequacy of these disciplines or its own incapacity to make use of them.

Our judgment is that one has to apply only the most elementary of the processes of historical and literary criticism to the present form of our Pauline epistles to discover how greatly complex they are, and how readily they may be analyzed. The criteria of syntax and diction are often sufficient to indicate disparity of materials; shifting of the fundamental situation contemplated, or vacillation in the connotation of terms may often betray complexity; arguments are at times painstakingly built up only to be destroyed by the addition of contrary points of view; the presence of absolutely contradictory conceptions is often determinative.

The primary reliance of the ensuing study is placed upon

what should be the most decisive consideration. It is the simple attempt to trace the order and progress of Paul's discussion; the primary situation from which he is arguing must always be kept in mind; any blurring of these circumstances must be noted and estimated; we must take account of the basic connotations of the terms employed, and of any vacillation or contradiction in the meaning assigned to them in the same context; the logical coherence of the discussion, especially any distortion caused by the introduction of alien points of view, whether they result from mere inadvertence as to the situation or premises involved, or whether they be adjudged purposeful attempts to modify the point of view which Paul is expounding, must be ever before us. In other words we must rely upon those features of clearness, appositeness, continuity, and consistency, the absence of which must result in non-sense.

This simple procedure should be carried out from a purely objective point of view, without any preconceived notion as to what is genuine, what spurious. But, as is inescapably true in any scientific inquiry, the point will soon be reached, especially so if most of the materials alleged to be Pauline are really his, that the general lineaments of his thought will begin to appear. When opposing points of view are encountered, as they most assuredly will be, those must be deemed genuine which are most germane to the context, i.e., most apposite to the fundamental situation contemplated, most coherent with the trend of the argument, most consistent in the connotation assigned to the terms employed, most in harmony with the axiomatic presuppositions from which the discussion is developed, or, in cases in which the immediate context is thought to make a judgment uncertain, most fully in accord with basic Pauline positions as learned from the study of all his writings.

As soon as one has begun to learn to distinguish between those materials which are genuinely Pauline, and those which must be judged to be interpolated into his writings, he will perhaps be struck with the frequency with which suspected materials cohere with what are known to be documents later than Paul, or with viewpoints which are characteristic of later developments in the life and thought of the church. Materials supposedly Pauline are often so similar to Hebrews that if found apart from their context they would unhesitatingly be assigned to that epistle. In many suspected interpolations we seem to be faced with both the circumstances and the doctrinal position thoroughly familiar in the Pastorals. Again, we find passages with such developed Christology and such semi- or quasi-gnostic coloration that they are much more nearly akin to John than to Paul. In other words many of the "difficulties" which we encounter in our "Pauline" literature seem due to forces which came to clear expression in the later strata of the New Testament. The Old Testament scholar will find the closest parallel to the situation obtaining in the developed Pauline canon in the Deuteronomic movement, which not only wrote its own book, but which also introduced Deuteronomic modifications into those already in existence. Ephesians is the Deuteronomy of the New Testament.

Another type of modification seems due to the use of the epistles in the worship, or the preaching, of the early church. The use in worship may be thought to have given rise to doxologies, and especially to the frequent use of "Amen." It may also have caused some slight modifications in arrangement, or in language, such as materials used for liturgy almost inevitably suffer. Use in preaching may be responsible for the frequent generalization which seeks to make the materials available for homiletic use in situations much wider than that originally contemplated, if not, indeed, entirely different from them. The marks of homiletic generalization should not be hard to detect.

While general indebtedness to those who have previously labored in the field of Pauline study will be everywhere evident, and is gladly and thankfully acknowledged, it has not been thought necessary or helpful to refer to their discussions. Of specific indebtedness there is very little; no use is consciously made of previous work.

It has seemed best to rely only upon simple procedures. More technical processes, such as word counts, or minute consideration of syntactical constructions, have been dispensed with. Greek has been eliminated as being unnecessary for those who use it, and of little value for those who do not. The phenomena seem clear enough, even in our English versions, although their inadequacies are, of course, pointed out where necessary.

It should be recognized that no analysis of such a complex body of material as our Pauline canon can hope to be final, or either complete or perfect in detail; it is hoped, however, that the complexity of our Pauline literature may be recognized, and that an approach, at least, has been made to the recovery of the historical Paul.

Perhaps it should be clearly said that any judgment that a passage is non-Pauline is not to be construed as a verdict that it is, because of that fact, of less value than genuine materials. While it is true that later developments in the New Testament are often of less value than earlier viewpoints, and while it would appear reasonable that modifications of Pauline materials would be upon a lower plane, such is not necessarily the case. Every passage must be judged upon its merits. Many will find in some sections thought to be non-Pauline materials of great beauty and power. Paul was not the only inspired man in the early church, nor the author of everything of value.

Chapter II

THE EPISTLE TO PHILEMON

NO BETTER introduction to the study of Paul's letters can be found than a careful consideration of his charming little letter to Philemon.

It is a true letter, having none of the marks which would characterize a document which we might call an epistle. It has grown out of a definite concrete situation, whose details are so clearly reflected that they can be recreated with certainty. We can learn from the letter itself that Onesimus, the slave of Philemon, had run away and had come to some city in which Paul was in prison. Here he had fallen under the spell of the apostle, and had not only become a Christian, but had entered into the closest of personal ties with Paul, who loved him as his own heart. But there were also very close personal relations between Paul and Philemon, the master from whom Onesimus had run away. Paul speaks as though he could count upon his obedience; he directs him to prepare a lodging for himself in the event of his release from prison; he even intimates that Philemon owes to him his very self.

It seems that Paul had decided that much as he would like to have kept Onesimus with him, he ought to send him back to his master. But this would create a situation whose tenseness we can hardly imagine. The offense of running away was a most serious one for a slave to commit, and the laws gave Philemon the right to inflict upon him a very severe penalty. For Paul to send Onesimus back to his master, especially with the request that his offense be condoned, meant that Paul was taking the risk of alienating Philemon, one of his dearest friends. It also meant that he was subjecting Onesimus to the gravest of personal danger.

In this situation of the very highest emotional tension, Paul has written a little gem of a letter. It charms us with its simple directness, and its limpid clarity of style. There is not the least tendency to obscurity of thought, to inconsistency in the connotation of terms, to fumbling in syntax, to digression from the question at issue. Paul does not exhibit any tendency whatever to stutter with words in the face of a situation which has stirred him to the very bottom of his being. But the very intensity with which he feels keeps him closely to the train of his thought and enables him to clothe it in simple and fitting words.

The salutation is a model of clarity and conciseness. It designates Paul as the writer, associating Timothy with him, Philemon, Apphia, Archippus, and the church in the house of one of them, perhaps Philemon, as the recipients, and adds the formal greeting, "Grace to you and peace from God our Father and the Lord Jesus Christ." Paul knew how to begin a letter.

He characteristically follows the salutation immediately with his thanksgiving for the faith which Philemon has in Christ and the love which he has for all the saints, to which thanksgiving he delicately adds the hint that the "sharing" of his faith should become effectual.

He then comes to the point; Onesimus has become his beloved child in the faith, and Paul would gladly associate him with himself in the ties of personal service. He could command Philemon to set him free, but he would not do that. He wished Philemon to have the experience of forgiving of his own free will the offense which Onesimus had committed. In that way Paul would not only win forgiveness, and perhaps freedom for Onesimus, but he would give Philemon the opportunity of experiencing the grace of Christ in his own heart. He could make effectual the sharing of his faith with Onesimus whom he would forgive, and welcome as a brother in Christ. Philemon's love for all the saints would thus be extended to include even the runaway slave who had, according to the standards of the day, so grievously wronged him.

The climax of the letter is a master stroke, both in conception, and in expression. With a simplicity and a directness born of the very intensity of his love for both of those who are involved, Paul writes, "If then thou countest me a partner, receive him as myself."

He who would understand Paul must make this letter to Philemon part of the most familiar furnishing of his mind and heart. It exhibits the apostle as one who could and did think clearly and in the simplest terms in situations of the very greatest emotional tension. It also reveals him as one who could write the very simplest, clearest, and most beautiful Greek. The playfulness of some of his expressions would be possible only to one completely at home in the medium in which he is expressing himself. The relevance of these considerations grows out of the fact that Paul is often represented to be one not at home in the Greek language, because some of the Pauline passages betray certain roughnesses of style, or monstrosities of syntax, or as one who could not maintain consistency of thought when face to face with a theme which stirred him profoundly. From the phenomena encountered in Philemon we shall expect Paul to be simple and direct and consistent in his thinking, happy in his diction, and skillful in his syntax. Explanations of abnormalities in syntax and infelicities in expression must be sought in factors other than Paul's logical processes or literary abilities.

There seems little reason to suspect later modifications of this epistle. It contained no doctrinal ideas which needed to be brought into line with later orthodoxy. There are only two places where any question needs to be raised. The first is in verse 9 where we find the only wavering in syntax. This occurs in the addition of the words, "being such a one as Paul the aged, and now a prisoner also of Christ Jesus." Taste is insistent in maintaining that the phrase adds nothing to the letter; it is indeed rather out of character with the simplicity, the rapidity of movement, and the forthrightness of the style. It adds two details which might be thought calculated to appeal to the pity of Philemon, Paul's age, and his present captivity. The presumption that his age was great enough to move Philemon to pity is out of harmony with all our other knowledge of Paul. The detail of his captivity may be learned from other references in the letter. This may be some scholion added by some lesser man to gild the lily. It were better left out.

The addition of "Amen" to the benediction in some of the later Manuscripts may be the result of the liturgical habit of concluding in this fashion passages read in church.

Chapter III

THE EPISTLE TO THE GALATIANS

THE Epistle to the Galatians, as it lies before us in the generally accepted versions, may be taken as typical of the letters ascribed to Paul, and in it may be observed most, if not all, of the phenomena of the literary process through which we think that the Pauline Epistles have passed.

There seems to be persuasive, if not convincing, evidence that Paul was confronted with a crisis in his relations with his Galatian converts, caused by the intrusion into his field of opponents who sought to discredit him and his work, and to win his converts away from his simple and dynamic gospel of faith in Christ to the utterly different gospel of dependence upon circumcision and the works of the law, and that to meet this crisis, Paul wrote a simple, burning letter directed solely to the point at issue, in which he sought to show the incompatibility of the two gospels, and insisted that the Galatians should choose between them.

But as it lies before us in our accepted versions, the Epistle to the Galatians lacks a great deal of being a simple and direct treatment of the point at issue with the Galatians. It has been glossed and modified at many points to bring it into agreement with later developments in the organization of the church, and especially to bring it into agreement with doctrinal viewpoints which became orthodox, but which do not at all represent the gospel which Paul preached to the Galatians, and which we shall endeavor to show, was the gospel he preached in all his missionary labors.

Although at times this glossing and modification has been done with some skill, making it impossible for us to be clear in our analysis, and certain in our conclusions, it has at other times been done in such a manner that it is comparatively easy to detect the spurious materials, and by removing them, to restore the simplicity and directness of the original Pauline passages.

Concerning Paul's relations with the Galatians, we can be certain only of the details which can be learned from the letter itself. We cannot fall back upon the account of any episode or episodes recounted concerning the missionary travels of the apostle in the book of Acts, because of the controversy as to which, if any, of the churches whose founding is related in Acts, are the churches to which the epistle is addressed. The solution of this problem could give no decisive answer to the question of the literary integrity of the epistle, nor to the equally important question of the nature of the gospel Paul preached in this field. It can, therefore, have but little importance for this study; it should be taken up in its proper place in New Testament scholarship, the study of the book of Acts.

From Galatians iv: 11-20, we learn that Paul's first ministry to them had been because of an infirmity of the flesh, although we are told nothing whatever as to what this infirmity was, nor of how it had been connected with the ministry to the Galatians. It is characteristic of epistolary materials that they should abound in references to situations so well known to both writer and reader that it is not necessary that there be supplied the details which would make them intelligible to readers to whom the epistle was not addressed.

But in spite of what must have seemed to Paul a great obstacle to his reception, a temptation to them to despise him, they received him with the enthusiasm and devotion properly accorded to an angelic visitant, or even to Christ himself.

But this cordial and loving relationship was at least threatened by the intrusion of others, whose zeal in seeking the Galatians did not grow out of any genuine interest in the Galatians themselves, but rather out of a desire to reduce them to a position of inferiority and dependence upon these new-comers. They even represented that Paul, by telling them what Paul thought to be the truth, was their enemy. So greatly had this troubled Paul that he speaks of himself as undergoing an anxiety which can be likened only to travail, but which he hopes will result in the birth in them of the Christ.

The impression gained from this passage is confirmed by other materials in the epistle. We learn that the early course of their Christian life had been quite satisfactory to the apostle. (iii: 1-5; v: 7.) They had been evangelized by the graphic presentation of the crucified Christ; through faith in him they had received the Spirit, with all its wondrous manifestations. And for a while, at least, they had been running well.

This happy relationship was disturbed by the intrusion of rival missionaries, or perhaps of those who were only proselyters, who sought to commit the Galatians to an interpretation of the gospel so different from that which Paul had preached that he can refer to it only as another gospel, a perversion of the gospel of Christ, or as no gospel at all. (i: 6, 7.) The details of this gospel, whose propagation was evidently coupled with an attack upon Paul himself, must be learned from a careful study of Paul's discussion of it, and his attempts to refute it.

They represented Paul as insincere, seeking the favor of men, preaching, perhaps in other places and circumstances, the gospel of circumcision, although denouncing it in the

Galatian field. They probably spoke of him as inferior to the leaders of the Jerusalem church, dependent upon them for the gospel he preached. And they may have represented him to be one who was glorying in the flesh of his converts, mutilated as it was in the rite of their circumcision.

The gospel these disturbers had preached to the Galatians may have been presented to them as the traditional gospel, preached in the Jerusalem church, and from this mother church handed down to all who were properly Christian, her daughters in the faith. It was, in their account, not only the true gospel, but also the historic purpose of God as witnessed in the Scriptures. These opponents of Paul are often spoken of as Judaizers. Their gospel certainly appears to be one strongly influenced by Jewish values, and committed to Jewish institutions. It stands in stark contrast to the gospel of grace and liberty. The obligation to receive circumcision was urged upon the Galatians. And the fulfillment of at least a portion of the works of the law, e.g., food regulations, or living as Jews, was definitely demanded of them. Other seemingly Jewish notes are the implicit raising of the issue of authoritarianism, and the apparent contention that only the sons of Abraham might inherit the kingdom of God.

The Epistle to the Galatians, as written by Paul, would be a true letter, growing out of this concrete situation, confining itself to the issues involved. Paul would have been too vividly intent upon meeting the menace of the conflict to be drawn into the discussion of irrelevancies, too deeply concerned by the threat to the spiritual life of his beloved converts even to be aware of extraneous matters which at other times might present themselves to the minds of those rereading the epistle, using it in their instruction of later Christians, and copying it for the edification of the churches.

At first sight, our letter to the Galatians does not seem the simple, direct, burning letter needed to deal with a crisis threatening not only the life of the Galatian church, but the future of the entire way of life that Paul was proclaiming. But as we study it more carefully we can see that such a letter must originally have been at the basis of our present epistle. Fortunately it is possible to see the places at which the primary situation is lost to view, and at which the train of thought turns to problems other than those which the apostle faced. By removing passages which are patently out of harmony with their context, and which do not function properly in the argument in which they are employed, we are enabled to recover a letter, all of which is germane to the situation from which it sprang, and in which the train of thought flows smoothly and effectively toward its goal. We cannot at all times be sure that the result will be the original epistle in its entirety, for intruded passages may at times have crowded out some genuine materials, but we will be left with a simple, sensible, and altogether adequate treatment of the question raised by the agitation which so vitally threatened the faith and the religious life of Paul's Galatian converts.

It is the purpose of this study first to attempt to follow Paul in his discussion of the situation confronting the Galatian church, and in his argument that the gospel of grace and faith is incompatible with the gospel of circumcision, and dependence upon law, to which his converts have been enticed, and then to take up in order each of the passages which seem to have been added to the original epistle, and to endeavor to show that they cannot be parts of the letter which Paul wrote.

After a conventional greeting from Paul and the brethren with him, wishing to the churches of Galatia grace and peace from God, and our Lord Jesus Christ (i: 1-3), Paul expresses his astonishment that his converts are so quickly removing from the grace of Christ to a different gospel. This is a perversion of the gospel of Christ; indeed it cannot be called a gospel, for there is no gospel other than that which Paul had preached to them. If Paul himself, or even an angel from heaven, should preach another gospel, let him be anathema. The gospel cannot be altered to please men, as they evidently charged Paul with doing. He who proclaims it is the servant of Christ, accountable to him alone. (i: 6-10.)

Any student of Paul will do well to pause to ponder the implications of this passage. For it pictures the apostle as not only acutely conscious of the divergence between his gospel and that other which his opponents are proclaiming, but as so sure that his interpretation of the gospel is the only one possible that he does not hesitate to call down the direst of maledictions upon the head of anyone who would proclaim another gospel, be that one himself, or even an angel from heaven. When we are faced, in writings attributed to Paul, with gospels diametrically opposed to the one basic to the argument of the Epistle to the Galatians many insistent questions press upon us. Did Paul then have no clear-cut understanding of his own gospel? Did he modify his understanding of Christ and of the Christian life? Was he really willing to be all things to all men, and is this passage to be taken as an exhibition of his willingness to go to any length to win the argument in which he is presently engaged? It is our conviction that there is a characteristic Pauline gospel which can be recovered in all of his writings, to which he held so consistently that he can be thought utterly sincere in his denunciation of all other gospels even to the point of malediction.

Paul held this gospel as a stewardship directly from Jesus Christ himself. God had set him apart from his birth, and had revealed his Son in him. His gospel had not come from men, and specifically not from the leaders of the Jerusalem church. He had been completely insulated from early Christians not only by the assiduous zeal with which he had devoted himself to the religion of the Jews, but by a hostility toward the new sect which had caused him to persecute the church beyond measure. (i: 11-14.)

His adherence to Christianity was the result of a spiritual experience. He did not then go up to Jerusalem to learn from the earlier apostles; he avoided all conference with men by going to Arabia. It was only after three years that he went up to Jerusalem for a fifteen-day visit with Cephas. Even then he saw none of the other apostles save James the Lord's brother, and his contact with the Jerusalem churches was so slight that they knew him not by face, but only by hearsay. (i: 15-24.)

Then after the space of fourteen years, which would seem to be reckoned from the date of this first visit, he again went up to Jerusalem. This was not to learn from the leaders of the early Christians, but to present them with an entirely different point of view from their own, to maintain this other viewpoint unyieldingly, and to win from them the right hand of fellowship; they acknowledged his call to the apostleship to the gentiles, and laid upon his gospel no restriction whatever. They did but urge that he remember the poor, which he had always been zealous to do. (ii: 1-10.)

We must keep before us the realization that the only importance for the argument of the Epistle to the Galatians of this insistence upon his independence of the Jerusalem leaders is its guarantee of the independence of his gospel, and its difference from their traditional interpretation. Once this slips out of the foreground, the argument is beside the point.

This independence is further shown by Paul's account of his controversy with Cephas at Antioch. He points out that he withstood Cephas to his face because he was wrong in withdrawing himself from the gentiles with whom he had been eating before certain ones came from James. It is evident that this had raised the question of the observance of food regulations, and this question is germane to the discussion only because it is also germane to the situation confronting the Galatians. But it had raised in the mind of Paul the much deeper question of the fundamental meaning of the gospel. Could men be saved by faith in Christ alone, or must they still depend upon the works of the law, at least upon those which had to do with the question of ceremonial purity?

So deeply is Paul stirred by his realization of the incompatibility of the two viewpoints, and of the bearing of the question upon the very foundations of his own faith and gospel, that he feels impelled to recount for the Galatians the full story of this historic dispute, (ii: 11-21). Cephas had proved himself to be wrong; for he had built up again that which he had destroyed. He had first repudiated the necessity of ceremonial observances, and had then, when challenged, reaffirmed it. He could not have been right in both positions. But in which was he wrong? It was also ridiculous that Paul and Cephas, both Jewish born, should forsake Jewish ways of life, and then should turn around and demand of gentiles those Jewish ways which they themselves had forsaken, because they had trusted in Christ alone for their justification. If they had sinned in forsaking the ways of their fathers, they had been led to this position by their faith in Christ, and Christ would thus have been made a contributing factor, or a minister to their sin. How absurd! how utterly impossible!

This contention with Cephas parallels so closely the controversy between Paul and his opponents in Galatia, and the question at issue affects so fundamentally Paul's conception of his gospel, from which he has already so vehemently insisted there can be no deviation, that Paul cannot allow the discussion to rest in any merely negative considerations, but is impelled to set forth for the Galatians, as he had set forth for Cephas, the essence of the gospel by which he lived, and which he preached to all. Those who have faith in Christ pass in their spiritual experience through a process of death-life. With Christ they experience by faith an identification so complete that they are crucified with him, and they no longer live. It is (the risen) Christ that lives in them, and the life they now live in the flesh, they live in faith which is in the Son of God who gave himself up for them. Righteousness is not through the law; for then the grace of God is vain, and Christ died for nought, (ii: 19-21).

Up to this point the argument of the letter has been very clear. Paul has shown that his gospel is not the traditional gospel derived from the leaders of the church at Jerusalem, but that on the contrary he has twice in conflict with them triumphantly maintained one utterly different from the one they preached. He has here set it forth in purely Hellenistic terms of identification through faith with a dying-(rising) Christ, in an experience of being crucified with him, and living henceforth a life of righteousness which results from the indwelling of Christ.

That this is the true gospel, although his opponents have bewitched the Galatians into forsaking it, Paul endeavors to establish by appealing first to their own experience, and then to the historic purpose of God as set forth in the Scriptures.

Their faith had begun when Jesus Christ had been vividly presented to them in his crucifixion. It was not through works of the law, but through their faith in what they had heard, that the Spirit had been given to them, and had exerted his powerful influence upon them. Was all this experience to be in vain? (How foolish we are in our interpretation of the Scripture or of Christian life when we lay the principal stress upon the hearing of faith rather than upon the mighty working of the Spirit to which the hearing of faith contributes!) (iii: 1-5.)

Paul turns from the appeal to their experience to a consideration of the historic purpose of God as set forth in the Scripture. The reckoning of righteousness to Abraham was the result of his faith, and it is they who have faith, rather than they who depend upon the observance of the law, who are the sons of Abraham. The Scripture, indeed, foresaw that God would justify the gentiles by faith, and preached the gospel beforehand to Abraham, "In thee shall all the nations be blessed." They that are of faith are blessed with the faithful Abraham, (iii: 6-9). (This is) in order that the blessing of Abraham might in Christ come upon the gentiles, and that we might receive the promise of the Spirit through faith. (iii: 14.)

Because of the importance of "justification," and of the "reckoning of righteousness" to any understanding of the Pauline gospel we might well pause here to inquire into the meaning of these terms. It is indisputable that the experience of Abraham is referred to as a "reckoning" of righteousness; it is equally indisputable that Paul is here reproducing the wording of the Old Testament passage utilized in his argument. The righteousness which comes through faith in Christ cannot be thought of as an "imputation," or as a "reckoning" of any kind or degree. It results from Christ living in us. It flows from the reception of the Spirit, and from his mighty effect upon us. The curse of the law comes from failure to do the things commanded in the law. They that are Christ's crucify the flesh with its passions and lusts. The fruits of the Spirit are found in actual love, joy, peace, goodness, and not in the "imputation" or "reckoning" of these qualities. In short, there is to be found in the genuine passages in the Galatian epistle no trace whatever of the idea of "imputing" or "reckoning" righteousness save in this color carried over from the Old Testament passage alluded to.

The argument is continued by showing that even in men's dealings with each other, a covenant is final, being subject to being neither voided nor modified. So the law, coming four hundred thirty years after the promise, could not make it of none effect, which is exactly what would have happened had the inheritance been of the law. But God granted it to Abraham by promise, (iii: 15-18).

The law was merely an ad interim provision, a tutor to lead us to Christ. But now the tutor is no longer necessary. All are sons of God, through faith, in Christ Jesus. All who have been baptized into Christ, have put on Christ. This has done away with all distinctions. There can be neither Jew nor Greek, neither bond nor free, neither male nor female, for all are one in Christ Jesus. And if we are Christ's we are Abraham's seed, heirs according to promise, (iii: 23-29).

Let us, then, stand fast in the freedom with which Christ

has made us free, avoiding the yoke of circumcision and of the law. Circumcision and Christ are mutually exclusive. Circumcision obligates one to the fulfillment of the entire law. There can be no half way measures. It severs from Christ. For in him neither circumcision nor uncircumcision is of any avail. All that matters is faith working through love! (v: 1-6.)

The Galatians had been running well, committed to the Pauline gospel of faith in Christ alone. This other viewpoint was not Paul's, (or not of God), but it would as leaven permeate the entire lump. But Paul does not think it will really come to this. He is confident that eventually the Galatians will condemn his opponents and follow him. The idea that he is preaching circumcision, and that they might depend upon circumcision, and yet follow him, is absurd. For if he were preaching circumcision, the offense caused by the demand that they take the cross and be crucified with Christ would be done away; he would no longer be so harassed. Let those who would be circumcised exaggerate it to the point of mutilation! (v: 7-12.)

The argument has come to rest. They must follow either Paul or his opponents. It must be Christ, or circumcision.

There remain to be urged upon the Galatians two practical considerations. Paul may have realized their urgency from his experience of the results of this utterly spiritual gospel of faith in Christ alone, which he encountered in all his missionary labors. Or he may have felt that they were specially needed in the Galatian field because of his knowledge of the state of affairs in these churches. The gospel of freedom seems to have brought with it the twin dangers of unbridled license on the one hand, and of an inflated self-esteem on the other, which might be joined with a censorious attitude toward one's neighbors.

Freedom must not be used as an occasion to the flesh. One of the manifestations of the fleshly spirit is an attitude of strife and hostility toward one's fellows. Faith works through love, and love makes us servants of each other. This would indeed fulfill the intent of the law. But if we bite and devour one another this must eventuate in the complete destruction of the group. It would seem that here the argument has been caused to deviate from a straight course, perhaps by the urgency of the rivalry and strife known by the apostle to exist in the Galatian church. (It is of course possible that verse 14 or even 14 and 15 may be later additions to the genuine epistle.) (v: 13-15.)

Freedom cannot be an occasion to the flesh, for he who is Christ's has shared in the crucifixion of Christ through the crucifixion of the flesh with all its passions and lusts, and has received the Spirit, which must from henceforth dominate his life. The flesh and the Spirit are diametrically opposed to each other. He who is dominated by the flesh cannot do the things he would. He who is led by the Spirit is not under the law. (v: 16-18.)

Here follow catalogs of the works of the flesh and of the fruits of the Spirit, (v: 19-24), in which the important thing is not the various items listed in each group, but the underlying conception that flesh and Spirit are vital forces which dominate life, and each of which produces its proper fruit in the life it dominates. Here is no thought of the "imputation" or "reckoning" of good or of evil. The flesh makes the life it dominates actually wicked; he who has been crucified with Christ has suffered with him the crucifixion of his flesh; he is free from its dominance; he has been imbued with the

Spirit; this functions as a vital power fructifying the whole of his life, and making it altogether lovely, pure, and good. They who practice such things as the flesh produces cannot inherit the kingdom of God. They who are led by the Spirit, live by the Spirit, walk by the Spirit. They who in Christ are free cannot use their freedom as an occasion to the flesh, because, by reason of the very fact that they are Christ's, they have been so closely identified with him that they live the Christ life.

The consciousness of being imbued with the Divine Spirit, or alternately, of having Christ incarnate within one, with the resulting experience of ecstasy or attainment, might well result in an inflated self-esteem, making one vainglorious, envious, or apt to challenge his brother. Especially would it make one conscious of failure or relative lack of attainment upon the part of the other. He who is truly spiritual will be humble, gentle with his brother, and will seek to restore him rather than to challenge him or to glory in his downfall. For he who thinks himself to be spiritual may be merely deceiving himself; his spirituality must be proved by the fruits of the Spirit in his own life. Bear each other's burden; this is the law of Christ; at the same time, be very sure of your own real character and attainment. (v: 25—vi: 5.)

The letter comes to a natural conclusion in a paragraph drawing a contrast between Paul and his opponents, and between the gospel each is proclaiming, (vi: 11-16). These opponents of his are not sincere; they do not themselves keep the law they would endeavor to fasten upon you. They do but desire to make a fair showing in the flesh, and to avoid the harassment visited upon those who preach the mystic doctrine of the cross of Christ, with its demand for the crucified life. While they glory in the flesh of their converts, Paul renounces all glorying save in the cross of our Lord, Jesus Christ, through which the world has been crucified to him, and he to the world. Circumcision and uncircumcision are nothing. All that avails is a radical experience of grace which makes one a new creation. Peace be upon all those who walk by this rule. They are the true Israel of God.

After asserting that henceforth no one should trouble him, because he is Christ's branded slave, (vi: 17), Paul concludes the letter with the benediction, "The grace of our Lord Jesus Christ be with your spirit, brethren." (vi: 18.) The "Amen" may be the result of the liturgical use of the letter.

It remains now to take up each of the passages which have been rejected, and to exhibit the grounds upon which each of them has been so dealt with. No analysis can hope to be final. It may well be that any one passage taken by itself might be so interpreted that it might be fitted into the thread of the letter. The evidence for glossing and for modification is of course cumulative, and as it becomes more likely that any one passage, or even more that any considerable number of passages are spurious, this in itself reduces the probability that the letter as a whole lies before us as Paul wrote it, and heightens the contrary probability that passages which seem awkward or incongruous are not parts of the original, genuine letter.

CHAPTER i: 4, 5.

In these verses we are confronted with the question as to what in a letter properly belongs in the greeting. Its function is that of placing the writer or writers in relationship with the readers, together with some more or less conventional formula of greeting. It tends to become formalized and stereotyped. This is no place to introduce theological discussion. Once the words of greeting are spoken, the greeting itself is finished. A glance at the salutation of each of the letters that have come down to us under the name of Paul will show that the almost invariable formula consists in the delineation of those from whom the letter is sent, Paul and his associates, the delineation of those to whom it is addressed, and the formal words of greeting. Titus is an exception, but the spuriousness of Titus is so generally recognized that this exception cannot be urged. Romans is the only other letter, apart from Galatians, in which we meet extraneous material in the salutation. This should cause us to subject the contents of this opening paragraph in Romans to the most careful examination. It will indeed raise the question whether in Romans we have a true letter, or a formalized "epistle." (See Rom. i: 1-7; I Cor. i: 1-3; II Cor. i: 1, 2; Gal. i: 1-5; Eph. i: 1, 2; Phil. i: 1, 2; Col. i: 1, 2; I Thess. i: 1; II Thess. i: 1, 2; I Tim. i: 1, 2; II Tim. i: 1, 2; Titus i: 1-4; Philemon 1-3.)

We further note that in Galatians alone is any material introduced into the salutation after the words of greeting, "Grace to you and peace from God, the Father, and our Lord Jesus Christ." If it were to be put into the greeting at all, this material should by all means have found its place before this stereotyped formula, which closes a greeting with the same uniformity and finality that "Amen" ends a prayer.

Our suspicions are further roused by the fact that this material is concluded with a doxology, which is complete even to the closing "Amen." This would seem to be evidence that a liturgical use has been made of at least this portion of the letter.

These suspicions are confirmed by the failure of our attempts to find echoes of the theological positions set forth in these verses in other genuine Pauline materials. They are rather the statement of an orthodoxy that later fastened itself upon the church.

We are first told that Christ "gave himself for our sins." This expression can be paralleled exactly only in I Tim. ii: 6, "who gave himself a ransom for all," and in Titus ii: 14, "who gave himself for us," and in Eph. v: 2, 25. It is apparently paralleled in Gal. ii: 20, where Paul is speaking of living his present life in the flesh "in faith in the son of God, who gave himself for me." But in this passage the idea of the self-giving of Christ is so rooted in the idea of our participation in the Christ life through mystic identification with him, that there can be no question of equating it with the same expression used in i: 4, where the context would demand that it be equated with snatching us out of this present evil world, rather than with identifying us in the life we now live in the flesh with the Christ who lives in us. Such a parallel amounts only to the use of the same words. The whole of their intent and meaning is different.

But even if we should not insist upon the use of the same wording, but should seek for the broader meaning of the clause under consideration, we would find that it is characteristic of the later strata of the New Testament, rather than of the earlier ones. The idea of a sacrificial, substitutionary death of Christ is written deeply into these later strata. In the Pastorals, Ephesians, Hebrews, and I Peter, this idea is very plain, and it is to be expected. But in the Synoptic materials, apart from the sporadic saying in Mt. xx: 28, Mk. x: 45, "to give his life a ransom for many," the teaching of the substitutionary death of Christ seems to be confined to

Eucharistic materials. These would very early be subject to liturgical, as well as to doctrinal development. In regard to the saying just quoted from Mt. and Mk. it is important to note that the Lucan parallel is to be found in a pericope which he has placed in his account of the Last Supper, (Lk. xxii: 25-27; John dramatizes it, in the same setting, into the story of the washing of the disciples' feet). Lk. gives for these vital words the variant, which has every appearance of being original and genuine, "I am in the midst of you as he that serveth." It is evident that this conception has only incidentally, indeed doubtfully, touched the Synoptic tradition, and that in the definite form of the broken body, and the shed blood. Only Mt. has the phrase "unto the remission of sins" (Mt. xxvi: 28). It is exceedingly doubtful whether it is to be encountered in the primitive tradition of the words of Jesus.

Parallels in John are only seeming. Giving one's life for one's friends, (xv: 13), and the good shepherd giving his life for the sheep are expressions of the love and faithfulness exhibited in the act of self-giving, rather than pronouncements of a substitutionary doctrine. The fact that in I Jn. iii: 16 we are exhorted to lay down our lives for the brethren, as he did for us, certainly excludes the idea of a unique redemption. The ascription of a cleansing function to the blood of Jesus is one point in which the First Epistle of John differs from the Gospel, (I Jn. i: 7). The remark of Caiaphas that it were expedient for one to die for the people referred in the first instance to the preservation of their political existence, and not to their salvation from sin. (Jn. xi: 50-52, xviii: 14).

It is evident that this idea of the substitutionary death of Christ has also been deeply written into the Pauline Epistles, as they lie before us. But in every case reasons can be found for regarding the passages in which this idea occurs with the strongest of suspicion. Such passages are Ro. v: 6, 8; viii: 32; I Cor. xi: 24; xv: 3; II Cor. v: 15, 21; Gal. iii: 13; I Thess. v: 10. Where the passages are not to be rejected, the connotation is such as to permit, if indeed it do not require, the meaning that Christ died for us that we might die with him, and rose that we might rise with him here and now in righteousness and in newness of life. The true Pauline conception of the meaning of the death of Christ is mystic, not substitutionary. (We must defer treatment of these passages in point to the study of the epistles in which they occur.)

In the words "that he might snatch us out of this present evil age," we are confronted with an attitude toward this world incompatible with Paul's idea concerning it, and with an interpretation of salvation utterly without parallel in the New Testament. The expression, "the present evil age" cannot be found elsewhere in our New Testament writings. At most we find inferences that this age, (or world), is transient and evil, and that its standards and motives should not govern us. But nowhere do we find it referred to as "this present evil age." The word for "snatch out" is found only in the Matthean tradition of the word of Jesus, which bids us to pluck out an offending eye, (Mt. v: 29, xviii: 9), and in Acts (vii: 10, 34; xii: 11; xxiii: 27; xxvi: 17), where it has the softened meaning of to rescue or to deliver. This softened meaning is quite inappropriate in the passage in Galatians under discussion. The fact that the dominant New Testament occurrence of this word is in the Book of Acts can hardly increase our confidence that this passage is Pauline.

We are here confronted with the starkest of apocalyptic conceptions of salvation. This present age is evil; it will continue to be evil; there is no use to hope that it can be improved;

the true Christian attitude is defeatism; stand looking up into heaven, awaiting the return of Christ; pray that he may snatch us out of this world with all its evil. On the other hand the whole outlook of Paul is suffused with the conviction that through identification with Christ the power of God, through the impartation of the Spirit, becomes available to us, making us triumphant over all temptation and limitation. We are more than conquerors; we are God's children: our lives are new creations; we can do all things through Christ. What worlds this is away from the hopeless, helpless attitude of dejected defeat, waiting for some manifestation of miraculous power to snatch us out of our weakness and our woe!

The note of predestination is struck in the phrase, "according to the will of our God and Father." That this note occurs in this passage, which is suspect for so many other reasons, will scarcely increase our confidence in the theory that Paul was predestinarian in his thinking. It must, on the contrary, cause us to subject all of the predestinarian passages in the surviving letters to the most careful scrutiny. The fact that the preposition for "according to" the will of God agrees with that used in Ephesians, (i: 5, 11), contrary to Paul's customary diction, may bear witness to the lateness and secondary character of this passage.

The more deeply the third chapter of Galatians is studied, the more difficult it becomes to escape the conviction that Paul's simple discussion of the relation between law and promise, in which he would be concerned with the bearing of the issue upon the Galatians' adherence to one or to the other as the basis of their Christian life, and not at all with ultimate and universal aspects of the problem, and in which he had merely pointed out the priority of the promise, its fundamental and ultimate place in God's purpose, and the entire lack of any conflict between law and promise, has been modified by the insertion of materials which raise the resulting question as to the ultimate character of the law. It is easy to see that the church would at some time or other be compelled to deal with this problem; it should be equally easy to see how inappropriate it would be to interject such considerations into the crucial battle in which Paul was engaged.

Not only is such discussion utterly unwise in a critical debate upon whose outcome hinges not only the loyalty of these Galatian converts to Paul, but that which was infinitely more significant to him, the genuineness and the power of their Christian life; but the solution propounded to the question of the relation of the law to the gospel, is thoroughly non-Pauline. The law is conceived as a necessary negative preliminary to the gospel. It could not make alive; it could but result in a universal sinfulness, thus creating the universal need of an atonement. This, of course, entirely disregards the historic application of the law to Israel alone; it proceeds from the point of view that all are made sinners by the law, whether they ever heard of the law or not.

It is of interest to note that both viewpoints are to be found in Romans, which apparently begins by attempting to assert a universal depravity which creates the universal need of an atonement, and which in v: 12ff involves itself in insuperable difficulties as it struggles with the necessity of establishing a universal sinfulness, while yet realizing that there really cannot be sin where there is no law. These materials in Galatians are unquestionably due to the influence which modified Romans in identical ways.

CHAPTER iii: 10-12.

These verses are undoubtedly genuinely Pauline, for they think of justification as determined solely by the question whether or not one does or fails to do the things that God commands. There is no question of "imputation" here.

They are just as evidently displaced from their proper context. If they are examined by themselves it is immediately evident that they discharge the logical function of supplying the proof of the general assertion "by the works of the law shall no flesh be justified." This they do beautifully by pointing out the ultimate principle of justification by law is through keeping its commandments; it is not a faith-law, but an obedience-law; it calls down a curse upon all who do not continue in all of the things that are written in the book of the law to do them. The premise that no one does this is assumed. If placed after ii: 16, these verses would make sense, supplying a cogent proof of the position there maintained. In their present position, they, together with verse 13, reduce the logical sequence of the passage to chaos.

CHAPTER iii: 13.

The reasons for the rejection of this verse are clear and compelling. It does not cohere with either the more remote or the more immediate context.

As to the more remote context, it places upon the death of Christ a substitutionary rather than a mystic valuation. We would have been accursed because of our failure to keep the law. But we are "redeemed," i.e., bought off, by Christ, who became accursed because of his having been hanged upon a tree. It is immediately evident that the one who wrote these words is thinking merely in terms of the avoidance of a penalty, and not in terms of an actual attainment by means of which we are enabled to keep the law. We are in the realm of bookkeeping, rather than in that of dynamic experience. No word is said either as to the mode of the functioning of this redemption, or as to its justification or validation. We are in the realm of thought, or in the period of the life of the church, when substitution has become a self-evident dogma, in need of neither support nor explanation.

There is an almost exact parallel to this expression in II Cor. v: 21, where, however, there is a most significant difference. "Him who knew no sin, he made 'SIN' on our behalf, that we might become the righteousness of God in him." This is vastly superior in religious value to the verse in Galatians, and incidentally much closer to the Pauline point of view; for it deals with the realities of sin and righteousness, and makes our righteousness, no "imputation" here, the end of the divine action. But there is no hint as to how God could make Christ to be "SIN," nor how the making of Christ to be "SIN," could eventuate in our righteousness. It is also instructive to note that the Corinthian material parallels the Galatian in the seemingly incidental fact that it is not integrated with its context by any connective particle.

The decisive argument for the rejection of Galatians iii: 13 is to be found in the impossibility of integrating it with its immediate context. It is not connected with this context by means of any connective particle. This may be thought to be a device to secure emphasis. It is far more likely that there is no connective particle because this verse is a gloss; it needed no connective particle, for it had no structural relationship whatever to the context in which it is now found, being originally written upon the margin by one dominated by the same substitutionary point of view which is set forth in Gal. i: 4a, perhaps as a homiletical reminder.

The logical chaos to which the whole passage is reduced by the inclusion of verses 10-13 may be seen by the simple attempt to follow the thread of thought through it.

Paul has been trying to point out that since the blessing came to Abraham through his faith, those who have faith are blessed with the faithful Abraham. Now those who were under the law fell under a curse through their inability to do the things commanded; Christ became a curse for us (viz., those under the law). The only possible result of this redemption would be to free those under the law from the curse of the law. Urging this upon the Galatians would be urging them to be under the law that they might share in the redemption provided in Christ for those under the law. Paul would thus at one stroke destroy all that he had been trying to build up in the entire course of his argument.

For this argument, as we have it in the present sequence of the material, proceeds to the amazing conclusion, not, as is alone logically possible, that Christ brings redemption to those under the law, but, most strangely! that this was in order that, or, brought about the result that, the blessing of Abraham might come upon the gentiles, who were not under the law, and that we, who, according to the whole argument of Galatians, must be taken as those whose religious life rests upon faith in Christ, and not upon any attempt to keep the law, might receive the promise of the Spirit through faith!

Many astonishing logical phenomena are encountered in this passage. There is first the pure non-sequitur in the idea that the establishment of the failure of the Jews must result in the establishment of the success of the gentiles. The negative premise that none could be justified through the works of the law can lead only to the negative conclusion that lawkeepers are accursed, not to the positive conclusion that the gentiles might receive the promise of the Spirit. The hopeless confusion of the passage is the result of the confusion in the connotation of the terms employed in the various steps of the reasoning. Paul's whole argument rests upon the distinction between the two classes, those who depend upon faith, and those who depend upon law-keeping. But this sequence of reasoning makes him establish a fact in regard to one of these classes, and then apply it to the other. For the construction employed in the beginning of verse 14, whether we are dealing with a construction of purpose, ("in order that"), or of result, ("so that"), or merely with a clause in rather loose apposition with the substance of the whole of the preceding context, ("that"), stringently binds the redemption wrought through Christ for those under the law with the attainment of those who have faith, that other class which, for the success of Paul's argument, must be so absolutely distinguished from those under the law.

Is it any wonder that so many have thought Paul is so hard to understand? If this whole passage, as it stands, must be accepted as genuine, we must conclude that Paul was devoid of any logical ability. Certainly we are here faced with the dilemma, either there has been some modification of original materials, or we have indisputable evidence of Paul's utter inability to do straight thinking in the most elementary terms.

Remove the spurious materials, and our dilemma is resolved. Paul stands before us as a clear and incisive thinker. God's original and unwavering purpose was to deal with all as he dealt with Abraham. This the Scripture had foreseen, preaching the gospel beforehand to Abraham. All that are of faith are to be blessed with Abraham, who had faith, so that upon the gentiles might come Abraham's blessing; so that we might receive the promise through faith.

It must be granted that if all of the original materials are present, and verses 10-13 have been interpolated without any excision, it is difficult to be sure of the grammatical construction with which verse 14 begins. If it be a construction of purpose. excision must have taken place; some premise may well have fallen out. But this must have been a positive premise; it must have had to do with the attainment of the gentiles, or with the gift of the Spirit through faith. But this may be a construction of result, or merely a substantive clause in rather loose apposition with its preceding context.

CHAPTER iii: 16b.

This material is evidently a gloss. As to the manner in which Scripture is quoted and interpreted it would much better stand in the Epistle to the Hebrews, than in anything Paul has written. It is characteristic of the Epistle to the Hebrews to introduce a quotation from Scripture with some such formula as "he saith," or "saying." See Hebrews: i: 5, 6, 8 (understood), 13; ii: 6, 12; iii: 7, 15; iv: 3, 4, 7; v: 5, 6; vii: 21; viii: 8, 13; ix: 20; x: 5, 8, 15; xii: 26. It is also quite characteristic of Hebrews to assign to the terms of Scripture arbitrary meanings whose sole justification is that they serve to establish a desired point of view. There are many indications that the Epistle to the Hebrews, as is the case with the Pastorals, is quite closely connected with the secondary and spurious materials in the Pauline letters.

It would seem that in this gloss we come to a dead end. Nothing is made of this proposed identification, but the argument immediately reverts to its proper channel by showing that God's dealing with Abraham was final, being subject to no subsequent modification. There seems to be an attempt to pick up the road that had come to a dead end in the reference in verse 19b to the seed to whom the promise has been made. This gives us the impression, if we take all this material to be genuine, that Paul was quite likely to go off on a tangent at any moment, and then to awaken with a start, and to go back to pick up the argument he had left in a suspended state of animation.

The utter incongruity of verse 16b with the context is evident from the fact that the entire course of Paul's argument is dependent upon his identification of the seed of Abraham, to whom the inviolate and unchangeable promise had been made, with those who have faith. Its identification with Christ reduces the argument to chaos and nonsense.

CHAPTER iii: 19-22.

Of this material, it would seem that verse 21a alone can be saved for Paul. It has the genuine Pauline fervor, and may well serve as the connecting link between verses 18 and 23. The fundamental conception of the law, and of its place in the Christian economy, as set forth in the remainder of the passage, is diametrically opposed to the position taken by Paul.

Paul is concerned to show that the law is not at all necessary in the Christian economy. It had at best but a temporary validity, and had the positive function of leading us to Christ. Until Christ came we were under a tutor. There is not the slightest suggestion that this was an evil estate, or that it eventuated in the condemnation of those therein. Although we were "shut up" in this estate, it was entirely natural, and was ordained not for the purpose of our condemnation, but of our being led to Christ.

The spurious material in verses 19-22 seems to be a theological expansion of this position, but from the later point of view of developed orthodoxy. 19b and 20 have long been a crux of interpretation. All of the permutations and combinations possible to mental gymnastics seem to have been brought to bear upon their elucidation. The difficulty in interpreting them grows out of the tension set up by the realization that if they be genuine, they must have some relation to the context, and fulfill some function in the argument in which they occur, which relation and function is not at all evident. The simplest explanation seems to be to take them as a double gloss, verse 19b from the point of view that would endeavor to venerate the law because of its mediation at the hands of Moses and the angels, 20 a countervailing gloss pointing out that the very fact of mediation introduces a note of disunity into religion incompatible with the unity of God. We are again at a dead end in the course of argument, for there is drawn from this profound discussion no conclusion which throws any light whatever upon any point at issue.

The fundamental point of view in regard to the law, (verses 19-22), is that it is a necessary negative preparation for the gospel. It was added because of transgressions. The best interpretation of this expression is "to make us transgressors," or to make transgressions actual. In 22 it is specifically stated that the definite function of the law is to shut up all things under sin. It may be remarked that this ignores the historic application of the law to Israel alone, and gives to this process of shutting up under sin a reference to all people, and to all of time. This tendency to generalization is widely characteristic of spurious materials in the "Pauline" writings.

It is quite evident that the syllogism lying at the base of this train of thought is constructed upon the major premise of later orthodoxy, that a universal depravity, and conviction of sin, is the necessary preliminary to any redemptive process. Universal damnation is the first step toward salvation. God sent his Son into the world to condemn the world that out of the depths of its miserable condemnation the world might lift up its voice, pleading for mercy. It is quite true that this is the thought underlying the early chapters of Romans as we have them. But this does not convince us that the thought is Pauline.

The introduction of this idea into the argument which Paul is utilizing stultifies it all. For the idea that the shutting up of all things under sin by the law was a necessary prerequisite to the giving of the promise by faith in Christ shatters the argument that the promise had been given to Abraham, and to his seed, which must be taken to mean those who have a faith like that of Abraham, four hundred thirty years before the law was given.

Chapter iv: 1-5; 8-10; 21-31.

It is exceedingly difficult to find in the fourth chapter of Galatians any materials except verses 11-20, and possibly verse 6, which are convincingly Pauline.

Verses 11-20 have the true Pauline and epistolary flavor. They so evidently grow out of the concrete situation, the relations between Paul and the Galatians on the one hand, and the Galatians and Paul's adversaries on the other, that they make no attempt to set forth clearly the details to which they allude, viz., the infirmity which had caused Paul first to preach the gospel to them. They have the simplicity, the directness, and the poignancy suited to the anxious and crucial discussion in which Paul is engaged. This same tone is resumed in the fifth chapter.

Verse 6, containing the idea that because we are his sons, God sent forth the Spirit of his Son into our hearts to lead us into the realization of our filial status, is quite in harmony with the fundamental Pauline idea of a present experience through the enduement of the Spirit. Verse 7, however, follows much more naturally upon verse 5, than upon verse 6. We are no longer bondservants, but sons, because we have been redeemed and have received the adoption of sons. It is redemption and adoption, and not the sending of the Spirit, that have made us sons. If verse 6 cohere at all with the context, it would much better come at the conclusion of the paragraph, following verse 7.

CHAPTER iv: 1-5; 8-10.

This material is a development of the position set forth in chapter iii: 23-26, from an entirely different point of view. The opening words bring an entire change of the stage setting. In ch. iii, verses 23-26, the minor child is merely under a tutor who is to lead him to Christ. But in the passage under consideration it is categorically stated that he differs no whit from a bondservant. This point of view is consistently maintained throughout the passage, for it is necessary that the child be redeemed and adopted ere he can be a child. Paul, having triumphantly asserted that we are sons of God is here made to say we must be redeemed and adopted, before we can become sons. The entire pre-Christian state, which in Paul's thought had been merely minority, is here transformed into bondage.

It is quite evident that this passage is both late and generalized. It comes from the time when the church no longer distinguishes between the pre-Christian state of Jews and that of gentiles. While Paul's difficulty with the Galatians necessitated a sharp distinction between the Jewish and the Hellenistic approach to Christianity, in this context the only distinction necessary is between the Christian and the pre-

Christian states, and the passage vacillates between a bondage under the rudiments of the world, and a bondage under the law. It is quite evident that the specific question to the fore in the Galatian difficulty, whether we are to be justified by faith or by the works of the law, especially circumcision, has slipped entirely out of focus.

There is utter confusion as to the nature of the bondage. In verses 3, 8 and 9, we were in bondage under the rudiments of the world, but in verse 5, we were in bondage under the law. There is an equally utter confusion as to those who are to be beneficiaries of adoption. We were in bondage under the rudiments of the world; God sent his Son to redeem them that were under the law; with the result that we, who were in bondage under the rudiments of the world, might receive the adoption of sons, which had been won for those under the law, not for those under the rudiments of the world. It is true that verses 4b, and 5a may be regarded as a not particularly intelligent gloss, the omission of which would eliminate this vacillation in terms.

But this omission would not bring the remainder of these materials into congruity with the Galatian situation. We must keep clearly before us that the question at issue is whether the Christian life is to be lived through faith in Christ, that is through a dynamic spiritual experience of identification with him, resulting in a life of righteousness through the power of the indwelling Christ or alternatively conceived, in the power of the Spirit, or through obedience to the demands of the law, especially circumcision.

But we are here confronted with the choice, not Christ or circumcision, but God or idols. The danger faced is not that which Paul is combatting, that they would embrace a perverted gospel and would adopt a spurious type of Christianity. It is rather that they who had been idolaters would revert to idolatry, and would go back to a bondage under the rudiments of the world.

It is important to note that verses 8-10 have a distinctly gnostic flavor. They had been in bondage under the rudiments of the world, which in Hellenistic syncretism, were the elements, earth, air, fire, and water. These were not thought of as physical constituents of the world, but as divine essences, and were worshipped as such. The path of deliverance is through knowledge. It was through their knowing God, or rather through their being known of God, that they were delivered from these weak and beggarly elements who were by nature no gods. They now wish to turn back to their previous state of bondage to these supposed dieties, evidently by the observance of days, and months, and seasons, and years.

It requires no great amount of penetration to realize that we are here face to face with "the Colossian heresy"! There, too, we encounter the rudiments of the world; there, too, we find the gnostic or philosophic approach; there, too, feast days, new moons, and sabbaths. The situation is essentially the same in both epistles, and it has nothing whatever in common with the danger faced by Paul that his Galatian converts would embrace a gospel of circumcision and of works, rather than one of faith and of grace through the power of the Spirit.

It should be needless to say that the encountering of a type of thought in Galatians similar to that found in Colossians does not necessarily validate this strain in Colossians as being either early or Pauline. It is equally permissible to draw the inference that Galatians has been subject to the play of the same forces as those met with in Colossians.

CHAPTER iv: 21-31.

If this material were found elsewhere than in its present setting, it would present few difficulties of interpretation. It would seem to be concerned with a controversy between Jews and Christians. It is at a comparatively late stage of the controversy, for the Christians have come to outnumber the Jews. The Jews still seem to be able to persecute the Christians, but the outcome of the controversy is certain, for it is not the Jews but the Christians who are to receive the inheritance, because they are the sons of the wife, and not of the slave, and hence are the true Israel.

The argument by means of which this position is established is Rabbinical, or allegorical, and would be of no use outside circles dominated by a Jewish point of view. It draws a contrast between two covenants, that of Sinai, or the law, and that of the promise; between two Jerusalems, that which now is, and that which is above. These are identified with the two wives of Abraham, Hagar, and Sarah. This identification is not only arbitrary, but historically it is definitely wrong. It is possible not only with equal arbitrariness to reverse the identification here made, but to point out that it was to the children of Isaac, and not to those of Ishmael, that the law was given. To reckon Sinai within the experience of the descendants of Ishmael is a palpable absurdity.

Here again the question is not a choice between two types of Christian life, but between Christians and Jews. This little allegory, beside being utterly arbitrary and historically absurd, is entirely beside the point which Paul is arguing. Could we save it for him, it would enhance our opinion of neither his spiritual insight nor of his Christian spirit. "Cast out the hand maid and her son, that is, the children of the Jerusalem that now is, the sons of the law" is at complete variance with Romans ix: 2, 3, "I have great sorrow and unceasing pain in my heart. For I could wish that I myself were anathema from Christ for my brethren's sake." In its dealings with the Jews the later church did not preserve Paul's attitude of brokenhearted grief!

CHAPTER v: 5.

This verse is not only a definite interruption to the continuity of thought in the context, but it introduces an idea of the function of the Spirit and of the nature of the Christian life diametrically opposed to that to be found throughout the epistle. For Paul, the Christian life is a present dynamic experience of the grace of God in the power of the Spirit. That which is contrasted with circumcision and the law is faith working through love. The function of the Spirit is to fructify our lives so that they do now produce righteousness.

This verse would seem to be interpolated by one who wished to counter the demand for a present life of triumphant righteousness. All that the Spirit can do, all that faith can do, is to give us a hope to wait for, a hope that eventually righteousness will be given us. There is in the Greek absolutely no hint that this righteousness depends upon any effort of ours. There is substituted for the present life of struggle and triumph, a salvation entirely futuristic, and passively received.

The omission of this gloss restores verse 6 to its proper function, the climax of the train of thought in verses 1-4.

CHAPTER vi: 6-10.

The entire spirit and content of these verses is manifestly late. Christianity is developed to the point it can be referred to as "the faith," and Christians can be spoken of as "the household of the faith." It further seems developed to the point that there are officially recognized teachers, with the equally recognized obligation of those taught to contribute toward their support. We shall hardly be sufficiently naïve to assume that this is justification enough for holding that the primitive Pauline church was organized with a professional class of catechisers or teachers. Where have these teachers been in all the critical struggle Paul has had with his opponents? If worthy, why has no appeal been made to their authority and example? If unworthy, why should they be supported or why have they not been singled out for instruction and rebuke? It is here, and here alone, that their existence can be suspected.

The whole passage reflects the generalization that so often characterizes homiletics, whether ancient or modern. Sowing to the flesh, and to the Spirit have no definite content. Equally generalized is the exhortation to "do good to all as you have opportunity." This should be contrasted with the definiteness of the materials found in v: 17—vi: 5.

The conception of flesh and spirit is also quite different from that in the context. For Paul flesh and spirit are forces that dominate life, and produce present and actual effects in life. But in this spurious material, they are rather soils in which seed may be sown. The result is, in due time, a harvest. The terms in which it is set forth lack the Pauline concreteness, idolatry, sorcery, enmities, strife, etc., longsuffering, kindness, goodness, faithfulness, etc. For these concrete deeds and traits are substituted the generalized abstractions, corruption and eternal life. Eternal life is a Johannine expression, and is a witness to Johannine forces playing upon the Pauline writings wherever found.

Here, too, is the same futuristic note found in v: 5. Life is a period wearily to be endured without fainting, for in due time, and only then shall we reap.

The Galatian situation is utterly lost in a hazy exhortation that has arisen not out of a sharp critical struggle, but out of the long pull.

Chapter IV

THE EPISTLE TO THE ROMANS

IT IS quite a simple task to recover from the Epistle to the Romans itself the principal elements in the situation which led to its writing. Nothing else can be known concerning it with any certainty, although there are many points of approach open to our speculative inquiry.

Paul tells us specifically that in pursuit of his calling as Apostle to the Gentiles he had labored in the whole field from Jerusalem even to Illyricum. He had often wished to visit Rome, that they might be comforted in each other's faith, or rather, that he might impart unto them some spiritual gift. But his way to them had been providentially hindered. Now his opportunity in the field in which he was laboring had come to an end, and he was under the necessity of proceeding to Jerusalem to bear to the poor among the saints in the mother church the great collection he had long been raising in their behalf among all his churches. But he still hoped that he would be able to come to them, and after a period of rest and mutual encouragement through each other's faith and Christian experience, he might be furthered by them in the journey which he contemplated making into Spain.

We have no certain knowledge as to the origin of the Roman church, nor as to its exact strength and influence at the time Paul wrote. Our knowledge of the relation of Rome to the empire, and of the amount of travel between the capital and outlying parts would lead us to expect that Paul would regard it as of the utmost importance that he have the sympathy of this group of Christians, and that his teachings should be clearly understood by them. We can understand how great had been his disappointment that he had been hindered from visiting them, and we can appreciate the eagerness with which he would avail himself of the opportunity to set forth with some fullness the gospel he had been preaching among the gentiles.

Our Epistle to the Romans is rightly regarded as the most important of the writings which have come down to us from the apostle. In sheer bulk, it is one of the longest. But its value to us depends much more upon the fact that in writing to a church which had no personal acquaintance with his preaching, Paul was under the necessity of setting forth more systematically than in other epistles, and with greater comprehensiveness, the gospel with which he had been entrusted, and which had proved to be the power of God in transforming the life of the ancient world.

It would seem that under such circumstances, Paul would be at his best. Since it was important that this most influential church should understand his gospel, Paul would write to them in terms they could understand. He who had forsworn all the devices of human wisdom that he might present Christ, and him crucified, would surely avoid all the dubious paths of subtle disputation so his readers should not be left bewildered in a maze of opposing theological points of view. The very fact that our Epistle to the Romans has given rise to so many radically different interpretations of "Paulinism," and is so far from being understood even to-day, should cause us to ponder the effect the reception of such an epistle would have had upon the Roman church. So far as the clarification of Christian thought is concerned, and the unification of diverse groups in the early church, the dispatch of such an epistle as lies before us could be nothing short of calamitous. Certainly many types of Christianity, from the most radical Hellenistic Mysticism, to the most conservative Judaistic Christianity, and the most thorough going substitutionary interpretations of redemption, find clear expression therein. We seem to face a most distressing dilemma, either that Christianity is not susceptible of a clear and intelligible exposition, or that Paul was incapable of understanding and expounding it. To many, of course, it will seem self-evident that inscrutability is a criterion of divinity, and that necessarily neither Paul nor anyone else will ever be able to understand or explain the gospel.

The phenomena presented to us by the Epistle to the Romans are fortunately capable of another and a much less dismaying explanation. Paul could and did understand his own gospel. He was not foolish enough to dispatch to Rome an epistle so ambiguous as to furnish the occasion of such endless and bitter disputes as might spring from the document so well known to us. Nothing is emerging with more clearness from our studies of the primitive church than the realization of the early diversity of Christian thought and practice, and the variety of the streams which ultimately converged and merged into the great river of Christian faith and theology. This diversity not only produced "sources" which looked at fundamental problems from the most contrary points of view, but very early developed a movement toward harmonization, which did not stop at the effort to legitimize its own points of view alongside others which it could not accept, but did not shrink from material modifications of inherited materials to bring them into line with what had become the orthodox pronouncements of the faith. Illustrations of this procedure can be freely supplied by all students of the process by which the gospels came into their present form, particularly the gospels of Luke and John.

That divergent viewpoints find expression in our epistle

will be abundantly demonstrated. Perhaps no competent scholar would care to deny that they are present. But since Pauline study has long been ruled by the more or less naïve assumption that all the materials that have come down to us in the major epistles are genuine, these complexities and contradictions have been taken to have been characteristic of Paul himself, an exhibition of the "manysidedness of the apostle's thought" which is the inevitable result of the inscrutability of his gospel.

The very importance of Romans for an understanding of Pauline thought and of Christianity itself should demand the most thorough investigation possible to determine whether the epistle as it lies before us is homogeneous, the product of the thought and preaching of one man, or whether there be evidence that the harmonistic tendency which later ruled the church has busied itself at the task of writing into this most important of Pauline letters viewpoints which were not only uncongenial, but even anathema to him.

For such an investigation there are available to us all the criteria and methods of historical and literary investigation. Their use is not only legitimate, but necessary. It is of the utmost importance, however, that the approach be truly inductive, and that the conclusions of the inquiry should be those dictated by the evidence presented by the phenomena encountered in the document, rather than those which grow out of subjective presuppositions, deductively enforced upon the understanding and interpretation of the epistle. The method upon which this study places its main reliance is that of an endeavor to keep steadily in mind the fundamental positions from which the argument of the epistle proceeds, and to estimate the congruity of a passage with these basic viewpoints, noting quickly any vacillation in the connotation of terms, or any modification of basic conceptions. These considerations are of particular importance when such topics are being considered as the basis and nature of the Christian life, or when the alleged vacillation or modification is in line with well known tendencies or movements within the early church as known to us from other sources.

It would seem important also to keep clearly in mind the only facts concerning Paul's epistle to the Romans which are known to us with any certainty, that is, that the apostle is writing a letter to a church whose members are unacquainted either with him or his message. While this cannot furnish us with certain criteria, its realization will enable us to reach judgments of greater or lesser probability as to what matters, and what tone or method of presentation, would be likely to have been included by the apostle in such a letter.

Our epistle readily breaks into three main sections. The second of these, chapters nine to eleven, is given to a discussion of the Rejection of Israel. This section seems to be independent of both of the others. It deals with a problem in the philosophy of history, or the philosophy of grace, and it is not integrated with either the situation known to exist in the Roman church, nor with the line of discussion running through the entire epistle. Whether it formed a part of the original letter of Paul to the Roman church or not, it may, at least for the purpose of study, be readily separated from it. These chapters deal with a single definite problem, and should present us with a homogeneous block of material. Such, however, is far from being the case. For in them, the argument proceeds from at least two fundamental points of view, one of which clearly appears to be tendentious.

Chapters twelve to sixteen constitute another separate section of the epistle. They are of a miscellaneous character; most of this material seems to deal with settled pastoral care of the church, rather than with the problem of establishing a favorable contact with a strange constituency. *excerpt from archives of Roman church.*

It is in the first eight chapters alone that we find material suitable to the declared purpose of Paul in writing to the Roman church, for in them alone does he attempt a systematic exposition of his understanding of the nature and basis of the Christian life, that is to say, of the gospel which he preached among the gentiles. In view of the importance that the Roman Christians should understand his gospel, and regard it sympathetically, it is in these chapters, if anywhere in the Pauline writing or preaching, that we should expect to find clarity, definiteness, the utmost possible simplicity, and above all an unwavering consistency in the exposition of a fundamental point of view. For if the trumpet give forth an uncertain sound, how would these Romans know what Paul thought or preached?

Even a superficial reading of these first eight chapters of the Epistle to the Romans should make evident what deeper study will insistently demand, that some analysis of these chapters, together with the elimination, or the virtual ignoring, of much material, must be made before any semblance of unity or consistency of viewpoint can be found. This analysis, together with the virtual setting aside of much material, is in fact made, even by the most casual reader, and is none the less actual because it is not consciously made. We merely attend to and stress those passages with which we are familiar, or with which we agree, while we are totally blind to all others, utterly oblivious of the fact that they deny categorically the fundamental presuppositions underlying the passages to which we do attend.

By some such process there has emerged what may be called the standard or traditional interpretation of the basic position of the Epistle to the Romans. It is that Paul first lays the foundation of the assertion of a universal sinfulness upon the part of both Jew and gentile, upon which he builds the assertion of the necessity of a blood sacrifice by virtue of which the "sinner" may be justified, that is "pronounced guiltless," and God may be justified in passing such a verdict upon him. No doubt many will be astonished to discover upon how little of the material such an interpretation rests, and how squarely it cuts across the tenor of much of the rest of these chapters.

When one regards chapters one to eight of Romans as a unit, and endeavors to discover a single theme running through them, it becomes evident that they are a discussion of the possibility of attaining righteousness, with especial reference to the means by which it may be attained, through the law, or through faith in Christ. In this discussion Paul holds that righteousness is attainable solely through faith in Christ; the character and content of that faith is specifically set forth; and because the law had been historically the means by which Israel had sought to obtain righteousness, and that, as she thought, in pursuance of God's revealed purpose, and in accordance with his solemn covenant, it must be shown that faith in Christ is not only God's real way of life, but that it is the realization of the basic intent of law and covenant, the substance of which they were but the shadow.

Fundamental to this discussion, in fact to Paul's purpose in writing to the Romans at all, was the exposition of that gospel which he held to be the power of God, that there was a righteousness which God had revealed, open to all alike upon the terms of faith in Christ, a faith which identified us with the dying Christ, in the crucifixion of the flesh, and with the risen Christ in rising with him to a new, Spirit filled life, in which, led by the Spirit, we fulfilled the ordinances of the law. In other words, Paul is here, as everywhere else, proclaiming the Galatian gospel, the one true way of life, than which there could be no other, even should that other be preached by himself, or by an angel from heaven.

Second in importance only to his purpose of proclaiming this one and only gospel, is the question of the relation of this gospel to the law, or rather to the historic attempt of Israel to attain to the righteousness of God through observance of the Mosaic Code. It was not only because Paul was himself a Jew, but even more because Christianity was an outgrowth of Judaism, that this question of law and gospel, of Jew and gentile, remained one of the most constant, and earnestly debated issues in the life of the early church. Much of the chaos which rules in the first eight chapters of Romans is due to the tension between opposing points of view which sought on the one hand to maintain the privilege of Israel, together with the superiority of her way of life, and on the other to establish the definitely Christian way of faith in Christ, and that in a clearly Hellenistic interpretation, as God's real and only requirement of man.

That this tension was particularly pronounced in the Roman church, whose Jewish sympathies must have been very strong, appears from even a superficial study of our present epistle. It is not at all difficult to establish from the epistle itself the intense interest in Jewish questions among Roman Christians. It has been thought that the church was made up principally of gentiles; Paul indeed speaks of having some fruit in them also, as in the rest of the gentiles. But the epistle is so saturated with Jewish valuations, and devotes so much of its content to the discussion of problems chiefly of interest to a Jewish constituency, that we must conclude that there was in Rome an intense interest in these Jewish questions.

This meets us in the very salutation to the letter, (i: 1-7), where great stress is laid upon the Jewish background of the gospel; it was promised beforetimes in the holy Scriptures through the prophets; Jesus was born of the seed of David according to the flesh. Since these matters are not introduced into the salutation of other letters from the hand of Paul, we must think that their presence here grows out of their importance, not to Paul himself, however great that may have been, but to those to whom he is writing.

The phrase in i: 16, "to the Jew first" may witness to the Jewish feeling of the Roman church; it may mean, "although you range yourselves among the Jews, rather than the gentiles, my gospel is still for you." It may have been added by some later hand as an assertion of the privilege of Israel. In any case, the Jew is given precedence over the gentile. Any comprehensive study of Paul's attitude and practice in this matter must reveal that he felt himself commissioned primarily, if not exclusively, to bear the gospel to the gentiles. Hence this reference must grow out of the interest of the Roman church.

In the latter half of the second chapter, and in the third, the argument is addressed specifically to the Jew. Its applicability to the Roman church would surely have been felt to be far stronger, if they felt themselves to be included in its reference, rather than excluded from it. Although the Jews are put into a subordinate position, it is suggested that their advantages had been very great. The appeal to the example of Abraham, in chapter four, who, although he was the father of the Jewish people, yet found justification through faith, rather than through the law with its accompanying circumcision, must have been much more persuasive if addressed to those whose basic assumptions were Jewish. Again, in chapter seven, we have a thorough discussion of the nature and status of the law. Although it is pointed out that it is ultimately inadequate, it is still spoken of as holy, just, and good. If anything could do so, this recognition of the goodness of the law would be calculated to soften what must to a Jewish minded group be the heavy blow struck by its rejection.

Chapters nine to eleven are given over entirely to a discussion of the problem of the Rejection of Israel. Keenly as Paul felt upon this question, its inclusion in Romans, certainly the great length at which it is here discussed, must bear witness rather to its importance in the eyes of the Roman Christians.

In chapter fourteen we encounter a discussion most easily understood against a Jewish background. While sabbatarianism is not necessarily involved, it is easily suggested by the question of the observance of one day above another; while the question of eating, or of abstinence, especially in connection with the definite statement that nothing is unclean in itself, cannot but recall those occasions in which Jewish dietary regulations had come into conflict with Christian principles, especially as those occasions had been related in the story of the encounter between Jesus and his Jewish adversaries, (Mark vii: 1-23), and also in the story of Peter's vision before going to preach to Cornelius, (Acts x: 9-16). We may readily understand that although these stories may have settled this question, or at least have reflected its settlement, so far as the church as a whole was concerned, it may still have persisted as a living issue in groups which were strongly Jewish in sympathy.

Christianity is categorically reduced to Jewish terms in xv: 8-13, where Jesus himself is said to be a minister of the circumcision for the truth of God, that he might confirm the promises given unto the fathers. The passage does, indeed, go on to say that in his name shall the gentiles hope, but this hope is defined as consisting in their subjection under Jewish rule, for there shall arise out of Jesse one to rule over them.

At this point of our study it need not be decided whether or not these passages are among the materials which have survived to us from the original letter of Paul to Rome. If they are his, they must testify to his conviction that Jewish problems were of great interest to Roman Christians; if, on the other hand, they have been added by later writers, their inclusion in our present epistle must bear witness to the persistence of powerful Jewish influences within the Roman church. This Jewishness of the Roman church would inevitably give rise to grave tension should Roman Christians be confronted with an essentially Hellenistic interpretation of the gospel.

Tensions in the early chapters of Romans have been widely and clearly recognized, but there has been no agreement in explaining them. These tensions have been taken by some as arising, not from specifically Roman problems, but from the great controversy between Paul and those opponents of his, commonly called Judaizers, who sought to wean his converts from faith in Christ and to cause them to adopt an essentially Jewish way of salvation. They think of Romans as having been addressed to no one church, but sent as an encyclical in which Paul sought to deal comprehensively and finally for the whole church with the entire question of the relation between Christianity and Judaism. This is in effect to recognize as fundamental to the epistle that which is merely its main subsidiary interest. Paul's fundamental purpose is the exposition of his gospel. In line with this mistaken interpretation of Romans is that most superficial estimate of the Apostle to the Gentiles which finds his chief significance in his liberation of the gospel from the shackles of Jewish legalism, which is a mere by-product of his essentially Hellenistic gospel. The stubborn fact apparently is that Paul wrote to Rome his own gospel, and that the tension was between his view of Christianity, and those which were held by the Roman church.

It would seem inadmissible to refer the tensions so evident in Romans to obscurities and contradictions in the mind of Paul. We are confronted with conceptions of the nature and basis of the Christian life, that is, with gospels, which issue from fundamentally different presuppositions, and which are incompatible with each other. Their presence is due to the conflicting currents in the thought and life of the early church which seem in Romans to have interpolated into an original Pauline epistle passages designed to supplement, or even to correct, points of view held to be inadequate or mistaken.

The salutation, (i: 1-7), is suspiciously long, diffuse, and encumbered with doctrinal matter. A study of the salutations of Pauline letters, and of what is properly included in a salutation, will lead us to challenge verses two to four. The function of a salutation is to establish relationship between the sender, and those who are to receive the letter; it adds a formal phrase to convey good wishes. In his surviving letters, Paul regularly adhered to this formula; none of them departs from it, even those whose authenticity may be suspected, with the exception of Titus, in which we find another long salutation largely given over to doctrinal elaboration, if not disputation, and of Galatians, where both the position of the doctrinal matter, after the salutation has really been finished, and the alien nature of the added material should lead to its unhesitating rejection. (See I Cor. i: 1-3; II Cor. i: 1, 2; Eph. i: 1, 2; Philippians i: 1, 2; Col. i: 1, 2; I Thess. i: 1; II Thess. i: 1, 2; I Tim. i: 1, 2; II Tim. i: 1, 2; Philemon 1-3.)

In all of these the salutation is brief, and contains merely the name of Paul, with those whom he wishes to associate with himself in the sending of the letter, the names of those to whom the letter is addressed, and the wish for grace and peace from God, the Father and the Lord, Jesus Christ. In many instances, Paul vindicates his apostleship, and thus his right to address them, by asserting that he is an apostle (called to be such), through the will of God. In Philippians he and Timothy are designated merely as servants of Jesus Christ, while in the Thessalonian letters, they have no designation at all. It is instructive to note that there is modification of this epistolary formula in the Pastoral Epistles. In I Tim. i: 1, Paul is an apostle "according to the commandment" of God, who is designated as "our Savior," and Christ Jesus, who is designated as "our hope." In II Tim. i: 1, Paul is an apostle through the will of God, "according to the promise of life which is in Christ Jesus." In Titus (i: 1-4), he is a servant of God, and an apostle of Jesus Christ "according to the faith of God's elect, and the knowledge of the truth which is in accordance with godliness, in hope of eternal life, which God, who cannot lie, promised before times eternal; but in his own seasons manifested his word in the message, wherewith I was entrusted according to the commandment of God our Savior." While we cannot here study this remarkable "salutation" in detail, we must remark that we have in it at least the hint of predestination, stress upon knowledge, the introduction of "godliness," a reference to Scripture prediction, a possible allusion to a mystery as long concealed, now revealed truth, and the definite Johannine expression of "eternal life."

The tendency to the elaboration of the salutation is the mark, not of a true letter, but of an "epistle," or of material used for the purposes of indoctrination and edification. The fact that Romans and Galatians, in their introduction of doctrinal matter into the salutation, do not agree with other genuine Pauline letters, but rather with the Pastorals, whose genuineness is so widely questioned, must cause us to look upon the doctrinal matter thus introduced with the strongest of suspicion. Such material would not occur to one who was on the point of writing a real letter, but at a time when the "epistles" were used as quasi-scriptural documents, their character as true letters would be lost sight of, and it would be a matter of indifference at what point doctrinal matter would be introduced.

In vss. 2-4 we meet with two definite points of view. The first is the endeavor to establish the Jewishness of the gospel. The gospel had been previously promised through the prophets in the Holy Scriptures. It had to do with Jesus, who was born of the seed of David according to the flesh. Christ is thus related closely to the fulfillment of Scripture and to the Jewish Messianic hope of a Son of David who was to come. It is quite interesting to note that such a viewpoint is in the Book of Acts made fundamental to the gospel which Paul preached, although no one would suspect it from Paul's own declarations. Nor does this point of view accord with the argument Paul later develops in this epistle to the Romans. For Christ is neither made to be the Messiah, nor is he the fulfillment of prophecy. The argument, so far as it contemplates the purpose of God for Israel, is that it has always been faith rather than law through which righteousness is to be obtained. By insisting upon the Jewishness of the gospel, this material in the salutation serves as a counterpoise to the idea later developed, that Jewish institutions and Jewish ways of life must be abandoned in favor of the gospel. It should be regarded as a Roman addition designed to soften the impact of Paul's Hellenistic gospel.

We meet with a second idea that Jesus was "declared to be the Son of God with power, according to the spirit of holiness, by the resurrection from the dead." This is to be regarded as a rudimentary Christology, later superseded by the mature development of Christian doctrine. It is frankly adoptionist, quite in line with the early Christology of the Roman church. There is, indeed, much Pauline color in its stress upon "power," and in its association of the resurrection with "the spirit of holiness." Christ, who was born of the seed of David according to the flesh, was established as the Son of God. The adoptionism of this Christology is obscured, perhaps dogmatically, by the translation "declared," although in the Revised Version, (American Standard), the translators are candid enough to call our attention in the margin to the fact that the meaning of the Greek is much stronger than a mere declaration of an existent fact. They suggest "determined." It was "by means of" the resurrection that Jesus passed the horizon of humanity, and became the Son of God.

While the evidence from this passage alone cannot suffice

to persuade us that these two dogmas, the Jewishness of the gospel, and the adoption of Christ, are not Pauline, their introduction into the salutation of a letter to a strange church, and their correspondence with viewpoints which may be demonstrated to have been characteristic of the Roman church, make it most probable that they are modifications of the original letter, which have been introduced by Roman thinkers to bring the original more into line with views held in the Roman church.

The deletion of these verses will leave us with a simple and appropriate salutation, quite in accord with the salutations found in most of the Pauline letters. In it there will be only the name and authority of Paul sending the letter, his justification for addressing the Roman church, the designation of those addressed, and the formal desire that they may have "grace and peace."

"Paul, a servant of Jesus Christ, called to be an apostle, separated unto the gospel of God, through whom we received grace and apostleship, unto obedience of faith among all the gentiles (or nations), for his name's sake; among whom are ye also, called to be Jesus Christ's: to all that are in Rome, beloved of God, called to be saints: Grace to you and peace from God our Father and the Lord Jesus Christ."

According to his custom, Paul follows the salutation with a paragraph (i: 8-15) in which he gives thanks for those things which he can commend in the life of those to whom he is writing. In this case it is their world renowned faith. But almost immediately he speaks of his constant prayer that he might come to them and preach to them as to others the gospel of Jesus.

Verse 14 seems somewhat curious in this context. Paul

justifies his ministry to them because he feels himself to be debtor to both Greek and barbarian, to both wise and foolish. He does not specify to which class the Romans belong. Is there here an implied rebuke, delicate in its sarcasm? You who think yourselves to be Greeks and wise are really barbarian and foolish. This may be taken to indicate a lack of tact upon the part of the apostle, whose presence is so abundantly evident in other connections, or it may testify to the existence in Rome from the first of an overweening pride and arrogance, which Paul felt that he must rebuke.

In this paragraph we find many of the most characteristic traits of Paul's writing. It is simple, direct, and clear. It grows so directly out of the concrete situation in which Paul finds himself that we have no difficulty whatever in reconstructing it. The sentences are short; there is no digression; no heaping up of relative clauses and participial constructions. This is Greek as Paul wrote it.

Verses 16 and 17 are almost universally taken to be the theme of Paul's letter to the Romans, although this insight is seldom rigorously applied. They are a simple and unequivocal statement of the nature and content of the Pauline gospel. It is a dynamic gospel, "the power of God." It is a gospel of faith. It consists in righteousness. It is of the utmost significance for the interpretation of Pauline thought that in this crucial passage Paul uses the word for "righteousness," and not the word for "justification." There is genius in the selection of the quotation from Scripture, "The righteous shall live by faith." Not "he who is pronounced righteous," but he who is really so. Not "shall be thought to live," but shall live.

Two features in these verses are worthy of discussion. The

first is the phrase, "to the Jew first," (i: 16). Upon the face of it, this phrase seems to be the assertion of the privilege of Judaism, of the precedence of Jew over Greek, and thus to be in line with the assertion of the Jewishness of the gospel, which we found to be a probable interpolation in the salutation. It may be an echo of the tendency of the book of Acts to make Paul preach to the Jews as long as they would hear him, and then turn in desperation to the gentiles only when it was evident that he had no further opportunity to preach to his own people. Unless it be here, there is no hint in Paul's own writings that such was his method. It is much more natural to see a reference to the historical sequence of Judaism-Christianity, and an assertion that even in Judaism salvation was by faith, in which righteousness was to be attained through the power of God. This is in line with the development of Paul's argument in chapter four. There is just a possibility that Paul is here referring to the Jewish sentiment which was characteristic of the Roman church. "You feel yourself to be Jews; but this gospel of faith, rather than of works, is still for you, for it is for Jews as well as for gentiles." But whatever may be the true meaning of this phrase, it is important to note that in it is raised the question of Jew and gentile, and that the precedence is given to the Jew.

The other feature in these verses worthy of discussion is the phrase "from faith unto faith," (i: 17). It is hard to find an intelligible meaning in this phrase. It is impossible to integrate it with the context. Neither here nor elsewhere is anything made of the concept that faith is the end, or issue of the Christian life, as well as its beginning. Its issue is righteousness. Paul's true thought is "by faith unto righteousness." It is by faith that we obtain the righteousness which God reveals. From whatever viewpoint it may be regarded, it would seem that the expression "unto faith" must be deleted. It may be thought to be an accidental corruption of the text. Whether it was so intended or not, the insertion of these two apparently harmless words functions as a total obscuration of two fundamental aspects of the Pauline gospel. The first is that faith alone is the basis of a righteous life. It tends to destroy the instrumental significance of the Greek preposition here employed, giving it a sense of spatial direction, "from—to," instead of "by means of," which is clearly demanded by the quotation, the righteous shall live by means of faith. It also tends to divert attention from Paul's insistence that faith shall issue in actual righteousness. For moral victory is substituted the theological abstraction, "from faith unto faith." It would seem to be of little moment whether the insertion of these words be accidental or intentional; they have no proper place in the development of Paul's thought.

In verses 18-32 we reach a passage which is crucial for the interpretation not only of the first chapter, but also of the entire epistle. It is commonly taken with iii: 9-18, and 23-26 as the fundamental standpoint from which Paul expounded his basic idea of salvation. Since verse 9 of chapter three says specifically, "We have before laid to the charge both of Jews and Greeks that they are all under sin," chapter i: 18-32 is taken to be a catalog of the sins of the gentile world, of which all gentiles are guilty. If there be any value in the methods and criteria of literary criticism, it would seem that the diction and structure of this material, as well as the fundamental viewpoint from which it is written, would cause us to regard it with the strongest of suspicion. We suddenly encounter a long string of alpha privative words, more than one to the verse. In structure the materials are argumentative, very closely knit together by the particles, "for," "because," "wherefore." The basic approach to religion and life is definitely intellectual. The gentiles ought to have known, for they had been given plenty of evidence, but they held or hindered (the translation is immaterial) the truth in unrighteousness. The invisible things of God, his everlasting power and divinity, are clearly seen and perceived, but men became vain in their reasonings, and their senseless heart was darkened. Wherefore God gave them up to a reprobate mind, because they refused to have God in their knowledge, but rather exchanged the truth of God for a lie. It is true that the result of this error was not only idolatry, but the most shocking and degrading immorality. But moral values are only the fruit, intellectual values are fundamental to both religion and life.

This does not seem to be at all the point of view from which Paul approached these fundamental questions. It was not the defect of the law that it failed to give adequate knowledge. On the contrary it enabled one to know and to approve excellent things. Its failure really lay without the sphere of the law itself, in the inability of the flesh to act according to the adequate knowledge which it gave. In other words, the fundamental religious problem was moral and spiritual rather than intellectual.

It is in the Pastorals rather than in the genuine Pauline epistles that we find this same intellectual approach to religion. Although the phrase is from Jude, religion is to the Pastorals "the faith once for all delivered to the saints," a body of truth traditionally preserved and mediated. Men are to come to a knowledge of the truth, which seems to be sound doctrine, over against which are questionings, fables, genealogies. The church is the pillar and ground of the truth. Repentance may be unto a knowledge of the truth; the Scripture makes us wise unto salvation. The Pastorals do, indeed, value morality, but it is apparently something to be added to sound doctrine, a knowledge of the truth. The same point of view is to be found in Second Thessalonians.

The affinity with the Pastorals further appears in that we have in I Tim. i: 9, 10, and in II Tim. iii: 2-4 catalogs of sins, or listed indictments similar to that found in Romans i: 29-32. The one in II Tim. iii: 2-4 is quite like the one in Romans, containing four identical items, "without natural affection," "boastful," "haughty," "disobedient to parents." There is also in the list noticed in II Tim. a very high proportion of alpha privative words.

Our suspicion of the genuineness of Romans i: 18-32 is confirmed by the fact that even this body of material seems composite. There is a complete break at verse 29. Up to this point the indictment is from the standpoint of natural religion. Failing to respond, primarily from the intellectual point of view, to the revelation of God in nature, that is, to the demands of natural religion, men have been charged with error, idolatry, and gross immorality. But in verse 29 both content and basis of the indictment have been radically altered. No longer in question are the unnatural, perverted, sexual enormities of verses 24, 26, 27; they have been replaced by a long list of moral derelictions, none of them sexual; no longer in question is man's failure to respond to the demands of natural religion; the demands are now those of revealed religion. These moral derelictions are violations of the ordinance of God. These verses are much more in keeping with the Jewish point of view in religion than are verses 18-28.

The connection of verses 29-32 with the sentence in which they occur is the slightest possible; they are a participial phrase, such as may be attached anywhere, followed by a relative clause.

These materials, Romans i: 18-32, exhibit the characteristics relied upon by form critics for recognition of the smaller units of which composite documents are made up. They are a boulder, whose substance and structure is so different from the stratum in which they occur that their disparity is apparent to the most casual examination. It will be shown by the subsequent development of Paul's argument that these materials are utterly incompatible with the line of thought basic to the early chapters of Romans. This incompatibility with Paul's train of thought, together with their affinity with later points of view, and with later materials, as found in the Pastorals, should be conclusive that they have been added by a later hand.

In chapter two, verses 2-10 seem to be a continuation of the Jewish point of view from which verses 29-32 of chapter one were written. They show also an affinity with the intellectual viewpoint of verses 18-28. It is a question of obedience to the truth, or obedience to unrighteousness. The Jewish flavor of the passage is seen in that its basic idea is that of rewards or punishments which are stored up to await the day of God's judgment. Anyone with Jewish sympathies could have written it. It is certainly incompatible with the idea that in Romans we have the assertion of a universal sinfulness, for verse 7 speaks of those who are patient in well doing, and verse 10 speaks of glory, and honor, and peace, to every man that worketh good. This in itself should be sufficient to dispose of the contention that in Romans i-iii Paul laid the foundation of a universal sinfulness upon the part of all. This material is not Pauline. It seems to be a homiletic gloss, tied in by "judge," and "judgment," and "practise such things." Its lateness should appear from its basically intellectual approach as seen in obedience to truth, in its stress upon corruption, and incorruption, and the Johannine expression, "eternal life."

It is in chapter ii that Paul begins the development of his theme, which has been greatly obscured by the presence of later interpolations. He rebukes the man who judges another, but practices the same things for which he has condemned this other one. A determination of the connotation of basic terms is here absolutely indispensable to an understanding of the passage. Who is it that condemns? and who is condemned? Having recognized verses 2-10 as a homiletic gloss and set it aside, we do not have to read far to discover that it is the Jew who condemns, and the gentile who is condemned. And the whole point of Paul's argument is that the Jew is not justified in condemning the gentile.

The Jew prided himself upon the fact that he was a Jew, a member of the chosen race; he had the law, thus knowing the will of God; he approved the things that were excellent. Because of all of this he set himself up as the teacher of all mankind. And the gentiles? This people who had not the law were accursed. But all this was not enough. It is not the man who has the law who is just before God; it is not he who is instructed out of the law, nor even he who in his arrogance and self-conceit attempts to instruct others. It is the one who does the law who is just before God. (ii: 17-25.)

And this leads Paul to what must have seemed to the Jew a most extraordinary statement. They would perhaps have been willing to follow him in his contrast between the outward insincere Jew who had all the external marks of Judaism, attendance upon the synagogue, circumcision, but who did not obey the ordinances of the law, and the one who was a true Jew. The whole tenor of the chapter forces us to see that Paul held that while there were some who were inwardly Jews, having a circumcision of the heart, not of the flesh, and who won the approval of God rather than of men, because of their real obedience to the commands of the law, still most of the Jews fell far short of reaching this high standard.

But into this discussion of the true Jew and the false, Paul has woven the statement whose acceptance must have seemed to the Jews like swallowing a camel, that although they did not have the law, the gentiles were not for that reason to be condemned; for God had given to them a law written in their hearts, which led them to the goal of a true righteousness, a doing of the thing which God demanded. (ii: 26-29.)

The real theme which Paul is discussing is the contrast between the false righteousness of the Jew and the true righteousness of the gentile. Although the Jew, from the standpoint of his possession of the law, felt himself so superior to the gentile that he could both instruct and condemn him, there was no respect of persons with God. But because the Jew did not keep the law he taught, his circumcision which he so greatly prized became as uncircumcision, and the name of God was blasphemed. On the other hand, the gentile, handicapped as he was because he did not have the law, still seemed to have been actuated by an inner principle which led him by nature to do the things which the law commanded. Not only did he by this win the approval of his own conscience, but his uncircumcision was reckoned as circumcision, and because he was a doer of the things which the law commanded, he was enabled to judge the Jew, who in spite of both the letter of the law, and of circumcision, was yet a transgressor of the law.

In all of this it should be abundantly clear that with Paul nothing can take the place of a real righteousness, which consists in an actual doing of the law. The only justification which he can recognize consists in being just. The modern interpretation of justification as being "pronounced righteous" must have been very pleasing to the Jew who would wish the external marks of God's favor to suffice, and to allow him to be pronounced righteous without having to meet the rigorous test of an actual conformity to God's commands. Morality is alike the most difficult and the most inescapable demand which religion makes upon man. To make Paul's idea of justification a verdict "not guilty," apart from the radical transformation of nature and conduct which would necessitate that verdict as the statement of a fact, is to give of him what he would call a slanderous report.

It should be equally clear that Paul's whole discussion is upon the basis of a present reality, not upon a judgment hereafter to be passed. Anyone could see the difference between the real Jew and the false, because the real Jew was a good Jew, who obeyed God's commands. And the same standard of present conduct values was to be applied to the gentile. There is not the slightest hint that distinctions among men rest upon unseen and undiscoverable tendencies, whose real outcome and effect can be seen only in the day of judgment. This consideration alone should place verses 2-10 outside the orbit of the chapter.

And even he who runs should be able to read this chapter with sufficient understanding to see that it does not grow out of a fundamental conviction that all, both Jew and Greek, are sinners. Paul is very careful to separate the good from the bad, the sheep from the goats. How could he be stupid enough to attempt such a thing if he were convinced that there were no sheep? It is impossible by any trick of exegesis to expunge from the chapter the basic idea that there were true, righteous Jews, who had won the approval of God, and that there were those among the gentiles who had put the Jews to shame, because they had kept the law. With this ii: 11-15 is in fundamental agreement; the gentiles had kept the law.

Verse 16, which attempts to make a unity out of the entire present passage can really do no more than to exhibit its disunity and the expedient to which one must resort to give it even the semblance of coherence. It has all the appearance of stitches inserted by a surgeon in the attempt to mend an almost hopeless laceration in the flesh of his patient. In verses 11-15 the contrast is between those who have the law, and those who have it not; these latter, the gentiles, act in accordance with an inner principle, and their conscience sits in judgment upon their actions. But verses 2-10 have been speaking of men living now lives of righteousness or wickedness which will ultimately be judged in the Great Day. Verse 16 apparently brings these two passages together. But it can do so only by suppressing the present witness of conscience in favor of the judgment as seen in verses 2-10. And while he is at it the editor has modified the Jewish color of verses 2-10 by making the judgment Christian rather than Jewish; the secrets of men are to be judged according to the gospel, but through Jesus Christ.

In the third chapter we have a continuation of the basic line of discussion. The Jewish attempt to attain righteousness has failed, but this does not mean that righteousness is unattainable. There is a true righteousness such as the gentiles have exhibited. But it is to be attained only through faith. The clarity and simplicity of the argument have been obscured by the intrusion of alien matter in verses 9-18, and 23-26. It is by no means certain that these alien passages have been merely inserted into Paul's original writing; there may have been some excisions as well as insertions. But after the insertions have been set aside, the remaining material still makes sense, and exhibits Paul's fundamental point of view.

The chapter begins with an evident answer to some one who objects to Paul's having set aside the privilege of Israel. What then was the use of being a Jew? or what was the advantage of circumcision? It was great. The Jew had been entrusted with the oracles of God. It was his want of faith (which must here have the connotation of obedience), which had made these privileges of none effect. God had been sincere. An examination of the entire question could but result in the decision that it was man's failure to obey that was alone responsible for his condemnation. It might thus appear that whenever the question of human transgression was examined the result would be the exhibition of human unworthiness, against which the purity and goodness of God would by contrast shine with all the greater brilliance. Would God in that case be justified in punishing the sinner? Would it not on the contrary be to his advantage to have a few sinners even in heaven to act as foils to his righteousness? Paul seems to have been quoted as saying that we should do evil that good might result. This whole point of view is blasphemous; all who so argue are justly condemned, (iii: 1-8).

Paul's basic viewpoint is clear. The law had been sincerely given. It should have been obeyed. It was solely the failure of man to keep the commandment that brought disaster. The discussion is resumed in verse 19, in which the realistic view is taken that the law had not been obeyed; no flesh was to be justified by the works of the law; the law had merely brought the knowledge of sin. That is to say, it had made very evident what was right and what was wrong. Ultimately it had failed, because it had not been obeyed. No other interpretation can be given to Paul's expression that some were without faith. This cannot mean that they did not believe what God had said in the law; otherwise the law would not have brought knowledge of sin. For if they had not believed what God had said in the law, every moral question would have been open to discussion. It is only when the law is regarded as the word of God that it can bring knowledge of sin.

Verse 19b is evidently a later universalizing gloss. The verse begins with the statement that we know that whatsoever the law saith it speaketh to them that are under the law, that every mouth may be stopped. The law had made very evident what was right and what was wrong, so that Jews, those to whom the law was given, could not plead that they had done the best they knew. There were no mitigating circumstances. But 19b utterly disregards the historic fact upon which 19a had insisted, that the law was given to the Jews. It makes it the function of the law to bring all the cosmos under the judgment of God. The failure of the Jew is broadened into the failure of all mankind, and even, to press the connotation of cosmos, of the heavens and all that in them is. From the line of argument it is quite clear that the law had not been given to the cosmos. What advantage had the Jew? He had the law, which set him aside from all. But this law was given to the whole cosmos. The Jew was then set aside from all by virtue of the fact that to him had been given a law which had been given to all. Is it any wonder that we still find Paul hard to understand?

It is in verses 21 and 22 that we reach the turning point in the argument of the epistle. It does not follow that, since the Jew has failed to obtain righteousness through the law, righteousness cannot be obtained. It is impossible upon the face of the argument Paul uses to interpret him as teaching that the utter failure of man is necessary before God can intervene for salvation. Righteousness has not been reached through law. Is there then no possibility of reaching it? The materials found in i: 18-32, iii: 9-18, 23-26, maintain that there is not. There is none that doeth good; sin has been laid to the charge of all. This is a complete denial of the Pauline gospel.

For essential to that gospel is the assertion that righteousness may be attained. God has revealed a righteousness apart from law. It is a righteousness which comes through faith in Jesus. It has been witnessed by both law and prophets; it has been God's unchanging way of dealing with men. It is available to all alike upon the same terms. There can then be no glorying or boasting, such as the Jew would be guilty of, "I belong to God's people; I have his law." For God is God of the gentile as well as of the Jew. He will deal with both alike; righteousness is possible to all who have faith. And God will justify both Jew and gentile by faith, and by faith alone, (iii: 21, 22, 27-30).

It should be impossible in this context to discuss justification by faith apart from the realization that the fundamental theme of the passage is that of the attainment of righteousness. Although the Jew did not attain righteousness through the law, it can be attained, by Jew and gentile alike, through faith. To anticipate further developments, it remains only to show that this has always been the way God has dealt with men, even under the covenant and the law, and finally to exhibit the nature of that faith through which we become righteous. It is an utter misrepresentation of Paul's basic position to hold that he teaches that the Jew has not attained righteousness; neither has the gentile; but God will "justify" unrighteous men. His position is rather that through faith both Jew and gentile may become righteous, so that "the ordinance of the law is fulfilled in us," (viii: 4).

The dogmatic assertion of the universal sinfulness of humanity and of the necessity of providing some other way than the attainment of righteousness for man's salvation is the burden of iii: 9-18, and of iii: 23-26. With these i: 18-32 may be integrated, while the gloss in iii: 19b looks in the same direction. iii: 9-18 are a most impressive catalog of quotations designed to show both the enormity and the universality of human iniquity. While it is no doubt true that there are some men whom this description might fit, it is absurd to think that it applies to all. It will no doubt be recalled that when Job remained adamant in the assertion of his innocence, his "comforters" were in their desperation, faced as they were with the necessity of upholding a universal theory in the face of a patent exception to it, driven to turn upon him and accuse him of the most absurd and revolting of crimes. By reason of its very failure to conform to reality dogmatism is frequently, through the necessity of its attempt to maintain itself, driven to the greatest of exaggerations. But even a theologian should realize that when he is in an argument driven to overstatement, this is an indication that his case is lost.

Verses 23-26 form the climax to the argument of the interpolated passages. There is no possibility of attaining righteousness, all have sinned. God must thus abandon his original goal of making men righteous, and address himself to making the most of the situation in which it has been found that his original purpose cannot be achieved. The crux of Paul's discussion is that God has revealed a righteousness which men may obtain through faith. But in this passage God is made to reveal his own righteousness. This consists in the fact that he has provided a propitiation in the blood of Jesus, by virtue of which he is enabled to pass over the sins done aforetime, and himself be just, the while he is justifying him who has faith in Jesus. (iii: 23-26.)

It will pay us to examine closely the presuppositions of this remarkable passage. Looked at from the standpoint of the orthodoxy which later came to rule the church, this passage is not at all remarkable. It is a simple, straight-forward statement of the position of the church that redemption is the center and the essence of Christianity, indeed of all religion. The essence of the Old Testament was not the commands of the law, but the institution of sacrifice, especially blood sacrifice; the central figure in the Old Covenant was not the prophet, but the priest. The benefit of the gospel is not to be found in righteousness, but in "justification."

But in the context in which it occurs, this passage is indeed remarkable; for it has modified, if not utterly perverted, the basic connotation of every term employed. This clearly appears when we examine the term righteousness. In Paul's discussion righteousness is something which the Jew had failed to attain through the law, but which God had made it possible for all to obtain by other means. Since that is not congenial to the dogma of universal depravity, this passage uses the term righteousness, but makes it apply to God, since it cannot apply to man. God showed himself righteous. For man, "justification" is substituted for righteousness, since it is self-evident that man cannot be righteous.

The perversion of the term "faith" is equally evident. In the Pauline discussion, faith is the means by which one may become righteous. But in this passage it has become "faith in his blood." This can mean nothing else than the acceptance of the substitutionary death of Jesus. God has provided a way other than righteousness. This seems to occasion some qualms of conscience in the mind of the interpolator. Can God be just, and yet "justify" man?

This discussion of the righteousness of God is entirely unnecessary from the Pauline point of view. It is very doubtful whether Paul could feel himself under the necessity of writing a theodicy, or "justifying" God. God's faithfulness has seemed to him so axiomatic that when it is questioned, he can but cry out, "God forbid!" There is a fundamental fallacy in every theodicy; and that fallacy does not consist in any error that may occur in the chain of reasoning by which we try to extricate God from his difficulty, or to apologize for his dereliction. The fallacy is to be sought in the train of thought which has led us to believe that God has been guilty of something reprehensible. God has never been in the well; all discussion as to how he got in, or who will get him out, is alike futile and stupid.

But it does not seem so to this interpolator. Except he had set forth a propitiation in the blood of Jesus, God could not have "justified" the one who had faith in Jesus. How different is the Pauline point of view! He has been talking of the attainment of righteousness. Although not attained by the keeping of the law, God has revealed a righteousness apart from law which is attained through faith in Jesus. Without anticipating the discussion of the sixth, seventh, and eighth chapters, in which it is pointed out what this faith in Jesus is, and how by faith in him, one becomes righteous, it is imperative here to point out that by faith we do attain righteousness. There can then be no problem in "justification," nor need it be apologized for. Our interpolator should have realized that what man will not do without rationalizing or making some excuse for, God will not do at all. The only thing that will lead God to pronounce a man righteous, is that, through faith in Jesus, he has become righteous.

It is hard to see how there could be more diametrical opposition in fundamental points of view than those contained in the main body of the discussion, and in i: 18-32, and iii: 9-18, 23-26. On the one hand it is maintained that man may become righteous, only it is insisted that this must be through faith in Jesus rather than by works of the law. On the other hand it is maintained that man cannot become righteous; all are sinners; there must be a blood sacrifice accepted by faith, by reason of which God can "pronounce guiltless." It would seem impossible to hold that both of these points of view were held by Paul. The establishment of either will necessarily exclude the other. Which is genuine must be determined by a thorough study of the Pauline gospel as set forth in each of his epistles.

In the fourth chapter the discussion basic to Paul's argument is again to the fore. In it we are dealing with both questions, those of race and of the means by which righteousness is obtained, the questions of law or faith, and of circumcision and uncircumcision. Abraham may be thought of both as the father of his people, and as illustrating the ideal in religious experience. Perhaps the former was of the greater importance to the Jew. He felt himself a child of Abraham, because of that fact he had the law, and in circumcision he bore in his very flesh the seal of God's covenant with his own. But for Paul it is as the ideal of a religious experience in which all may share that Abraham's real importance appears.

Paul's appeal to the experience of Abraham has greatly obscured the whole question of "justification by faith," although it seems that this obscuration has been quite unnecessary. The confusion has been added to by interpolated materials, the removal of which will greatly illumine the whole problem. In the passage from Genesis to which Paul appeals, there are two points, one of which is vital to his entire position, and the other of no significance whatever. As we "interpret" Paul, we are so true to his thought that we lay very heavy emphasis upon the point to which he has himself attached no significance, the while we make nothing of the point for whose sake he has cited the passage.

Paul's entire point is that the religious experience which came to Abraham came before he was circumcised. In circumcision we are at once face to face both with Jewish pretensions, and with the question of justification by works of the law. When the spurious materials have been recognized and removed, it will be seen that the whole chapter is given over to the assertion that blessedness came to Abraham by virtue of the faith which he had before he was circumcised; that circumcision, far from being the means by which he attained, was merely the seal of the faith which he had had while he was still uncircumcised. It follows that circumcision is not necessary, otherwise the promise would have been of no effect, and that, therefore, the blessing of Abraham is not confined to his children, who like him are circumcised, but that the promise is sure to all who walk in the steps of that faith which he had while still in uncircumcision, even to us "who believe on him that raised Jesus our Lord from the dead, who was delivered up for our trespasses, and was raised for our justification."

It is by no means accidental that we have in verses 24 and 25 an allusion to the content of Christian faith, nor that this content finds its central emphasis in our faith that Jesus died and rose again, and that his death was for trespasses, while his resurrection was for "justification." This is another diametrical contradiction of the idea in iii: 23-26 that the death of Christ availed for justification. Paul is still wrestling with the problem of convincing the Jewish minded Roman church that the type of righteousness characteristic of the gentiles is legitimate.

In the passage in Genesis to which Paul alludes, there is another point to which Paul has attached no significance, but which commentators both ancient and modern have singled out as the essence of his purpose in making the allusion. This is that Abraham's faith "was reckoned for righteousness." It is unquestionable that the Old Testament language does contain the word "reckon." But it should be equally unquestionable that Paul makes no point whatever of this "reckoning." He is entirely concerned with the priority of the promise to the law, not with the process by which Abraham became righteous. It was by faith, but there is no attempt here to explain the nature or the content of faith, nor to explain how faith can issue in righteousness. The content of faith is alluded to in verses 24 and 25; it is fully expounded later in the epistle.

Verses 4-8 undoubtedly contain a modification of Paul's argument from the later point of view which we have found to be expressed in iii: 23-26. In what is the essence of Abraham's experience to be found? From all that Paul has been saying up to this point, namely that righteousness is to be attained, but through faith, not by works, we must see the essence of Abraham's experience in the attainment of righteousness through faith. But in the material quoted in verses 7 and 8 from the 32nd Psalm, the essence of Abraham's experience is in the forgiveness of sin. This is as alien to the purport of the account given in Genesis of Abraham's experience as it is to the tenor of Paul's argument. There has been a rather clumsy attempt to integrate the quotation with its context in the introductory formula, "Even as David also pronounceth blessing upon the man unto whom God reckoneth righteousness apart from works, saying, Blessed are they whose iniquities are forgiven, etc." Upon examination it appears that there is no connection between the material quoted, and the situation to which it is made to apply other than the occurrence of the word "reckon." By means of this quotation the interpolator has attempted to write the definition, "Righteousness consists in the forgiveness of sin." This is a perversion not only of the Pauline conception, but also of the Psalm from which the quotation is taken, which reads, "Blessed is the man to whom Jehovah imputeth not iniquity, and in whose spirit there is no guile." There is no question here of "justifying the ungodly," but it is assumed that the Lord recognizes the purity of heart of the one with whom he is dealing. Iniquity is not imputed to him, because in him there is no guile. The Psalm ends with "But he that trusteth in Jehovah, lovingkindness shall compass him about. Be glad in Jehovah, and rejoice, ye righteous; and shout for joy, all ye that are upright in heart." Here trust in the Lord seems to make men happy and good; righteousness does not consist in the forgiveness of sin.

The incompatibility of this quotation from the Psalms with its context is shown by the awkwardness with which verse 9 follows upon verse 8. When discussing the forgiveness of sin, there is neither Jew nor gentile; there are only sinners. The real point at issue is whether Abraham attained by reason of circumcision, which is closely associated with the law, or without circumcision and the law. Verse 9 follows directly upon verse 3. To Abraham it was reckoned for righteousness. The important point is "Was this blessing due to faith? or to law? May it accrue only to those who are circumcised? or to the uncircumcised as well?"

From this it should appear that verses 4 and 5 are probably also interpolated. A case might be made for verse 4 as part of Paul's argument, but verse 5 is certainly alien. For the interpolator has given his hand away by referring to Abraham as an ungodly man. It will be objected that this verse is not thinking of Abraham at all. Probably not; but Paul was. It is characteristic of annotators to forget the point at issue. The verse is written from the later generalized theological point of view, "All men are sinners; faith consists in believing upon him that justifieth the ungodly; the result is the forgiveness of sins." It is only by forgetting Abraham and his experience entirely that such a point can be made.

Verse 15 is quite evidently alien to its context. Verse 16 follows immediately upon verse 14; the elimination of 15 giving continuity and sense to the passage. What was it that made it possible for all, Jew and gentile, the circumcised and the uncircumcised, to become heirs? Simply the fact that when Abraham attained it was prior to circumcision and the giving of the law; hence these could not be required for the attainment of righteousness. Any discussion of the nature and function of the law is quite incompatible with the discussion of the case of Abraham, for whatever the character of the law may be, it was at the time of Abraham non-existent. Perhaps the best that can be said for this verse is that it has been displaced. It would cohere much better with the material in v: 12-21.

It would appear that in verses 17-22 there is an attempt to explain the nature of faith. This paragraph is in reality a little midrash on the birth of Isaac. It is most suspicious to find God referred to as one "who giveth life to the dead." The next item "calleth the things that are not as though they were" is entirely congruous with the discussion of the birth of one not yet conceived. But giving life to the dead would never have been suggested by the circumstances of the birth of Isaac. It might well be taken from the genuine Pauline definition of faith which occurs in verse 24, our faith is in him who raised Jesus from the dead. The Pauline connotation of faith in the resurrection of Jesus will appear later. Resurrection in this passage is merely the illustration of something impossible.

This paragraph is an example of Christian Haggadah. It is redolent of a crude or degenerated type of faith. Faith is believing what God says, especially if it is hard to believe. The harder it is, the greater the faith. Faith can reach its climax only in the acceptance of the impossible. Hence the building up of the insistence upon the physical aspects of the miracle. Abraham was about a hundred years old; and

Sarah had long since passed the climacteric. It was the impossibility of the thing that made it divine. But Abraham wavered not through unbelief, but waxing strong through faith he was "fully assured." It should of course be entirely unnecessary to point out that this view of faith has nothing whatever in common with the faith which is "believing upon him that justifieth the ungodly." This annotator has at least not blundered into making Abraham an ungodly man. Verse 22 is a crude and violent attempt to bring the argument back to the track it has long since jumped.

The genuine Pauline argument finds its fitting conclusion in verses 23-25, and chapter v: 1, 2a. The meaning of Abraham's experience is not confined to Abraham; it was rather typical of the experience that may come to all of us, irrespective of law and of circumcision, by sheer faith in him who raised Jesus from the dead, who was delivered up for our trespasses, and raised again for our justification. Being therefore, (because Abraham was "justified by faith," or because "Jesus was delivered up for our trespasses and raised again for our justification"—the latter can certainly not be excluded), justified by faith, we have, or should have, peace with God through our Lord Jesus Christ, through whom we have access by faith to this grace in which we stand. This is an accomplished fact; there is no hint that we have merely the expectation of something which shall happen to us in the future.

Practically the whole of chapter v must be pronounced spurious. Verses 1, 2a, may well be Pauline. They speak tranquilly of a present experience of grace and peace. But in verse 2b, there is a violent swinging away from the orbit of Pauline thought. There is, first, the definite substitution of hope for grace. There is no real meaning in present experience. All religion can do is to help us bear the afflictions of the present knowing that they are the first step of a process which leads through tribulation to steadfastness, through steadfastness to approvedness, through approvedness to hope. The pessimism of this point of view should be quite evident; we are pilgrims through a sad and weary land; all we can have here below is hope, and the Spirit to shed abroad the love of God in our hearts.

The difference from the Pauline conception of the function of the Spirit is too clear to be mistaken. In Pauline thought the Spirit is the power that dwells within us, and gives the power of triumphant attainment. The fruits of the Spirit are love, joy, peace. Here there is no hint of power or of attainment.

The love of God is manifested in that Christ died for us. This is built up to a rather labored climax by a discussion of the relative merits of dying for the righteous, the good, or the sinner. It is not at all like Paul thus ploddingly to strain after effects.

It will be seen that the fundamental point of view which gives us the key to the interpretation of this passage is that of the interpolated materials in iii: 9-18, 23-26. We are sinners; we are justified by his blood, which God has set forth as propitiatory; we were enemies, but we are now reconciled to God through the death of his Son. There may be a faint Pauline coloring in the expression "we shall be saved by his life." But this expression has been buried so deeply beneath the accretions of the passage that there is not the slightest hint that we are saved by his life by virtue of the fact that by identifying ourselves with him we live the new, spiritual, righteous life, which corresponds to his risen life. This passage is typically sub-Pauline because it reproduces Pauline phraseology, with no understanding of Pauline meaning, but rather with the effect, whether intentional or unintentional, of an utter obscuration or denial of Pauline connotation.

It should be noted that one of the unfortunate distinctions in the interpretation of Pauline thought, that between justification and salvation, may derive some help and comfort from this passage. Being now justified, we shall be saved. Perhaps a stricter analysis of the material would reveal that it also holds that "being reconciled, we shall be saved." It would, therefore equate justification with reconciliation. But, since "justification" is supposed to have to do with God's attitude toward us, that is, he pronounces us not guilty, while "reconciliation" is supposed to have to do with our attitude toward God, this seeming equation of justification with reconciliation can but introduce confusion into the interpretation of "Paulinism."

This passage has seemed to pervert the basic connotation of every term employed. Salvation is not the attainment of righteousness, but deliverance from the wrath to come. It does not consist in a present triumphant victory over evil but merely in the hope that after the tribulations of this life there remains an expectation of the glory of God. We are to be saved by the blood of Christ, not through mystic identification with him. The function of the Spirit is not to be an indwelling power that makes for righteousness, but merely to shed abroad in our hearts the love of God. This would appear to refer to an emotional, rather than to a dynamic experience. Faith does not even appear in the entire passage.

All of this is a far cry from the discussion basic to these early chapters of Romans, that is that righteousness is to be attained, but not through the Jewish method of works, which had signally failed, but through faith in Christ.

If v: 12-21 had been found adrift upon the stream of tradition, we should be much more likely to have referred it to Hebrews, rather than to any Pauline document. It has the same interest in typology, and the same quite modest degree of intellectual penetration. The attempt to reduce it to logical consistency is hopeless. What its author is trying to establish is something like this: Men are sinners by the very fact that they are human; Adam was a type; or rather he was so closely united physically to his descendants that they inherited his sin. Hence all participate in Adam's sin, and in death, which is the consequence of sin. Christ is likewise a type; or rather men are so closely united to him, it would seem also physically, that they share in his righteousness, and in life which is the consequence of righteousness.

But this line of reasoning, simple, clear, and compelling, if the premise of physical participation is granted, labors under serious difficulties. There is an irreconcilable conflict between the idea that death is the consequence of sin, and all are sinners, and the idea that sin is the transgression of the Mosaic law. Before Moses there was no law, and therefore no transgression, and therefore no "imputation" of sin. But they were all sinners, anyway; they died, therefore they must have sinned; but they couldn't have sinned, because there was no law. In other words, they were sinners without sin, guilty without guilt.

There is the further hopeless difficulty that if we are to make Christ the source of righteousness as we have made Adam the source of sin, all must necessarily share in the righteousness of Christ, even as all have shared in the sin of Adam. There is, of course, a minor premise whose inser-

tion will enable us to escape one horn of the dilemma, only to
impale us remorselessly upon the other. If we make this participation in the benefits of Christ to depend upon our own
choice of faith, it will follow that only those who have faith
in Christ will share in the justification of life which came
through him. But that will destroy the parallel between
Adam and Christ, for the sake of drawing which the whole
passage was written. For then only those could participate
in the guilt of Adam who through their own choice followed
in his steps. There can be no parallel between that which is
on one hand universal, and on the other limited. Nor can
there be any parallel between that which is automatic and
physical, and that which is due to spiritual choice.

Our author has tried to make the benefits of Christ even
greater than the curse which came through Adam. The effect of Adam's sin was universal; it extended to all mankind.
But while sin abounded, grace did much more abound. The
implications of the universalism of righteousness and justification cannot be dodged by pleading that our author refers
to "the many" as sharing therein; for it is also "the many"
who share in the taint of Adam. "The many" were made
sinners; "through one trespass unto all men to condemnation," "even so through one act of righteousness unto all men
to justification of life."

A slight rectification of our passage is possible by regarding the references to the law in vss 13 and 20 as secondary.
This is possible, and would relieve us of one of our embar-
rassments. But it would not seriously affect the main argument. Through Adam all became sinners, and thus suffered
death; through Christ, all enter into righteousness and life.
Of course death still reigns over all mankind, after Christ

as well as before; men still die; but such a slight detail ought not to be allowed to affect a theological argument.

There are some features of this paragraph which echo Pauline thought. The idea that Christ was obedient, and that we may share in his obedience, resulting in righteousness, is thoroughly congenial to Paul. It must be noted that the work of Christ is made parallel to that of Adam. In the case of Adam there was transgression, the disobedience to God's command; this is paralleled in the life of his descendants by their disobedience to the law. In the case of Christ there was an act of righteousness, which must be interpreted as keeping God's command; this will be paralleled in the life of the faithful by their obedience to the law. There is in the context no justification whatever for interpreting Christ's "act of righteousness" as consisting in his death. In verse 13 there is talk of "imputation" of sin. But it is here alone that such an idea occurs. Men *are* sinners. There is no hint that righteousness is "imputed." Men are made righteous. While we have no reason to suppose that Paul thought that all men were sinners;—this is definitely countered by his basic argument in chapter ii from the fact that there were both good Jews, and good gentiles—; this conception of righteousness as real, and not "imputed," is in agreement with his thought.

But there are features which compel us to regard the passage as spurious. The whole style, the construction and elaboration of the argument, is much closer to Hebrews than to anything Paul has written. The conception of the work of Christ as bestowing a gift to be passively received, rather than as enabling us to achieve an experience in which we may participate in the power of grace as manifested in the Holy Spirit, is fatal to the theory that the passage is Pauline. In line with our adverse verdict is the occurrence of the defi-

nitely Johannine expression "eternal life." Every supposedly Pauline passage in which this expression occurs is strongly
suspect. The passage may represent the reworking of a Pauline original. But in the form in which it lies before us it
seems to be greatly modified.

In those portions of chapters six to eight which are deemed
genuine, we find the climax to the line of thought pursued
through the early chapters of Romans. Righteousness may
be attained, but only through faith in Christ. What, then,
is the nature of that faith in Christ through which we become righteous? Here follows the full exposition of what
that faith in Christ is, and what it accomplishes in the life of
him who has faith. This is the very core and essence of the
Pauline gospel, which must be found to be the power of God
unto salvation.

We have judged the closing paragraph of chapter five to
be the reworking of a Pauline original. This judgment is
confirmed by the apparent reference in "the abounding of
grace" to the preceding context. The very posing of the
question, however, "shall we continue in sin?" shows that
Paul was not obsessed with the idea that the very being human was also being sinful. Men may sin, or they may not.
But for the Christian, continuing in sin has become impossible because of the very nature of the experience by which
he became Christian.

How does one become Christian? What is faith in Christ?
Paul's fundamental understanding of the work of Christ and
of the nature of the Christian life rests squarely upon the
central teachings of the mystery religions, with their myth
of the death and resurrection of the dying-rising Savior
God, and their equally fundamental conception of mystic

enthusiasm, that is, that the believer may participate so fully in the nature and experience of the God that he becomes one with him. We become Christian by dying and rising again with our dying-rising Savior.

Completely possessed with this conception Paul argues from it; (vi: 1-14): how can the Christian continue in sin? Does he not know that he has participated so fully in the death-resurrection of Jesus that it must henceforth dominate his life? In baptism, we were baptized into his death. We died to sin. But that is merely the first step in an inseparable process. We must share also in his resurrection by being raised to a newness of life.

There is a reality in the spiritual experience of everyone who has faith in Christ that corresponds to the death-resurrection of Christ. We are united with him in the likeness of his death. Corresponding to the death of Christ upon the cross is the fact that the old man has been crucified with him; the body of sin has been done away. Corresponding to the resurrection of Christ is the fact that we enter upon a new and righteous life. Even so, as Christ died to sin, but lives to God, must we die to the weakness and wickedness of our fleshly lives, and as alive from the dead, present ourselves unto God, our members becoming the instruments of his righteousness. We are not under law, but under grace. In this context, grace must refer to the power of a dynamic spiritual experience by which we have become one with Christ in his dying-rising again.

vi: 15-23 is a digression from Paul's line of argument, in which other values are substituted than those which he employs. This represents the degeneracy of sub-Pauline thought. It rejects Paul's radical conception of sharing in the death-resurrection of Jesus by dying to sin, and "walking about" in newness of life, in favor of the master-servant relationship. We are servants either to sin or to righteousness. Instead of the transformation of life there is the conception of the proper reward which accrues to each type of servitude. The wages of sin is death; the free gift of God is eternal life. Death-life is not a creative experience through which we pass, but rather the end of different types of living. Our sharing in the death-life experience of Christ has been suppressed; this later thinker has eliminated the "mystery taint" in Paul's thinking. How, then, does one become Christian? By hearty obedience to a traditional type of teaching, because of which God will "give eternal life." We are submerged in the point of view of the later orthodoxy of the church, some features of which find their clearest expression in the Pastoral Epistles, to which the passage under discussion is very closely akin. Here again, the Johannine expression, "eternal life," is found. This merely confirms our verdict, reached upon other grounds, that the passage is spurious.

In vii: 1-4, there is a resumption of the argument much more in the Pauline strain. For there is here both the utilization of death as the effective means of attainment, and the definite idea that we are to be joined to Christ both in his dying to sin, and in our living in righteousness. There is, however, some obscuration in that it is not the one who dies who is freed from sin, but his wife, who through his death is freed from the "law," in this case her bond to her husband. If this passage is eliminated, vii: 5 seems to join directly upon vi: 14. vii: 1-4 may be merely a rather unskillful attempt at illustration of Paul's principle, that we are through death freed from law and sin, which as a gloss later found its way into the text. But it is so closely akin to Paul's fundamental point of view that no decisive pronouncement against its genuineness may be made.

Verses 5 and 6 of ch. vii pick up the thread of thought found in vi: 12-14. Sin is not to reign in our mortal body; when we were in the flesh the passions of the flesh wrought through our members with fatal result. But we have died to the flesh, to the law, and to sin; as alive from the dead, we are to live a new, a spirit dominated life, which will be righteous.

All of this discussion as to the attainment of righteousness by means other than the Jewish law might have seemed to Paul likely to have raised the gravest of misgivings in the Jewish-minded Roman church. What, then, was the meaning and purpose of the law? The Jews had always prized the law as God's best and greatest gift to man. But now it would seem that it had been a handicap; it had had a fatal result; it was positively evil. Was the law sin?

There has been much debate as to whether vii: 7-25 is autobiographical. Fortunately it makes no material difference in the interpretation of Romans whether Paul is here describing his own spiritual experience, or whether he is describing the spiritual pilgrimage of Everyman, or rather of every sinner. In any case he is setting forth his basic conception of the cause and cure of sin.

It should be evident at once that Paul did not regard sin as a taint of human nature, inherited from Adam, corrupting all mankind. Sin is the failure to do what we know we ought to do. Before one knows the law, there is no possibility of sin; it is only when law has made plain the difference between right and wrong that sin is possible.

Paul would probably consider the Jewish law, that is, its moral rather than its ceremonial aspects, as the best and clearest revelation man had ever had as to the nature and content of morality, although it does not appear that he thought man had no other valid moral insight. The law was holy, and just and good. This much, at least he could share with the Jewish sympathizers in the Roman church. It could lead man to the knowledge of goodness; further, it might even quicken his aspirations to yearn for that goodness. It was not the reason for sin. It ought to have been an aid to righteousness.

The cause of sin is the weakness and corruption of human flesh. It is the sinful passions, working in the members of the flesh, that lead to sin. We know what is good; we strive to do it; but in spite of our good intentions we are overpowered, and dragged into transgression. The law may be thought of as a force, ruling the inner man, or the mind, tending toward righteousness; but it is overbalanced by another law, for sin may also be thought of as a force, dwelling in the outer man, the members, the flesh. The result is: (verse 25b must evidently be placed before verse 24), I of myself with the mind, indeed serve the law of God: but with the flesh, the law of sin.

Some may detect an inconsistency in Pauline thought as he struggled with the question of the ability of man to attain righteousness. The impression given by the passage under discussion is that by very reason of the fact that he is fleshly, man cannot obey God's command even when he understands it, and wishes to obey it. Does Paul, then, after all, believe in the universality of human guilt? There are many indications, some of which we have already discussed, that Paul could not subscribe to this view of human nature. We must not forget that in the second chapter Paul has argued from the fact that there were true Jews, obedient to God's law, whose circumcision was of the heart, and whom God approved. There were also gentiles, who had the work of the law written on their hearts, who won the approval of their consciences, and whose uncircumcision, because they kept the law, put to shame the circumcision of the Jew. In his discussion of the Rejection of Israel, we shall find passages which may legitimately be interpreted from the viewpoint that Paul felt that under the law Israel had had her chance. She not only might have kept the law, but she ought to have done so. Is Paul hopelessly confused?

This is admittedly a difficult problem, but there are many approaches to it which will at least mitigate its difficulty, if indeed, they do not enable us to find a solution. One means of approach is to raise the question, "Of whom is Paul writing in this seventh chapter of Romans? Is he writing of himself, or of some other man?" If this chapter is taken as Paul's spiritual autobiography, the difficulty vanishes. "I am not speaking of all mankind, but this is what I found in my own experience." It is not certain that we have here a record of Paul's own experience. To build upon this chapter our fundamental conception of Paul's character and moral struggle is most precarious. A similar approach is to find in this discussion an analysis of the spiritual experience not of Everyman, but of the sinner. In discussing the origin of sin it would be foolish to discuss the spiritual experience of a righteous man. Another illuminating approach is to regard Paul as here speaking from the standpoint of Christian thought. Since Christ has come it is possible for all to share in his death-resurrection, and to live a spiritual life. The question as to what we would be if Christ had not come has no relevance now that he has come.

The true approach to this problem and its probable solution is in the recognition that basic to Paul's thinking there was a very simple though vital distinction. This was between self-righteousness, and the righteousness that came from God. Israel indeed failed to keep the law, but this was because she sought to establish her own righteousness. Abraham, on the contrary, trusted God. It would appear that the attainment of righteousness had always been a spiritual matter, a dependence upon God, coming through faith. Those who had sought to attain righteousness in dependence upon themselves were thrown back upon the flesh, which proved inadequate. But an experience of moral victory, or of spiritual power, had always been available through faith. The promise was sure to all, and Abraham should have been the father both of the circumcision and of the uncircumcision.

But of whomever Paul is speaking in this passage, with the Christian the case is clear. So long as we are in the flesh, so long as our lives are dominated by the flesh, we cannot please God, we cannot do his will, we cannot attain unto life. But is there no escape? Wretched man that I am, who will deliver me from this body of death? The climax is found in the triumphant shout of victory, Thanks be to God, through Jesus Christ. There is deliverance; it is through Christ.

Now it is vital to our interpretation of Paul that we pay particular attention to the nature of that deliverance, and to the means through which it is achieved. Paul does not here repeat his discussion of the means through which the Christian is delivered from the body of death. He has made that so abundantly clear in the sixth chapter, verses 1-14, that repetition is here unnecessary. We already know that through faith the Christian is so closely identified with Christ that he shares his death-resurrection experience. The body of flesh is done away, because the old man has been crucified with Christ; we are no longer the prey of the sinful passions working through the flesh, for Christ died to sin, and rose to live henceforth the spiritual life. We are joined to him in the likeness of that resurrection, which is for us "walking about in newness of life."

The salient fact in regard to the nature of the Christian life is that it is no longer dominated by the flesh, or by the law of sinful passion that works through the flesh; it is dominated by a new and stronger law, that of the Spirit of God. (viii: 1-4.) For God had taken hold of the problem of sin at the crucial point. He had dealt with sin in the flesh. He had sent his Son in the likeness of sinful flesh that he might condemn sin in the flesh. It is interesting to see how fully Paul's central and dominant mysticism illuminates this passage. What does it mean to condemn sin in the flesh? Judgment has been pronounced upon it; but what was the sentence which the judge imposed? In the absence of specific formulation of this judgment by Paul himself, we are thrown back upon the context for its reconstruction. It seems, "Sin shall no longer have power over the man who has faith in Christ." The basis of that power has been destroyed because the flesh has been done away in our dying with Christ. For the dominance of the flesh is substituted the dominance of the Spirit, by virtue of whose leading "the ordinance of the law is fulfilled in us." Righteousness is actually attained; there is no question of "imputation," or of "justification" in the sense of "pronouncing righteous." If he who has faith is "justified," this must mean that through the power of the indwelling Spirit he has become righteous. That there can be no condemnation to those who are in Christ Jesus does not flow from any gracious act of God's unmerited favor, but from the recognition of the fact that the entire basis and character of the life has been changed. Condemnation has become impossible; it would be unjust and absurd.

It is difficult to determine just how far the current of Pauline thought continues in this eighth chapter. Certainly through the fourteenth verse, with the possible exception of verse 11, the argument continues from the same basic point of view. Those that are in Christ are no longer in the flesh, whose mind is enmity toward God, and whose end is death. They no longer mind the things of the flesh, but the things of the Spirit; for the Spirit (the Spirit of God, and the Spirit of Christ, and even the indwelling Christ himself seem indistinguishable in Pauline thought), dwells in them, and leads them. If we have not the Spirit, we are none of his. But if Christ is in us, we have been identified with him in his death-resurrection experience, the deeds of the flesh have been put to death, and we live, because of righteousness. Those who are led by the flesh, live after the flesh; but those who are led by the Spirit, live after the Spirit; they are sons of God. (viii: 5-14.)

Verse 11 may be interpreted wholly within the meaning of the context in which it appears. It speaks of the indwelling of the Spirit as a fact of present experience. And that indwelling Spirit shall give life to our mortal bodies, manifestly by leading us in the paths of righteousness and of life. The only difficulty is in the characterization of our bodies as "mortal." This may convey a suggestion that the significance of the resurrection of Christ for the Christian is to be found in reference to immortality, rather than in reference to morality. If that is the meaning of the verse, it must be regarded as a gloss, interpolated by someone wishing to find the meaning of our sharing in the resurrection of Christ in the fact that like him we shall "be raised up in the last day." This conception is Johannine, rather than Pauline; it represents a total perversion of Paul's idea as to the significance of the resurrection of Christ for the believer, at least as Paul has been expounding it in this passage. It is interesting to note that sub-Pauline perversions have often a decidedly Johannine flavor.

It is certain that in verses 17-30 we are thrown violently out of the orbit of Pauline thought. It may be questioned whether the divergence does not begin with verse 15, or even verse 14. Verse 13 forms a fitting and natural conclusion to the line of thought thus far followed in this chapter. Verses 14-16, 26-28 constitute a discussion of the function of the Spirit in the hearts of Christians. The one thing which in them the Spirit does not do is the thing upon which Paul has insisted, empower them to live righteous lives. But, to take verse 14 as belonging to this passage, he witnesses to our sonship to God by making us realize within us a filial relationship, if indeed he does not actually make us God's children. He coöperates with us in all good things, especially in prayer, making intercession for us with groanings that cannot be uttered.

Verses 29, 30 abruptly change the reference from the Spirit to God. They appear to be a homiletic development, largely from details to be found in this context, of "What it means to be called according to his purpose." Foreknowledge and foreordination have not been remotely suggested in the course of Paul's argument; calling appears in verse 28; sonship to God in verses 14 and 16, but here weakened to "being conformed to the image of his Son," "justification" is apparently a faint echo of verses 1-12, and "glorification" of verses

18-23. It is tempting to see here the outline of an early Christian sermon jotted down upon the margin, later to creep into the body of the text. It has all the marks of the homiletic mind.

It is in verses 17-30 that we are farthest from the mind of Paul. He has been talking of the realization of Christian experience in a present glorious triumph over the weakness and sinfulness of the flesh. But this passage proceeds from the point of view that there is no present reality in religious experience. Grace must be abandoned for hope. And hope cannot refer to the present. There seems a polemic spirit, almost a cantankerousness in verses 24, 25. "In hope were we saved; hope that is seen is not hope." There can be no present attainment; we can only patiently await.

It is in this spirit that verse 17 makes the transition from the idea of present sonship, witnessed by the Spirit in the heart of the Christian, to heirship, that is to a status in which we must await the consummation of God's dealing with us. Our relationship to Christ is that we are now sharing his sufferings; it is only in the last day that we may share his glory. Completely obliterated is the essential Pauline position that we share his death in the death of our flesh, his resurrection in a newness of life.

Whereas for Paul the religious question had seemed personal and moral, for the author of these verses it is cosmic and physical. Paul had found the defect in the weakness of human flesh, this writer finds it in a fundamental subjection of the whole of creation to vanity. We have previously encountered pessimistic views of human nature and human life, quite out of harmony with Paul's triumphant optimism, but this passage would extend this pessimism to the whole of that creation which God had pronounced very good; it is groaning and travailing, awaiting the revelation of the sons of God, in which it will apparently have an automatic share. It will be delivered from the bondage of corruption into the liberty of the glory of the children of God. It is hard to attach any real meaning to this phrase.

But what all this will mean for men is made very evident. They must await their "adoption." This ought to mean their becoming the children of God. But it is categorically stated that it means "the redemption of the body." It is hard to see how thought could move upon a greater scale to the attainment of a lesser result. The spiritual bankruptcy of the passage is complete.

A final item is the function of the Spirit in this grandiose scheme. In Paul the enduement of the Spirit has been the climax of the entire process of identification with Christ. The Spirit has become the effective force that dominates life and makes it righteous. But here the Spirit is given as a sort of first-fruits, as a token of some greater thing which God shall ultimately do for us, which has proved to be the redemption of the body.

It is hard to see how there could be greater divergence from fundamental Pauline thinking than we encounter in this passage.

In viii: 31-39 we come to the conclusion of the entire discussion. An analysis of this material will reveal that most of it might properly grow out of the line of thought Paul has been pursuing, while other details have apparently "come in besides."

Proper to the argument are the ideas that God has not spared his Son, but gave him for our sakes, to die and to rise again, so that nothing can ever separate us from the love of Christ. All of this reflects the color of Paul's central mystical conception of the Christian life as one of union with Christ in his essential experience of death-resurrection. It is because of our union with him in his dying-rising, with its implications for our moral living, that no one can bring any charge against us.

As contrasted with this triumphant outcome of our endeavor to attain righteousness, and the assurance that comes from the consciousness of our inseparable union with Christ, of what account are the vicissitudes of this earthly life, especially those which Paul has encountered in his troublous ministry? What though it had brought hardship and want, persecution and suffering, and even threatened death itself? For Christ's sake, he was willing to face danger and death constantly, and to be even as a sheep designated for the slaughter. In all these things he was conscious of an abundant victory through him who had loved him.

All this is essentially Pauline, for it is characteristic of his thought to be conscious of present triumph, not to think he is merely enduring misery and defeat in the hope of something that is later to come.

In verse 34b we encounter the items of Christ's Session and Intercession. These have at no place figured in Paul's discussion as to the possibility and means of attaining righteousness. They do figure prominently in Hebrews, and in the later creeds of the church. Intercession amounts to a denial of Paul's fundamental thesis that by identification with Christ we put off the deeds of the flesh, and in the power of the Spirit, fulfill the ordinance of the law. Intercession is rather a part of the depravity-redemption complex, which has, indeed, often been intruded into Romans, but which has been shown to have no place in Paul's discussion. These are items as congenial to Roman thought as they are uncongenial to Paul's thought. It is easy to see how they would have been added as the epistle was used for the purposes of edification in the Roman church. It would be unnecessary to intercede for one who is more than victor.

The color of verses 38 and 39 is utterly different from that of verses 35-37. Instead of the background of the vicissitudes of a missionary ministry, so vividly real to the apostle, we have here a quasi-gnostic enumeration of forces hostile to the soul. Life and death are personified; they are joined by angels and principalities, the ascendancy and declination of the heavenly bodies, while all the other unknown and non-existent figments of the pseudo-philosophic imagination are lumped under the head of things present or to come, or any other kind of creature.

This also must be judged to have "come in besides." When Paul has been doing his best to account for the origin of sin and failure, and to explain how they may be overcome, there has not been the slightest hint that all these dread specters of the cosmos have been even in the background of his thought. This passages coheres with the interpolated passage in viii: 17-25, rather than with the Pauline viewpoint.

It may be illuminating to observe that while Paul has been saying that none of the vicissitudes of life can separate us from the love of Christ, this passage changes the statement into nothing in the cosmos can separate us from the love of God. It would indeed be splitting hairs to find evidence of interpolation in the mere change from the love of Christ to the love of God in Christ. But the change may be considered significant when it occurs in connection with material which differs totally from its context not only in the vocabulary employed, but also in the basic point of view from which it approaches the problem of human misery and blessedness. These are for Paul connected with the moral struggle; for this interpolator with the cosmic process.

Chapters nine to eleven constitute a homogeneous unit, which has no vital relation to either the preceding or the following materials. It is given over entirely to the discussion of a single problem, The Rejection of Israel. But it has at least this in common with the remaining portions of the epistle. It is definitely complex; the original Pauline materials have been overwritten from other, presumably later, points of view. Once this has been recognized the task of analysis is very simple and easy. One has only to keep clearly in mind the fundamental connotation of terms, and the basic premises from which different passages argue. The various threads are distinct, and are indeed so highly colored, that distinguishing them from each other presents a relatively simple problem.

If the section is read as a whole, without too much attention to detail, one may be left with the vague feeling that "all's well that ends well." Israel is not, after all, to be ultimately lost. But when one gives heed to the detailed explanations that are advanced as to why Israel has been rejected, he will be left in hopeless confusion. The quotations from Scripture present a problem in themselves. So long as the materials are thought to be unitary, it seems impossible to find in the use of the Scriptural materials very much insight. It is only as we realize that our chapters incorporate in themselves divergent points of view that we are enabled to see that each quotation from Scripture is to the point, and cogent.

The inclusion of the discussion of the Rejection of Israel in an epistle to the Roman church, and especially the length at which it is debated, cannot fail to throw some light upon the interests of the Roman church, if not upon the type of Christians in its membership. Since the question does not grow directly out of Paul's discussion found in the previous chapters, its occurrence here, and especially the great emphasis given to it, must be due either to the great place it held in Paul's thought, or to its intense interest for Roman Christians. There is no evidence from Paul's other writings that this was a consuming interest of his; the conclusion seems inescapable that there was in the Roman church an insistent interest in the fate of Israel. This would hardly be an idle curiosity; it must have been felt to have urgent meaning for the Romans themselves. Either the church was composed largely of Jewish Christians whose allegiance to Christ had not destroyed their loyalty to their own nation, or it was made up of gentile Christians, who for one reason or another felt an intense sympathy with the Chosen People. The Jewish interest of the Roman church is unmistakable.

Paul begins the discussion of the Rejection of Israel (ix: 1-9) by affirming with his characteristic poignant simplicity his own heartbroken grief that his kinsmen according to the flesh had been cast away, even wishing that he might himself be anathema, if only they might not fall short. They had had every advantage; theirs was the adoption, theirs the glory, theirs the covenant, theirs the giving of the law, theirs the service of God, theirs the promises, theirs the fathers. And to crown it all, Christ after the flesh himself was one of the Chosen Race. For them to be rejected would seem to make meaningless all that had led up to the coming of Christ;

it would seem that even the word of God had come to nought.

But this is by no means the case. For with his characteristic consistency Paul reverts to one of his basic axioms, with which every student of Pauline thought must be thoroughly familiar. God had from the beginning intended that the children of Abraham should be, not those in whose veins flowed the blood of the patriarch, but those in whose hearts lived his faith. For the inheritance was not to be to all of his children, but only to the children of promise. For in the very words of the promise itself it was pointed out that *Sarah* should have a son.

We may pause to observe the insight and skill with which Paul quotes from Scripture. How closely and brilliantly the light is focussed upon the one point in the verse which has appositeness and cogency! *Sarah* shall have a son. In this one expression we may see foreshortened all of God's dealings with his own.

The very words with which verse 10 begins, "and not only so," should put us on our guard. It is the beginning of a long detour, from which we return only in verse 24, if indeed, not in verse 25. There has probably been some elision, as well as the evident interpolation. We know from Galatians, (iii: 6-13), that Paul made of Isaac a type of all the children of promise, and that he realized that the children of promise, being all who shared in the faith of Abraham, might include gentiles as well as Jews. He has evidently been following out this thought in this context, for the quotation from Hosea establishes what would otherwise be an incredible thought. Those who were not the people of God were to become his own.

Disregarding for the moment the two quotations from Isaiah in verses 27-29, we have the explicit statement that it was the gentiles who had attained, and not Israel. And it is unequivocally stated that the cause of Israel's failure is solely because they sought to obtain righteousness by works, and not by faith. A stone had been laid in Zion; those who built on it by faith should never be put to shame. But it had become a rock of offence, not because of what the stone was, but because of their attitude toward it, and because of the use they made of it. In Paul's thought this rock was undoubtedly Christ; before the coming of Christ it was the possibility of faith in God and in his promise. For the purpose of God had ever been essentially the same.

By disregarding the interpolations in chapter x we see that Paul had consistently carried out this argument that Israel might have attained by falling in with the provisions that God had made for them, but that they had failed because, for all their zeal, they had really been trying to establish their own righteousness, rather than that righteousness that comes from humble dependence upon God. (x: 1-3.)

We are faced with a vexing question as to what Paul really took to be the meaning and purpose of the law. We are already familiar with the thought elaborated in chapter seven that all that the law could do was to bring knowledge of sin; it could quicken aspiration, but it could not provide the power for its realization. But the whole tenor of this passage is that the law was not in vain. In it God had sincerely provided the means whereby Israel could obtain righteousness. The fault was not in the law, but in the use Israel made of it.

God had intended that the law should be kept. For in Deuteronomy (xxx: 11-14) we read that no one need ascend into heaven, nor cross the sea to bring the commandment near them, for the word was near them, in their mouth, and in their heart, THAT THEY MIGHT DO IT. We are driven by the use Paul makes of this quoted material to understand that he thought that Israel might in the law, had they only had the right attitude toward God, have obtained the righteousness which God intended. True, there was in the law no power to enable them to obey it. Neither was there sufficient power in themselves. No one can establish his own righteousness. But had they depended humbly upon God in faith, they would have found in him all the power they needed to obey the law.

In the light of these considerations we may try to interpret verse 4, and to assess its genuineness. It can be made to bear such a meaning that we may ascribe it to Paul. If genuine it must mean that salvation was essentially the same for Israelites as for Christians; it was a matter of faith in God. For Israel righteousness came through dependence upon God for the strength to do his will as it was revealed in the law. For Christians it comes through faith in Christ. If this verse have any application to Israel it must mean that we see in Christ the illustration of that which alone can save, the attitude of faith. But the more we think about it the more evident becomes its inapplicability to Israel, and the necessity for searching for some meaning which will allow it to apply to Israel at all. On the other hand the more do we see its naturalness from the point of view of established Christianity. Since Christ has come it is quite natural for Christians to assume that in Christ we have the "end" for which the law was given. This is typical of the way in which Pauline "difficulties" vanish when we realize how easily homiletical glosses, jotted in a matter of fact way in the margin, ultimately crept into the text. This proves to be a gloss natural to the Christian preacher, but utterly out of place in the discussion of the historical problem of what God had intended for Israel in the giving of the law. If Greek usage throw any light upon the question at issue it strongly speaks for this verse being a gloss. The participle representing "that believeth" is in the present. If it were intended to refer to past as well as present, the aorist would be expected.

So far the argument is clear. Israel had had her chance. In the law God had provided the way of righteousness. If only Israel had trusted in him instead of in themselves, they would in him have found the power to obey the commandments, and all would have been well.

When, after another detour, we pick up the thread of genuine Pauline material (x: 19-21), we learn that Paul must again have pointed out that the gentiles had attained where Israel had failed. This Paul had unequivocally asserted in chapter ii, verses 14, 15, 26, and 27. It was clearly set forth in the Scripture, for Moses had said that God would provoke them to jealousy with that which was no nation, while Isaiah had said that God was found of them that sought him not, but that He had unavailingly stretched out his hands all the day to His own disobedient and gainsaying people.

In the genuine materials of chapter eleven the final thought is added. The stumbling of the Jews has resulted in the salvation of the gentiles, and it is hoped that this will provoke the Jews to emulate them in a like faith. The chapter begins with the assertion that God had not cast off his own people, to which Paul himself belonged. (xi: 1.) Verse eleven continues that the result of their fall has been the salvation of the gentiles, to provoke the Jews to jealousy. Despite the grief in his heart caused by the refusal of his own to accept Christ, Paul has magnified his ministry to the gentiles in the hope that this may hasten the day when the Jews will emulate their faith. So the believing gentiles will be the first fruit whose holiness will leaven the lump, until it is all holy; they will be the root, whose faith will ultimately give life to the branches, the Jews. (xi: 11-16.)

No more materials may with any certainty be claimed for Paul. The rhapsody in verses 33-35, whether it be the outburst of Paul, or added by a later hand, is an altogether fitting conclusion to the line of thought which Paul has been pursuing, that, in spite of its seeming incredibility, God's dealing with Israel, leading them at long last to faith in Christ, if only through emulation of the despised gentiles, is an exhibition of a wisdom of God which the human mind can hardly trace out, to say nothing of presuming to have conceived it.

Verse 36 is in all probability a liturgical addition, witnessing the end of a section in the lectionary when the epistles were read in worship.

Our study has thus revealed the genuine materials to be ix: 1-5a; 6-9; 24-26; 30-33. x: 1-3, (possibly 4), 5-8a, (with the exception of 6c and 7b), (perhaps 11-13), 19-21. xi: 1, (perhaps 2a), 11-16, (perhaps 33-35). In them Paul has set forth clearly, simply, and consistently his explanation of the Rejection of Israel. God had always intended, alike in Christ, and in the law, that men should attain righteousness through faith. Israel failed because they trusted in themselves rather than in God, in works, rather than in faith. Had they trusted in God, they might have kept the law, and fulfilled God's demands. It is the gentiles who really attained righteousness, and their success would ultimately provoke Israel to abandon their trust in their own righteousness of works, and to turn to God's ultimate purpose for all, righteousness through faith in Christ.

From the viewpoint of Jews, or Jewish sympathizers, this solution of the problem was utterly unacceptable. In it Paul had been completely true to his fundamental positions. There was only one gospel, one way to attain righteousness; this was the way the gentiles had taken, faith in Christ, identification with the dying-rising Savior. The church was unwilling to accept Paul's thinking even in such a practical, and apparently non-theological a problem as that of the Rejection of Israel. Paul's simple exposition of the matter was therefore modified by the introduction of two corrective ideas. Israel was not to blame; it was all God's fault. And, anyhow, God had never intended to save more than a part of Israel. Fortunately, these corrective ideas of predestination, and of the remnant philosophy, are easily recognized and segregated.

The first suspicious material to be encountered is ix: 5b, "who is over all, God blessed forever, Amen." This is to be regarded as a liturgical gloss or addition, growing out of the use of the epistle in worship.

The Jew, or the Jewish sympathizer, would naturally object to any solution of the problem of the Rejection of Israel which placed the blame for this calamity squarely and solely upon the Jews. In ch. ix, verses 10-23, (or 24, which may be an editorial ligature), we have the vehement retort that Israel was in no wise to blame. The responsibility was God's alone. It was due to the inviolable choice of his sovereign will. God had always done as he would; he had called and he had rejected whom he pleased. It were silly to think that man's response of faith could have any weight, for God hardened whom he would. And certainly no heart that God had hardened could ever make the response of faith.

The example that is chosen is, from the standpoint of logic, altogether admirable; but from the standpoint of morality and conscience, horribly deplorable. Paul had chosen Isaac as the example of God's dealing with men, for the whole account of the birth of Isaac had turned upon Abraham's response of faith. But for the predestinarian annotator the perfect example is to be found in Jacob and Esau. For in this case there is no question of parental attitude, and it is insisted that the children had not developed to the point where they could do either good or ill. The omnipotence of God is arrayed not against the weakness of infancy, but against the utter helplessness of children yet unborn. What could the prophetic indignation which denounced in unmeasured terms the barbaric warrior who committed the heinous sin against humanity of ripping open women with child have found to say of a God who was "willing to show his wrath, and to make his power known" by invading the sphere of prenatal life to visit destruction upon developing lives still alike utterly helpless and entirely undeserving of such severity?

The case is not helped at all by the ability of this predestinarian annotator to support his position from Scripture. God's dealing with Pharaoh may be cited to prove that God had intervened to harden his heart, so that he could not comply with the demand to release the Israelites. From the standpoint of bigoted nationalism it is quite understandable that God should have hardened Pharaoh's heart and then gone ahead to visit upon him the direst of calamity. But theology cannot be written from this point of view! We can hardly escape the feeling that it was not fair to deal thus even with a grown man.

The argument is carried on by bringing in the analogy of the potter and the clay. It may be remarked that here our materials suddenly exhibit some of the characteristics of the diatribe, heretofore lacking in the genuine Pauline portions. It is true that the clay has neither the heart to feel the injustice of arbitrary dealings, nor the moral stamina to protest any outrage that might be inflicted upon it. But no one who has known the love of God manifested in Christ, or for that matter even in the act of creation, wherein he has made us like himself, can ever find a true analogy of the relationship between man and God in the figure of the potter and the clay. Man is not insensate clay; he is the child of God. Can we not hear Jesus say, "Which one of you, being a father, could exercise a potter's seeming irresponsibility in dealing with the child of his love?"

This may be a Jewish passage; it falls far short of the ultimate insights of Christianity. He who would claim this passage for Paul would render no service to the great apostle. It is dominated by the hateful spirit of later Judaism speaking in the words of Malachi, "Jacob have I loved; but Esau have I hated!" Christianity is not the lineal prolongation of Judaism. It is what it is because of its ability to winnow the grain from both Judaism and Hellenism, not only discarding the chaff, but adding to the best of both Judaism and Hellenism its own superior insights. Too much stress is placed upon the Jewishness of Paul. Jew he was, but he followed Judaism only so far as his insight and conscience would allow.

Nor did the annotator render any service to the Scripture

by using it to support his revolting doctrine. The concept of irresponsible arbitrariness is not rendered any more acceptable to the enlightened conscience by the fact that it was shared with this predestinarian annotator of Romans by the author of one section of the book of Exodus. To some, the questioning of Scripture would seem just as blasphemous as the questioning of God. But neither the Scripture nor God could wish to be exempt from the demands of conscience. The doctrine of the altogether otherness of God reaches the very climax of its absurdity and its unacceptability when it would even intimate that God is free from human goodness, and that deep revulsion from heartless cruelty is foreign to him. If in the deepest and best of our nature we are not like God, the whole concept of his revelation of himself in Christ is a hollow travesty. It is a mistaken and unchristian reverence which bows down before each passage of Scripture as an inscrutable and unchallengeable revelation of the unchanging truth of God. He who is our Master said, "Moses indeed said unto you, But I Say." To him the saying "It is written" was by no means the conclusion of the discussion. He fully realized that there might be some mitigating circumstance or some lack of insight which might cause any passage to fall short of the complete expression of ultimate truth. For a Jew the citation of Scripture might be conclusive; for a Christian it can never be final.

This passage must be rejected as Pauline, not because of its bigoted Jewish nationalism, nor because of its abhorrent predestinarianism, but simply because it tears down the argument which Paul was so carefully constructing. He is trying to establish the fact that Israel was rejected, and the gentiles were accepted, because Israel steadfastly refused to accede to God's pleading that they manifest the faith by which the gentiles had attained. This passage overlooks God's pleading; it denies the possibility that Israel might have attained. They are rejected simply and solely because God had hardened their hearts and made any other course impossible.

In verses 27-29 of chapter ix, we have another attempt to modify the rigor of Paul's indictment of the Jews. The appeal is here to the familiar doctrine of the remnant. History had shown that not all of Israel could survive, but that only a remnant had been left. This was plainly written in the book of Isaiah, whether as a genuine prophecy of what should take place, or as a pseudo-phophetic vindication of what had happened. This is a complete solution of the problem, and if it be Paul's, most of what he seems to have written in these chapters is sheer waste.

There are two considerations overlooked by those who would consider these verses to be genuine. The first is this completeness with which their point of view disposes of the problem. The second is that with Paul it is not a question of fractions of the Holy People, of which the greater is lost, while the lesser is saved. It is Israel as a whole that is lost, and the gentiles who are saved. It is not the bulk of Israel that is to be provoked by the attainment of the remnant; Israel is to be provoked by that which is no nation. Had Paul held to the idea of the remnant he would naturally have looked to it as the leaven which would ultimately permeate the whole. But the question of the loss of Israel, and the attainment of the gentiles, not only dominates the whole tenor of the discussion; it comes to categorical statement in ix: 30-33.

This idea of the remant is interpolated into chapter xi. Here it is combined with the idea of predestination previously expounded. This may prove that both strains are due to the same interpolator. Or it may show that the interpolation in chapter xi is a later reworking, attempting to combine the two viewpoints. In that case the ligature is to be found in verse 5, in which the ideas of the remnant and of election are combined. Rather striking is the different attitude taken toward the remnant in ix: 27-29, where the stress is placed upon the tiny portion of Israel that is left, and here, where it is pointed out that in the days of Elijah there were seven thousand who had not bowed the knee to Baal. Paul has taken the matter too seriously, more are saved, after all, than one might think!

In this passage, xi: 2, or 3-10, (2a may well be Pauline; it is suspicious only because of the expression, "whom he foreknew" which may be an editorial coloring to tie the passage in with the predestinarian materials), the contrast is not between Israel who failed, and the gentiles, who obtained, which is so characteristic of the entire epistle, but between Israel and the election. In verse eleven the genuine contrast between Israel and the gentiles reappears. Materials from Isaiah and from the Psalms are utilized to establish the idea that any failure to attain is to be attributed solely to God, who had darkened their eyes and bowed down their backs. (xi: 9-10.)

The remnant philosophy has again touched xi: 25 and 26, combined again with the predestinarian concept, where a part of Israel had had the misfortune to be hardened, while all of the Jews will ultimately be saved. But in verses 28-32 it is quite evident that the question concerns Israel as a whole.

The doctrine of the remnant is to be unhesitatingly and decisively rejected as Paul's solution of the problem of the Rejection of Israel. It is in violent conflict throughout with both its immediate, and its more remote context. It does not at all represent Paul's view of the situation obtaining in the past or in the present. It is Israel as a whole, in his thinking, which has failed to attain the righteousness of God, and which is now rejecting his persistent pleading. And as he looks to the future, he sees Israel as a whole, and not even an overwhelming majority of the Chosen People, abandoning their self-righteous method of works, and turning in humble trust to God's appointed way of faith.

But these two corrective considerations, of the remnant, and of predestination, are not the only forces which have modified these three chapters. For chapter x has been deeply modified by the later situation in the developed evangelistic mission of the church when missionaries are sent to preach the word of faith; men "hear" and "believe"; they "confess," and "are saved." The point of departure is found in 8b. Up to this point Paul seems to have been arguing that Israel might have attained righteousness through the law, which was not far off, but was near, in their mouth, and in their heart, (that they might do it). But in 8b the attention is shifted from the question of Israel and the gentiles to a situation in which missionaries are going abroad on a generalized evangelistic mission. It is no longer a question of the attainment of righteousness through obedience to God's commands. But "salvation" comes to men as a gift from God; it comes to all who will "believe," and "confess," and "call upon the name of the Lord." The evangelistic mission has been thoroughly organized; the missionaries are subsidized. In verses fourteen and fifteen we encounter the exhortation of one intensely missionary minded that the church do its duty in the sending of preachers, lest the whole evangelistic mission collapse. Verse 18 may be interpreted as the boast of the infant church, much exaggerated, of course, that this mission had extended into all the world.

One of the clearest instances of modification in these chapters is to be found in the somewhat ill-tempered Jewish rejoinder in xi: 17-24 to Paul's idea that the gentiles, through their faith, would be the first fruits, which might ultimately leaven the lump. They would be the root, which would ultimately give life to the branches. By no means! says this annotator. The Jews are the root; the gentiles are but the branches of a wild olive tree grafted onto the genuine stock.

It is a pathetic comment upon "scholarship" in the Pauline field to recall how commonly these verses are made the basis for the dictum that Paul was a city man, not versed in practice of horticulture. Anyone who knows anything at all about grafting should know that it is the cultivated branch that is grafted upon the wild stock.

But to accept this interpolation as genuine will be to bring against Paul a charge far more serious than that of an appalling ignorance of horticulture. He will also have to be charged with an inability to carry forward from one verse to the next the fundamental connotation of a term basic to his argument. In verse 16 the root is to be taken as the gentiles; in 17-24, the root is to be taken as the Jews. In verse 16 the branches must be taken as the Jews; in 17-24 the branches are the gentiles, unnaturally grafted in, later to be broken off.

Nor can this change in context be taken as mere inadvertence, or "inconsistency." The new connotation in verses 17-24 is assigned in the deliberate attempt to destroy Paul's entire argument that the gentiles are the ones who have really exemplified God's purpose in the attainment of righteousness through faith, and that the Jews must emulate them if they are to attain. It is an endeavor to assert Jewish values as over against Paul's charateristically Hellenistic interpretation of the gospel.

Unless verses 33-35 be thought of as Paul's own outburst of reverent praise in view of the strangeness of God's dealing with Israel, as well they might be, we must find the conclusion of Paul's discussion of the problem of the Rejection of Israel in xi: 16. Verses 25-32 have some faint reflection of the Pauline viewpoint. In them there is the same optimistic estimate of the ultimate fate of the Chosen People. There are in these verses, however, many objectionable details. A "mystery" would seem to be interpreted in intellectual terms. It is something of which men had been ignorant, which is now explained to them. This conception of mystery is frequent in "Pauline" writings, but it is not Pauline. The conception of salvation is redemptionist, rather than Pauline. Paul's whole discussion has turned upon the attainment of righteousness, presumably through obedience, the power for which comes through humble trust in God. But here it would seem that there can be no attainment. God is "to take away their sins." Since the wording of the parallel member is "to turn away ungodliness from Jacob," it might be urged that the writer is thinking of freeing Israel from actual sin, rather than from its consequences. But the connotation intended in the quotation becomes evident when the writer goes on to expound its meaning to be the showing of mercy upon the part of God, and the obtaining of mercy upon the part of man. Verse 32 lines up definitely with all the interpolated depravity-predestinarian-redemptionist materials in its explicit assertion that "God shut up all unto disobedience that he might have mercy upon all." This is the categorical denial not only of Paul's assertion that the gentiles, who had

not the law, had still by nature fulfilled its requirements
(ii: 12-14, 26, 27), but also of his teaching that there can be
no condemnation to those who are in Christ because the ordi-
ance of the law is fulfilled in those who are led by the Spirit.
(viii: 1-4.)

The third section of our present epistle to the Romans is
found in chapters xii-xvi. These chapters are quite miscellaneous in character. There is in them little that can with
any confidence be ascribed to Paul. Most of their contents
is much more in keeping with the settled pastoral care of the
church than with a letter sent for the purpose of establishing
a personal contact to a church which the author had never
visited, and of acquainting its membership with a teaching
with which they evidently did not agree. Roman these chapters seem. The Jewish interests are quite to the fore. They
read like excerpts from the archives of the Roman church.

Verses 1 and 2 of chapter xii incorporate a spirituality
which accords well with the spirituality of Paul, but a close
analysis will exhibit traits both of vocabulary and of content which make it improbable that they are genuine. It
is easy to read into them our own realization that religion
must issue in conduct acceptable to God. But these verses are
saturated with gnostic and intellectualistic rather than with
moral values. Our "reasonable" service, while it might be
thought of as a walk holy and unblamable before him, appears from the development it receives in the second verse to
be thought of as a renewal of the "mind" which does not
"conform" to "this age." It would of course be entirely
wrong to see in the reference to "this age" any necessary allusion to the "two ages"; whatever the reference of "this

age" may be, we are not exhorted to conform to "the age to come."

It seems that there is an effort to produce a forced connection between these verses and their context. I beseech you -"therefore." But to what does this "therefore" refer? Because of the use of the term "mercies" it might seem that it refers to the mercy God has showed to the gentiles, and which he will subsequently manifest to Israel as well. Or there is a possible connection with the main argument of the first eight chapters. If this be intended the connection is improper, because in those chapters Paul has based the Christian life not upon any mercies which God has shown, but upon a dynamic experience of identification with the dying-rising savior which transforms life. This distinction between mercy and grace as the basis of the Christian life is one of the best indications of the genuineness or spuriousness of materials in the "Pauline" literature. The effort to force a connection with the context seems to betray the hand of an editor who knew that he was dealing with diverse materials.

In xii: 3-21 the intellectualistic and gnostic color of verses 1 and 2 is completely lost. "Thinking" here has nothing to do with "renewing the mind" or "conforming" to anything. It refers solely to the opinion one may hold as to his value and function in the church. We are to have regard for ourselves only as we fulfill humbly and diligently the function which God has assigned to us for the upbuilding of his body, the church.

In its beginning this passage rests upon the fundamentally Pauline figure of the body made up of different members, each contributing its characteristic service to the whole. It may be either the survival of a genuine bit of Pauline mate-

rial, or more likely it is the faithful employment of Pauline
terminology by one who has encountered a similar problem,
and who uses Paul's well known figure in its solution. The
style lacks Paul's usual vividness and sparkle. But the main
consideration which leads us to regard this passage as secondary is that there is not the close connection between these
"gifts" and the Spirit which was basic to Paul's thinking.
We have gifts which differ according to "the grace given
unto us," and we are to prophesy "according to the proportion of our faith." This passage would seem to fit in with
an age in which the vivid experience of the presence of the
Spirit in the life of the Christian had faded into the background. But this should not be insisted upon.

The stylistic phenomena of the passage, however, are such
as are encountered not only in no other Pauline writing, but
seldom if ever elsewhere in the New Testament. Beginning
with verse 6 there is an almost total lack of any finite verb.
We encounter a monotonous succession of participial expressions, where we would expect imperatives or other finite forms
of the verb, whose absence is made up for in the English
translation by the liberal use of italics. In verse 15 we encounter two infinitives used with the force of imperatives.

Such stylistic usage is a marked peculiarity into which one
is not at all likely to lapse unless it be habitual. It strongly
bespeaks another author. It may be urged that Paul is here
making use of parenetic materials current in the early church.
But it has not been established that there were parenetic materials which exhibited such stylistic peculiarity. It is, of
course, reasonable to suppose that parenetic materials did circulate in the church at a later date. Their existence and their
use in epistles is evidenced by the use of the "Haustafeln,"
in Col., Eph., and I Peter. But it seems a violent assump-

tion that such materials were pre-Pauline. This would seem to overlook Paul's truly pioneer status in Christianity, and the length of time necessary for these materials to crystallize, to circulate, and to win such a status as would cause them to be utilized in epistles. This seems to be rather another instance which exhibits the influence which preaching and exhortation have exercised upon the present form of our documents.

These materials are also much better suited to the pastoral care of the church than to the introduction to a definite group of one who wished to make a favorable impression upon them. For while the passage may seem upon first reading to be merely general exhortation one soon sees that there is quite a grave situation in the background. For there seems to be the same disunity in the group that had obtained in Corinth. Only here it seems to have taken the form not only of a pride which unduly exalted self and despised one's fellow, but of a spirit of strife which went so far as to do evil to others, and which must be exhorted to allow the Lord to take vengeance unto himself. (vss. 16-21.) It would have been most inappropriate, and it might well have been very unfortunate, for an outsider to take a hand in such an acute situation. Paul might well have reconciled the Romans to each other, but only by aligning them in a common enmity toward him, which would have been fatal to his purpose in writing to them.

Chapter xiii: 1-7 seems certainly Roman, but hardly Pauline. Its burden, too, is a matter which would concern one responsible for the care of the church, but which would be inappropriate for one writing for the first time to a strange group. It probably comes from the time when the church had to come to terms with its environment, and to decide what should be its attitude toward the powers that be. It is, of course, a passage growing out of the long pull. There is a natural reflection of the Roman situation, where the church was confronted with such overwhelming force that any attitude other than unquestioning submission would have been immediately and certainly fatal. If the question of the worship of the emperor is in the background it is quietly and prudently evaded by the admonition to render honor "to whom honor is due." Each Christian must thus make up his own mind what is right. There are other indications that this moral relativism was a Roman point of view. (See ch. xiv.) Stylistically, the passage is labored and repetitious, far from the sprightly movement of Pauline writing.

In xiii: 8-10 there is nothing which would force us to deny the passage to Paul. The interpretation of the law in moral rather than in ritualistic terms, and the conception of love as the active course which rules out all harmful actions, is quite in harmony with Paul's basic teaching that the Christian life is one of actual righteousness, wherein we fulfill the ordinances of the law. But there is nothing characteristically Pauline in the paragraph. It might be written by any one dominated by fundamentally Christian attitudes. It seems a natural expansion of the thought that we should render to each his due, which is after all only that we should love everyone.

It is impossible to read verses 11-14 of chapter xiii without sensing the thrill of apocalyptic expectation. Salvation is nearer than when we believed; the dawn is already lighting up the portals of the east. Anyone who would from this passage attempt to establish the apocalyptic coloring of Paul's thinking should note well that it is interlarded between the discussion of the Christian's relationship to the powers that be, which relationship would be vitally affected by any expectation of the nearness of the end of all things, but in which there has not been even the slightest hint that since this is for such a short time it may safely be put aside as unimportant, and a discussion of the observance of days and dietary regulations, which is equally untouched by any realization of the shortness of the interim in which these questions are to be thought of. The argument of such a one would seem to be that the thinking of Paul is dominantly apocalyptic because only three verses in all of these contiguous chapters are tinged with apocalyptic coloring.

An attempt to understand the fundamental ideas of these verses will show us how far they are from the presuppositions of Pauline thinking. They suffer from the defect of a futurism which regards salvation, not as the immediate fruit of a present dynamic experience, but as something which will ultimately be manifested, whose coming is at some definite point in the future, which is now imminent. Paul's basic figure of our relationship to Christ is that we are identified with him in his dying-rising experience. He dwells in us. But here the basic figure is the putting on and off of armor or clothing. We are to put off the works of darkness; we are to put on the arms of light; we are to put on the Lord Jesus Christ. This is a decided weakening of the vividness with which Paul thinks of our intimate oneness with Christ. There is an equally diametrical opposition in the ways in which the flesh is conceived. With Paul the flesh itself is evil; the only remedy is death. With this author it is not the flesh that is evil, but only its lusts. The flesh is not to be crucified; its lusts are merely to be left without any provision being made for them. Not only is the remedy that is proposed milder, but the fundamental conception from which the remedy is prescribed is utterly different.

It must strike the careful student of Paul how often the passages which have an apocalyptic coloring must be rejected, not at all because they are apocalyptic, but because they modify or deny Paul's most basic conceptions.

An uncritical reading of chapter xiv might leave one under the impression that the question under discussion is the familiar one of things offered to idols. For there seems to be the same attitude that whatever may be the right and wrong of the matter, we must beware lest the enjoyment of our liberty lead to offending our brother, or even to destroying him. The resemblance, however, is only superficial. For it is not a question of eating meat which has been consecrated by sacrifice to an idol, but of eating any meat at all. It is vegetarianism as over against the eating of any flesh whatever. With the eating of meat is conjoined the drinking of wine. It would seem that there were some teetotalers in the early church.

Here the curtain is lifted to give us a glimpse into what is perhaps an otherwise unknown nook in the life of early Christianity. Controversy seems to be raging over the drinking of wine and the eating of meat. Coupled with this is the observance of days. One thinks at once of Jewish ideas of Sabbatarianism and of dietary regulations. But there is no indication that the Sabbath itself is definitely in question, and we are not confronted with Jewish regulations, for these distinguished between meats that were clean and those that were unclean, while here all meats are questioned. He that is weak eats "garden-stuff." This may be merely the manifestation of those forces which seem widespread in the early

church which created the demand for asceticism and the observance of days. In other words this may be the local variation of the "Colossian heresy," whose Jewishness may be very
greatly overestimated.

It is of the greatest interest to observe how the situation
is met. Fundamental to its solution is a conception which
may be thought to be essentially Jewish. We stand before
God as a servant before his master. Everything we do must
be well pleasing to him. For everything we do is unto him,
and ultimately we must stand before his judgment throne.
Whether we live or die, we are the Lord's; we live unto him,
and unto him we die. Were it not for the gloss in verse 9
perhaps no one would suspect that we have here any reference
to a life beyond this life. Dying is merely taken as the ultimate in human life. Nothing in human life is without reference to God, not even the curtain which is its close.

Verse 9 must be taken as a gloss, for it thrusts Christ
into a context which has been speaking only of God. Christ's
death and resurrection (the Greek word is merely "lived";
the meaning of resurrection is possible, but not necessary in
this context) were to the end that he might rule over both
the living and the dead. This is a far cry from the question
of the eating of meat and the drinking of wine, which might
indeed have meaning for the living, but scarcely for the
dead. This is an exhibition of the way in which later thought
both Christianized and generalized our documents.

One of the most striking characteristics of this chapter is
its moral relativism. There is nothing unclean in itself, but
things are clean or unclean to us as we regard them. One
must be assured in his own heart as to the cleanness or uncleanness of anything, as to the rightness or wrongness of
any action. Faith is thus not the action by which we identify

ourselves with the dying-rising Lord, as in Paul; it is rather the ground of conviction from which motives rise, and actions spring. Because of this moral relativism it is quite possible that we may do something which is right, because we are assured that it is right; our brother, however, may be destroyed by doing that very same thing which is right for us, because it seems wrong to him. Sin would appear to be the violation of our deepest moral convictions, whether or not they be mistaken. This leads to what may be a later homiletic gloss "Whatever is not of faith is sin." Asceticism and the observance of days thus become the sacred duty of those to whom they appear to be right.

The only certainly Pauline color in the chapter seems to be the conception that the upbuilding of the group is paramount to the insight and liberty of the individual. Far more important than the insistence upon our rights is our influence upon our brethren.

There is neither continuity nor coherence in chapter xv. Verses 1-3a form the conclusion to chapter xiv. Verses 3b and 4 are a remarkable digression. Christ is, in the approved Roman fashion, held up to us as an example. This is in the context a most unfortunate illustration, for the discussion has been dominated by the idea that we are not to be guided by our own ultimate insights but by the scruples of those around us, ignorant and mistaken as these often are. This would suggest that Christ guided his life by the scruples of his neighbors. It was only by characteristic homiletic generalization, losing sight entirely of the specific situation under discussion, that this illustration could ever have occurred to the commentator. The quotation from Scripture is equally unfortunate, for it has completely forgotten the idea that Christ governed his life by the ideas of those around him, substituting the idea that the reproaches of those that reproach the Christian fell upon him.

In verse 4 the capacities of the homiletic commentator are given full play. He has forgotten all about the immediate situation in which an intelligent Christian is face to face with mistaken scruples held by his weaker brethren, and is expounding with complete independence a subject in which he is interested, but which has no connection whatever with the context, "the misery and sorrow of human life." Seen through dark glasses, the whole meaning of the Scriptures is immediately apparent. They were written that through the patience and the comfort of the Scriptures we might have hope! How much is here made of the fact that the Scriptures were written for our instruction; how glibly is it assumed that nothing stands therein but comfort and patience! All of this stems from a generally pessimistic view of human life as a weary journey through a vale of tears in which religion's only function is one of palliation and anaesthesia; its ultimate function is to lead us at last into a better, brighter realm.

This is the counterpart of the doctrine of depravity in our estimate of human nature. Such pessimistic views of human life and human nature are possible only when we deliberately close our eyes to the beauties and joys of life and to the nobility and heroism of human character. God's world is good and we are like him. How little of God's word have these pessimists read! But all of this pessimistic estimate is spun out of the adverse connotation of the one word "reproaches." Indeed, we at last see some light on the question why such a quotation from Scripture was ever made in this context. The text has grown out of the sermon, rather than the sermon out of the text. The quotation was brought in to give the preacher the pretext for his sermon. How little have preachers changed in all the history of religious effort!

It should go without saying that anyone who has even glimpsed Paul's fundamental teaching that the Christian life is one of victorious achievement and of blissful oneness with Christ will immediately perceive that such a pessimistic estimate of human life, and such an appraisal of the meaning of Scripture must be anathema to him.

In verses 5, 6, and 7 we see an editor doing the best he can to restore some order to the chaotic material which lies before him. From verses 3b and 4 he draws the characterization of God as a God of patience and comfort, while from the discussion of chapter xiv he draws the exhortation to unity in Christ to the glory of God. To this he adds the exhortation to receive each other as Christ has received them, repeating for good measure, "to the glory of God."

In verses 8-13 we have a bit of material to which the criteria utilized in Form Criticism may well be applied. It is entirely distinct from its context, and is rounded off by a benediction. An editor has endeavored to force an integration with the context by the use of "for." But that it is forced immediately appears from any attempt to understand this new material in the light of the previous discussion. The Roman Christians have been exhorted to cure a disunity among themselves which grew out of the fact that some had been offended by conduct upon the part of their fellows which violated scruples which admittedly rested only upon their own limited point of view. This had in turn caused the more liberal to despise their narrower brethren. They were to receive one another in spite of these differences caused by narrow scruples. But in this paragraph any difference in

Christians is racial. It is a recurrence of the old question of Jew and gentile; and it is written wholly from a Jewish point of view.

There is the categorical assertion that the whole meaning of Christ is in relation to Judaism. He is a minister of the circumcision. He came merely to confirm the promises made to the fathers, who are in this connection undeniably the Jewish fathers. It is true that the gentiles are to rejoice in his mercies; these must be mercies manifested in Christ's being a minister of the circumcision, and in his confirmation of promises made to the fathers. Any extension to the gentiles must arise out of their relation to the Jews, out of their inclusion in the Holy People. This comes to explicit statement in the quotation from Isaiah. One shall arise out of Jesse to rule over the gentiles, and in him shall the gentiles hope! This is a characteristically Jewish view of the blessedness that shall come to the world when all shall have come under Jewish domination.

Again in verse 13 we find the work of an editor who has done the best he could with his diverse materials. The question of Jew and gentile is discarded and there is expressed the generalized and spiritualized hope that the God of hope fill them with all joy and peace in believing, that they may abound in hope in the power of the Holy Spirit. One should not overlook the trifling detail that the ground of hope held out has been the establishment of the basically Jewish character of all of God's purposes and dealings with men. As to Pauline coloring this verse does speak of joy and peace, and does mention the power of the Holy Spirit. But it is essentially un-Pauline in making hope God's greatest gift to men.

Any connection verses 8-12 may have with the context is with the materials in verses 14-32, with which they are in basic opposition. Paul is going to speak of the dedication of his ministry to the gentiles, and of the genuineness and power of their religious experience. The Jewish sympathizer to whom verses 8-12 are due has thought it wise to slip in first his own categorical assertion that Jewish values alone are valid in religion.

It is in xv: 14-32 that we have genuine epistolary materials, entirely apposite to the concrete situation out of which the letter grows, and wholly appropriate to such a letter as Paul would be writing to the Roman church. Its thought is altogether coherent with the line of discussion which we have been able to disentangle from our present "epistle." It is a powerful confirmation of the thesis that Paul has been writing to this Roman church, so thoroughly Jewish in sympathy, to commend to it his own characteristically Hellenistic interpretation of the gospel.

Perhaps sarcastically, he begins by assuring them that he is persuaded that they are filled with all goodness and wisdom. But he must remind them of the grace that was given him to be a minister to the gentiles. It is his glory that the offering of the gentiles was acceptable to God, being sanctified by the Holy Spirit. For they have attained that righteousness from God, evidently apart from law, which consisted in their being obedient in word and deed in a dynamic experience of spiritual power accompanied by signs and wonders. Here is the characteristic Pauline gospel, empowered in the Holy Spirit, and eventuating in present obedience.

It may be objected that Paul is speaking of his ministry rather than the life of his converts, as being endued with spiritual power, and manifested in signs and wonders. While this may be a possible construction of the Greek it is by no means necessary. And it would in no degree minimize the contrast between the gentile and the Roman types of Christianity which Paul is drawing, entirely to the advantage of the gentile or Hellenistic type.

Paul concludes this portion of his letter by pointing out the extent of his field of labor, which has many times hindered his plan to come to them, and repeating the hope that the way may soon be open for him to visit them. But now, although his present opportunity in the district in which he is at work is at an end, which they might think would make it possible for him to come to them, he must go to Jerusalem to deliver the collection which he has taken up among his churches for the relief of the saints. He hopes that they will join with him in prayer that he may be delivered from disobedient Jews, and that his ministration may be acceptable to the Christians. This is a definite indication of the strained feelings existent between Paul on the one hand, and both Jews and Jewish Christians on the other.

Verse 33 is a simple, appropriate, and perhaps Pauline conclusion to the letter.

The entire sixteenth chapter must be rejected, for in it we are in neither the world nor the mind of Paul. Prisca and Aquila we know, but we do not know of any occasion upon which they risked their necks for the apostle. Neither do we know of any captivity shared by Andronicus and Junias. It is most suspicious to find so many listed as *kinsmen* of the apostle. They are Andronicus, Junias, Herodian, Lucius, Jason and Sosipater. It is commonly explained that they were not really his relatives, but that they were Jews, to all of whom Paul felt himself related. But every one of these Jewish relatives has a Grecian name. Nor is there any evidence that they were Jews, except that this assumption would solve a very embarrassing problem. But when we learn that Andronicus and Junias were not only relatives, but were of note among the apostles, and had been Christians before the author, presumably Paul, our credulity is strained beyond the limit of endurance. Moreover, the writer was so closely associated with Rufus that the mother of the latter might be spoken of as also his own.

If we could regard this material as genuine it should be a sufficient comment upon the value of "Luke" as a historian to remark that we have here the survival in written form of a "source" dealing with many dear to the apostle and closely associated with him in his work, and by blood, and alluding to a crucial experience in his career, of which not the slightest trace is to be found in the book of Acts.

And certainly the acceptance of this material as genuine should forever settle the question of the place of women in the life and even in the ministry of the Pauline church. Phoebe is definitely made a "deacon" in the church in Cenchrea; Prisca is spoken of as his helper; Mary, Tryphena, Tryphosa, and Persis are spoken of as laboring in the Lord, Mary and Persis abundantly. In the light of these definite assertions such a passage as I Cor. xiv: 33b-36 is clearly impossible. This is not Pauline material, but it should be sufficient to establish the fact that if Paul denied to women a place in the ministry the early church did not follow him, and that some early editor did not feel it inappropriate to ascribe to Paul, or at least to include in the Epistle to the Romans, this material which speaks of six women as helpers, and as having a more or less abundant place in the ministry.

There is little doctrinal material in the chapter but such

as there is has no Pauline color; it coheres much more closely with the Pastorals than with genuine Pauline materials. Christianity is a teaching which they have learned. From schismatics and heretics they are to withdraw. There is no attempt to define the errors of these disturbers, nor to confute them. But in the spirit of Jude and the Pastorals they are merely denounced. They are described as of smooth and fair speech, and as serving their own belly. In the days of an established orthodoxy such a procedure would be sufficient; but in the pioneer days of the Apostle to the Gentiles, when the church was moving toward an understanding of its basic beliefs, some discussion of opposing points of view, so characteristic of Paul, would be called for. This denunciation and excommunication of the heretic came to be standard practice in the later church; it is far from the intelligent and purposeful way in which Paul dealt with his adversaries. Verse 20 may have an apocalyptic significance, but, occurring as it does in this context, it hardly furnishes support for the view that Paul was apocalyptic in his thinking.

It should not be overlooked that in 20b we have a benediction such as those with which Paul often closed his letters. This, as is the mention of Timothy in verse 21, may be a quasi-Pauline touch, designed to create a presumption of Pauline authorship. Tertius is often thought of as the scribe who has written the whole Epistle to the Romans; he may in reality be the author of this little letter commending to some unknown church, or even to the church at Rome, Phoebe, the deaconess of the church at Cenchraea.

Verses 25-27 are recognized as spurious by many scholars. With this verdict we must concur. The textual phenomena connected with these verses alone are sufficient to raise the gravest misgivings as to their genuineness. Their content is definitely non-Pauline. In them we see what the church finally did with the idea of a mystery. Paul undoubtedly understood the term as having reference to the story or "myth" of a dying-rising Savior, with whose supreme and crucial experience we are so closely identified that we become new creatures, and participate in the divine nature. But this later, non-Pauline view, regards a mystery as something long concealed, now revealed. This gives heed solely to the esoteric and intellectual phases of a mystery to the entire exclusion of its "mystic" character, so fundamental and characteristic in genuine Pauline thought.

Chapter V

THE FIRST EPISTLE TO THE CORINTHIANS

PAUL is thought to have written at least four letters to the Corinthian church. Of these letters two have until recently been thought to have come down to us in our canonical First and Second Corinthians. Taken together they are much more considerable in bulk than the remains of his correspondence with any other group. They range over a wide variety of topics, and give us our most detailed knowledge of conditions in the life of the Pauline church.

They can also furnish us with much instruction as to the development through which the originals of the Pauline epistles have passed, and as to the character of the present documents which lie before us in our canon. It is generally admitted that our First Corinthians is not the first letter which Paul wrote to the Corinthian church. For in I Cor. v: 9, he states, "I wrote unto you in my epistle to have no company with fornicators." Many scholars think that this epistle, or a part of it, has survived in our II Cor. vi: 14—vii: 1.

It is also quite commonly held that our II Corinthians is not in the form in which it was sent by the apostle to the Corinthian church. Apart from the question as to whether vi: 14—vii: 1 is or is not a part of the first letter Paul wrote to Corinth, many scholars have felt that in our II Corinthians there are at least portions of two letters which formed part of a long correspondence. In II Cor. ii: 4, and vii: 8 there are references to a severe letter which was written with many tears, which caused great sorrow to the Corinthians as well as to Paul, but which seems to have succeeded in winning them back to their allegiance to the apostle. It is thought that this painful letter, or part of it, is to be found in II Cor. x-xiii, while chapters i-ix constitute still another letter which Paul wrote to the repentant church after his disciplinary or threatening letter had had its desired effect.

However that may be, it is interesting to note that the phenomena exhibited by our II Corinthians have led even conservative scholars to the conclusion that there has been some manipulation of materials surviving in Corinth, whether that manipulation be accidental or purposeful. There are strong indications of complexity in the makeup of the present epistle. It is pure assumption that the manipulation which is supposed to have combined parts of two or three letters in II Corinthians, violating their chronological order by putting a later letter first, and burying deep in the epistle at least a fragment of the first letter of all those which Paul had addressed to the church, has been confined to the Second Epistle to Corinth. If there has been rearrangement of Corinthian material, why should it be thought strange that there should have been rearrangement of Roman, Galatian or Philippian material? It is also pure assumption that an editorial activity which did not hesitate to make even drastic changes in order would not have dared to make changes in content. Or, if not editorial activity be presupposed, but it be held that such changes as have occurred have been accidental, and that the present form of our epistles just grew up, it would be difficult to see why such a purposeless assemblage can be assumed to have excluded all extraneous materials.

It is the viewpoint of this present study that the phenomena exhibited by II Corinthians may be observed in greater or lesser degree in nearly all the letters which have come down to us under the name of Paul. None of them, with the possible exception of Philemon, represents a single letter, but all of them are collections of materials accumulating over long periods of time, in which we have to deal not only with fortuitous, often unfortunate, arrangements of genuine materials, but also with extraneous materials which have grown up either through the use of the original epistles in preaching and the instruction of converts, or through the deliberate attempt to modify the Pauline teaching in the direction of harmonizing it with the views which had become orthodox in the later church. Once the naïve assumption that the canonical letters represent the epistles as Paul actually wrote them to his churches is given up the way will be opened to a new understanding not only of the work and teaching of Paul, but of some of the developments in early Christianity.

It is not our intention to write a commentary on First Corinthians, but merely to try to follow its course of argument, noting disarrangements and alterations, in an attempt to recover as much as possible of the original, and to recognize modifications of Pauline teachings and developments in Christian history and doctrine.

The saluation i:1-3 is a simple greeting specifying Paul as the author, associating with him Sothenes the brother, naming the saints in Corinth as the recipients, and using the customary formula, "Grace and peace to you from God our father, and the Lord Jesus Christ." In this salutation Paul has asserted his apostleship through the will of God, but has introduced no doctrinal matter. Even this salutation has been modified, however, by the addition of "with all those who call upon the name of our Lord Jesus Christ, in every place, their Lord and ours." This is highly inappropriate in a letter sent to the Corinthian church which deals with some very personal and embarrassing questions not at all suited to an open letter. It is thoroughly natural when the letter has become part of the possession of the entire church, and is used in the instruction, not only of Corinthians, but of all who call upon the name of the Lord.

Paul's customary thanksgiving for those things which he could approve in the life of those whom he addressed, follows hard upon the salutation, (i: 4-9). It, too, seems to have been modified by the gloss found in 7b, 8, which has taken the whole edge off Paul's characteristic conception of the Christian life. Disregarding this mutilation, we find Paul thanking God for the grace given them, which has assured that they are enriched in all utterance and knowledge, falling behind in no gift, and concluding with his confidence in the faithfulness of God which has called them into "fellowship" with his son Jesus Christ. The meaning of this is crystal clear to the student of Pauline thought; Paul has consistently made the Christian life to consist in our sharing in the life of Christ, dying with him to the flesh and to sin, rising with him to newness of life, and living with him, and in him, from day to day. This "participation" in Christ is parallel to enrichment in utterance and knowledge, and attainment in every gift. Into this context is thrust the contrary idea that the Christian life is a waiting for a future salvation, to be revealed in the days of our Lord Jesus Christ, the essence of which is to be that we are to be found unreprovable in the judgment assumed to be part of that revelation. "Fellowship" with Christ would thus be made to mean that no charge could be brought against him; while "participation" in Christ is excluded. This latter, the denial of the mystic meaning of Christianity, is probably what the glossator intended.

The remainder of the first four chapters is mainly taken up with Paul's attempt to deal with the disunity in the church of which he has learned from certain of the household of

Chloe. It appears that factions have developed in the Corinthian community, parties having grown up about different leaders. It is commonly held that there are four of these parties, those of Paul, of Apollos, of Cephas, and of Christ. It soon appears, however, that there are but two, at least but two to which Paul thinks it important to devote much of the discussion. These are the parties of Paul and of Apollos. The Christus party has bulked much more largely in the discussion of the epistle than it does in the epistle itself. The four chapters revolve around the twin centers of Paul and Apollos on the one hand, and the pride of wisdom on the other.

Paul very greatly deprecates the tendency to form a party under the banner of his name. It seems that he has done all in his power to prevent the rise of such a party. He has been particularly careful not to baptize his converts, lest this constitute a mark which might set some apart from others whom he had not baptized. His whole interest had been in preaching the gospel, not in the wisdom of words but in power. (i: 10-16.)

The trouble appears to have arisen out of the "wisdom" which characterized the preaching of Apollos. It is not important to decide whether this refers to the content of his gospel, or to the oratorical ornamentation of his discourse. At any rate, there were those who were comparing him with Paul, to the disadvantage of the apostle.

Paul's dealing with the ensuing problem seems to consist principally in the elaboration of two assertions. The first is the disparagement of what the world would call wisdom in favor of a true wisdom, which consists in a spiritual experience of power by which we become like Christ. The second is the abjuration for himself, and for all true ministers of

Jesus Christ, of any place of pride or prominence; the insistence that he and Apollos are but equal fellow workers in the same cause, and that the ministry is a stewardship to be fulfilled in hardship, in sorrow, and in utter self-abnegation.

Paul insists that any dependence upon wisdom will make void the cross of Christ. For religion consists in an experience of power and not in anything that the world would call wisdom, whether that refer to a content of esoteric knowledge, or to any sophisticated rhetorical elaboration of discourse. No type of wisdom suffices for a knowledge of God. The intellectualistic approach to religion is forever futile. The wise, the scribe, and the disputer of this world alike stand discredited. God has made foolish the wisdom of the world. He has chosen to save the world through what the world would call foolishness, the preaching of the cross. (i: 17-25.)

As a comment on this Paul calls attention to the fact that God had not built the Corinthian church out of material which the world would have chosen, the upper classes, the wise, the strong, the noble, but rather the weak, the base, the despised; so that there would be no occasion for any human pride, nor for any boasting of the flesh. And so his gospel which he had preached among them had not been such a gospel as the world would have chosen, excellent in its form or content; it had been alone the word of Jesus in his crucifixion, so that their faith might not rest upon the wisdon of men, but rather upon the power of God. (i: 26—ii: 5.)

Drawing, it seems, upon the phraseology of the mysteries, Paul then asserts that he does have a wisdom to preach to the fully initiated. For God has revealed it through the Spirit. The Spirit alone can reveal true wisdom. This follows necessarily from an understanding of what this wisdom is. As the depths of human nature can be known only by man's own spirit, so can the ultimate realities of the divine nature be known only by the Divine Spirit, and they can be made known by him alone. This is not information to be imparted, but an experience to be shared. He who has not the Spirit of God ministering in his heart, the natural man, has no conception of this divine truth, for it can be imparted only to those who have the Spirit, or it can be apprehended only by spiritual means. Tying this in with Paul's fundamental teaching as to our mystic participation in the dying-rising of Jesus, we see how this wisdom, mediated in the power and demonstration of the Spirit through the foolishness of preaching a crucified Christ, can reach its climax in the assertion that we have the mind of Christ. By sharing in the climactic experience of his life and death, we have become like him. Paul has thus destroyed the possibility of any pride in human wisdom by holding up the soul searching challenge to become one with Christ through the crucifixion of the flesh with all its pride and wisdom. (ii: 6, 10-16.)

It is of the utmost import to note the impact of the mystery religions both upon the Corinthian Christians and upon Paul himself. Both seem strongly influenced by them. The difference is that the Corinthians seem to conceive a mystery in the terms of a content that can be known; they are spiritual, they are wise, they know. But for Paul a mystery is ever a spiritual experience we share. It is the dying-rising of the Lord. No one can justify the claim that he is initiated by passing an examination; he is still a babe unless he has attained an experience whose fruits are manifested in his living. This contrast between the basic conceptions of the Corinthians and Paul is clear in his insistence that he must judge their progress in the mystery by their conduct. While there still exist strife and divisions among them, this is conclusive evidence that they are not yet fully initiated. To have the mind of Christ, one must be like Christ. (iii: 1-4.)

This, then, is the true wisdom which Paul preached; he came among them with no self-confident assurance, trusting to his own knowledge, or to his own ability to preach; but in weakness, in fear, and with trembling, he told here, as in every field in which he worked, the simple story of how Jesus had died and had lived again, and how we through faith in him may take our cross, putting to death the old man, and putting on the new in holiness and righteousness before him. And in humble wonder he had seen that in Corinth as elsewhere, the power of the Spirit had taken hold of those who in humble trust in God had tried to become one with Christ. They lived anew, and the fruits of the spirit filled life with everything lovely and of good report. (ii: 1-5.)

In the face of this divine process what is any man? Who is Paul? Who is Apollos? Each is but a minister through whom they believed. It was the activity of the Spirit of God in their hearts as a consequence of their faith that had produced the wondrous result. Do we not see it in all our living? Man can but plant and water; God alone can give the increase. Spiritual growth is divine, miraculous, as is the increase in nature. It is immaterial who plants, and who waters. Both the planter and the waterer are mere helpers; neither of whom contributes the essential part of the process. Every helper in their growth has been a subordinate, each equally important. Paul and Apollos are merely equal subordinates in the great process of their spiritual growth. They are the husbandry of God. (iii: 5-9.)

So let all pride be put aside, whether upon the part of the minister, or upon the part of the Christian. If anyone think himself to be wise, let him become a fool, that true wisdom may be his. For God has taken the wise in their craftiness; he knows the reasonings of the wise, that they are vain. Let no one glory in men, either in his own wisdom, or in the minister whom he is following. The only important thing is their spiritual attainment, which comes from God, and to which all things contribute, whether Paul, or Apollos, or Cephas, or anything in this life or the next. All things are yours, as ye are Christ's and Christ is God's. (iii: 18-23.)

As for himself, Paul is not in the least concerned what men may think of him, or what place they may assign to him. He is a steward of the mysteries of God, and his sole concern is that he may be found faithful in the eyes of him who has entrusted the stewardship to him, and who alone can judge him. (iv: 1-4.)

These things, so clear in the figure of husbandry, Paul has applied to himself and to Apollos for their sakes, so that no one of them be puffed up for the one against the other. (No satisfactory meaning can easily be found for the expression "that in us ye might learn not to go beyond the things which are written." Any meaning assigned to the phrase must be such as will allow it to fit in with the creating of division by one thinking he has exceeded his fellow.) (iv: 6.)

How silly are these divisions resting upon pride! For each one of them is what he is by virtue of what he has received, not of what he is in himself. God has given all the increase, to him alone be glory, and honor and praise. (iv: 7.)

Paul brings the argument to a close by an appeal which must surely have melted every heart. He contrasts the arrogance of their pride in what they think they are with the almost infinite cost at which he, and other ministers of the gospel, have brought to them the word of life. They think they are wise, they are strong, they are honored, they are full.

But those who have ministered unto them have done it at the cost of labor, of suffering, and of want. They are like those who have been condemned to death, bringing up the rear of some triumphal procession, a spectacle exposed to the scorn and callous contempt of all men. "Even unto this present hour we both hunger, and thirst, and are naked, and are buffeted, and have no certain dwelling place, and we toil, working with our own hands: being reviled, we bless; being persecuted, we endure; being defamed, we entreat; we are made as the filth of the world, the offscouring of all things, even until now." (iv: 8-13.)

It will, of course, have been noted that in our exposition of Paul's argument, we have omitted several passages. This has been done because they were not germane to the discussion, and, it would seem, must be excluded by the sense and purpose of the argument itself.

In chapter i, verse 30 seems quite suspicious. It is entirely unnecessary to the context. By its omission verse 31 serves as a quotation clinching the thought of verse 29. Verse 30 thrusts a generalizing summary into the course of a fast moving argument. Wisdom is thoroughly germane to the context. In the addition of righteousness, and sanctification, the glossator is fairly close to the context, and to the mind of Paul. But in the insertion of "redemption," he has introduced a concept which is completely alien, if not to the mind of Paul, at least to the present discussion.

In ii: 6-9, it is quite evident that extraneous material has been added, but one cannot be certain of the precise point at which the genuine materials break off. Judging alike from the construction of the Greek, and the course of the argument, the most satisfactory solution of the problem seems to be to find in the placing of "wisdom" in 6b in apposition to "wisdom" in 6a the device employed by the annotator to tie in his materials with those of Paul. If no genuine materials have been omitted, we should read, "We speak wisdom, however, among them that are fullgrown (vs. 6a) (instead of fullgrown, we should translate, "perfect," or "fully initiated"), for God has revealed it unto us through the Spirit." (vs. 10.)

In the excluded materials, the expression, "a wisdom not of this world" fits in perfectly with what Paul has been saying, but could easily be supplied by anyone wishing to make his materials conform to the setting. No serious objection could be raised to the quotation in verse 9, for it does but bear out the idea that the true wisdom proclaimed among the initiates was beyond human comprehension; it must be prepared by God himself. But Paul's thoroughly spiritual and beautifully logical argument is altogether distorted by the introduction of completely alien points of view. There is the idea that a mystery is something hidden, now revealed. This is the standard interpretation of a mystery upon which the church ultimately settled. How alien it is to this context is immediately apparent when we reflect that this stresses the content which is once hidden now revealed, an idea which Paul is categorically denying. To this is added the idea of predestination which frequently is intruded into Pauline arguments. Here it is pure excess baggage. In the eighth verse we see the climax of the idea that a mystery is occult esoteric knowledge. We know something which even the dread spirits referred to as "the rulers of this world" do not know. To allow that "wisdom" is of such character would demolish the whole argument upon which Paul rests his case, that wisdom is not anything known, but is experience mediated in the power of the Holy Spirit, whose possession is not at all to be tested by what we know, but by the quality of our conduct. The contrast between the Pauline and the non-Pauline ideas of a mystery could scarcely be more clearly pointed.

In chapter iii: verses 10 through 17 are not apposite to the discussion Paul is conducting. He has been pointing out that he and Apollos are but helpers in a process in which that which is most vital is the activity of God himself. To illustrate this he turns to agriculture, making of himself a planter, of Apollos a waterer. Now he does not insist that the planter is of more consequence than the water boy. On the contrary he maintains that neither of them is more important than the other. Both are equal before God. The only thing that matters is the crop. The Corinthians are God's husbandry.

This basic idea may equally well be illustrated by the figure of a building. Many workmen labor in building, but their effort is but the carrying out of the plan of the master builder who in this context is necessarily God. Paul may have added to "Ye are God's husbandry," the additional figure, "Ye are God's building."

But in verses 10-15 we have a little homily on "building" conceived from quite a different point of view. It may well come from the period of heresy in which the author considers himself the master builder laying the true foundation, but looks askance at the work which others are erecting upon it. Whereas for Paul the master builder must be God, and the structure the people, in this paragraph the master builder is thought of as Paul, or more likely under the type of Paul the teacher who wishes to see all teaching conform to his own, and the structure is the type of teaching these others are doing. Some is good; some is bad. Never mind, the fire will come and prove the work, burning up the wood, hay, and stubble, and allowing only the materials of genuine worth to remain. Perhaps the builders themselves will be saved, but all of their mistaken or vicious works will perish.

In the rejection of this material the most vital consideration is not to be found in the altered connotation of the terms "Masterbuilder," and "building," although this alone should be decisive. Its rejection is compelled by the consideration of the effect the understanding of this little parable must have had upon the troubled faction-riven life of the Corinthian church. For the point of this homily is the distinction between the builders, and the type of work they are doing. Instead of making all equal before God, of equal importance for the work, the attainment of the Corinthians, it clamors, "Judge between us builders; commend or condemn the work we are trying to do. Decide which of us is the master, or which ones of us are building worthily upon the true foundation." This could but have intensified the divisions in the church. It would but have furnished each faction with a stout club with which to belabor his opponent. Especially would it have encouraged the adherent of Paul to say "Paul laid the foundation in this church; he is the master builder: Apollos has come in later; his work is stubble, and will be burned!" It would thus have been fatal to the result Paul was trying so hard to achieve.

In verses 16 and 17 we find a bit of material which may well be Pauline, but which has no place in this context. It fits in beautifully with the discussion of the holiness of the body, which is the dwelling place of the Holy Spirit, and thus the temple of God, which is destroyed by fornication. These verses, if genuine, have been displaced from some such discussion as that in vi: 12-20. Their presence here is a testimony to the fact that our present epistle has been modified at least by the displacement of some of its materials.

In chapter iv, verse 5 seems to be a typical homiletic gloss. Paul has been asserting his lack of concern in any judgment the Corinthians may pass upon him, deprecating the partisanship which would arise from such comparative judgments. He is concerned merely that he be faithful to the stewardship entrusted to him by the Lord, who now is judging him, whether day by day he be faithful to his trust. This concept has great value in dealing with the situation before the eyes of Paul, the partisanship which is dividing the Corinthian church. But when that situation had died down, and the epistle is used in the edification of a wider circle, the idea that the Lord was daily judging Paul as to whether he had been faithful to his entrusted task would have but slight application to the lives of those who were then being instructed. It is therefore generalized into the judgment that would be passed upon all, which would take account not only of the faithfulness with which they had carried out assigned tasks, but which would include every hidden thing of evil, even the most secret counsels of each heart. This would, of course, be in the great day "when the Lord should come."

We should pause to estimate the light which this passage throws upon the supposed "apocalypticism" of Paul. It does, indeed, speak of the judgment in the day the Lord comes, but it gives no indication of the imminence of that day. It does not appear to be part of Paul's argument, but a homiletic generalization, intended to make the materials suitable for exhortation in a later day when the primary situation has lost its meaning. It can lend no support to the theory that Paul was apocalyptic in his thinking.

Verses 14-21 of this fourth chapter seem to be genuine.

They give us a true appreciation of the simple directness and heart-moving poignancy with which Paul wrote. But they are not at all germane to the situation which lies back of these first four chapters. For they do not deal with the question of factions which has arisen out of the rivalry of parties aligning themselves under the banners of Paul and Apollos, which Paul has sought to solve by pointing out that he is not one whit more important than Apollos, but both are equal fellow workers under God. This passage makes Paul infinitely more important than any other who is presently in question, and urges their allegiance to him, and to him alone. Its effect in the situation contemplated in the immediate context would be disastrous. But this material belongs unquestionably in some situation in which Paul's authority has been flouted, in which he has had to send Timothy to try to win back their allegiance to him, and in which he has had to make use not only of passionate pleading, but also of threats of vigorous action. It is surely much better to see in the placement of this passage the evidence of accidental disarrangement, or of bungling editorial activity, than it is to think of Paul as having no more sense than to conclude his masterly argument for unity in the Christian church upon the basis of the equality of the ministers in question with this passionate paragraph pleading for their allegiance to him alone. It would reduce Paul's logic to something of this order, "Apollos and I are of equal consequence, but I am of far more consequence than he!!"

In chapter five we have an illustration of the characteristic directness with which Paul dealt with a situation arising in the life of one of his churches, and also an illustration of how Pauline materials were modified by later influences.

Setting aside the spurious passages we learn that Paul had heard of a shocking case of immorality in the group. Someone had run off with his father's wife, presumably his own step-mother. And the Corinthians were puffed up over it, rather than mournfully removing the offender from their midst. If verses 3 and 4 are regarded as genuine, Paul speaks of himself as though having been present with them in spirit, and passing judgment upon the offender. This judgment must be his exclusion from the group. This appears not only from the illustration that a little leaven leavens the entire lump, so that if he were left among them, this brazen offender might infect all of them with his own impurity, but from the definite injunction with which the chapter reaches its climax, "Cast out the wicked man from among you."

It should be easy to recognize the modification in verses 7b and 8 for what it is, a later homily attempting to utilize the passage in general Christian instruction. It is to be hoped that the circumstances under which Paul wrote would not face many preachers. Seldom does one have to deal with a case of incest between a man and his father's wife. It is also to be hoped that there would arise few occasions upon which one would have to preach upon having to put some brother out of the church. The situation must therefore be generalized and spiritualized. The idea of leaven must be taken out of its context in which it means some wicked brother whose continued presence in the church might contaminate the whole group. The lump must no longer mean the church. But let the leaven be taken to signify malice and wickedness which is to be found in every life, and instead of the lump which is the church, let the contrast with the leaven be found in the unleavened bread, which is to be thought of as sincerity and truth. And so the figure of leaven permeating a lump is lost in the wholly different conception of the leavened and unleavened bread, which necessarily suggests the Passover. This must be given a Christian connotation, "Christ is our Passover"; he has been sacrificed for us. Thus, from a most unpromising start has been evolved a sermon which might be preached on any Sunday, but which is most appropriate during the Lenten season. The wicked man, his wicked deed, his demoralizing influence upon the church, and Paul himself, have all passed completely out of focus.

There is certainly a further modification in verse 5, if it do not extend to verses 3 and 4. These latter verses seem rather too heavy and involved for Pauline writing, and do not add much to the thought of the passage. It is quite possible that they are genuine and grow out of the fact that Paul felt so deeply the disgrace that had been brought upon the church that he thought of himself being present in spirit, joining in a congregational meeting which had judged the offender. But the church seems to have had no idea of condemning him, but rather to have been puffed up over his action. But whatever may be our decision in regard to verses 3 and 4, verse 5 must be decisively rejected. Any judgment which Paul has in mind seems to be that the offender must be removed from the group. This interpolation introduces ideas which later become familiar, but which have no application to the case in question.

Where Paul has been thinking of the purity of the church this verse is thinking of the salvation of the soul. It is frankly from the redemptionist point of view. Paul says we must save the church; this annotator says we must save the sinner's soul. The means of salvation is passing strange. It is to deliver the offender to Satan for the destruction of the body. When is the offender to be thus delivered? now, or in the day of judgment? What does the destruction of the body mean, the death of the offender? In that case how silly to talk of excluding from the church a man who is already dead! Or should we interpret the destruction of the body in the true Pauline sense of the crucifixion of the flesh? In that case the sin would be purged away, and there would be no further need for talk of excluding the brother from the church. There does not seem any reasonable meaning to attach to this phrase which would allow it to apply to the case of the incestuous man. It is, however, crystal clear when looked at from the later Catholic or orthodox conception of the salvation of the soul, almost certainly from the point of view of purgatory. Purgatory without bodily pain would be of little use to frighten the sinner; it is through the intensification of pennance to the point of destruction of the flesh that sins may be atoned for. And so the case may be dealt with by the pronouncement of the sentence of excommunication which will condemn the offender to purgatory until the flesh is destroyed, so that the soul may be saved. How far this theological development is from the specific case in which this flagrant sinner must be removed from the group lest he contaminate the church!

It is worth remark that Paul realizes fully that the church cannot withdraw from the world; it can only exclude flagrant sinners from its membership. This would tend to invalidate the materials found in II Cor. vi: 14—vii: 1.

The materials in vi: 1-11 are highly questionable. It has just been categorically asserted that the church judges those within its own body (v: 12). vi: 1-8 deals with the abuse of Christians' suing their brethren at law in the pagan courts.

It may be fairly doubted whether in the brief time which must have elapsed since Paul had organized the Corinthian church sufficient causes could have arisen to have created this situation in which the habit of Christians' haling their brethren into law courts had amounted to a scandal. This is, of course, possible, but all the probabilities are against it. However we may decide in regard to verses 1-8, it is quite evident that verses 9-11 do not cohere with their context. We must keep clearly in mind that the discussion has been concerning the practice of Corinthian Christians' seeking redress in pagan courts for offenses which their fellow Christians have committed against them. But in verses 9-11 we have a catalog of offenses of which thievery, reviling, and extortion, possibly adultery, could be causes of litigation, but in which idolatry, drunkenness, self abuse, and certainly covetousness could not be made a cause of action at law. Besides, while 1-8 contemplates the continuation of offenses which might cause Christians to proceed against their brethren, verse 8, indeed, categorically asserting that they are now wronging each other, 9-11 on the other hand states that while such offenses have characterized the Corinthians, now they have been washed clean, they have been sanctified. The offenses no longer exist; there are no causes for litigation.

The very phraseology with which verse 9 introduces the following material should put us on our guard. "Or know ye not?" "Be not deceived." These phrases are reminiscent of the diatribe, and suggest preaching rather than an epistle. It is not contended that Paul shows no evidence of being influenced by the diatribe, but merely that this phraseology which suggests preaching should raise the question whether we are not here really dealing with a homily? In fact we are here confronted with a later homily upon the pre-Christian and the Christian states of believers. Previously they had been idolaters, sexually abnormal, thieves, covetous, drunken, but now they had been washed (in baptism?), sanctified, and justified (which here must mean to make righteous, not to account righteous), in the name of Jesus, and in the Spirit of God. The primary situation in which brother sued brother in pagan courts has been entirely forgotten.

The discussion in verses 12-20 reverts to the question of fornication, dealt with in chapter v, but interrupted by the discussion of litigation in pagan courts, and the little homily in verses 9-11. This paragraph presents us with many difficulties. If the material be genuine it is obvious that it is not preserved in its original connection. It will also appear that it has been glossed or modified. It is hard to conceive that Paul would have admitted that fornication could be "lawful," but was to be avoided merely because it was not "profitable," or because he did not wish to be enslaved to it. As a matter of fact, the condemnation of impurity proceeds from the viewpoint that it is essentially wrong because of the unity that exists between Christ and the Christian. Here we have at least the echo of Paul's fundamental teaching that the Christian becomes one with Christ, or that the Spirit dwells in him. His body, therefore, is a temple of the Holy Spirit, and any impurity will defile that holy place. We must, therefore, glorify God in our body, (by keeping it pure). Personal purity thus becomes very much more than expediency; vastly more than avoiding the domination of evil. One suspects that varied materials have somehow been joined together.

The fourteenth verse is a patent modification of the Pauline point of view. It is questionable whether a reference to the resurrection be in order at this place. If it did occur it would have been part of Paul's usual teaching of mystic unity; we become one with Christ through sharing in his experience of dying-rising again. As has frequently happened in the Pauline literature the mystic interpretation of the resurrection of Christ, that we should share in it by being raised to a new life of righteousness, is destroyed by substituting the meaning that as he lived again, so should we be raised to a life beyond the grave. It is, of course, conceivable that this might be made the basis of an argument for personal purity, that immorality is unworthy of one who is to live forever. But it is not so argued here. The burden of this passage is that the Christian has been joined spiritually to Christ; that the Spirit has taken up its abode in his body; and that therefore impurity will defile the temple of God, which the Christian has become. In other words, the basic point of view is genuinely Pauline; this non-Pauline interpretation of the resurrection, that it guarantees us immortality, is completely without the orbit in which the thought is moving.

We must also set aside verses 19b and 20a, "and ye are not your own; for ye were bought with a price." It would be hard to conceive a more abrupt, a more violent change of figure. The whole argument has been from the basic Pauline conception of our unity with Christ. But suddenly the figure changes to that of a slave who may not do what he will, because he has been bought with a price, and belongs to another. It goes without saying that the argument of the passage might have been, "We may not be impure, because we belong to God, and he does not wish us to be." But this point of view touches the paragraph only here. Its impropriety to this context appears from the fact that the paragraph concludes, "glorify God therefore in your body." This conclusion is entirely apposite to the argument from the mystic unity of the Christian with Christ. It has no meaning whatever from the interpolated point of view. This same expression, "ye were bought with a price" appears in vii: 23, where it coheres with the context, but where the whole passage in which it occurs must be judged to be spurious.

In chapter seven we have a turning point in the construction of the epistle as it now lies before us; for in it Paul seems to take up certain questions concerning which the Corinthians had written to him. It is impossible to say how far the treatment of their questions continues. It may be that they had asked only concerning marriage and sexual relations; it may be that everything which follows this point grows out of their inquiries. It is hazardous to form any opinion in regard to this question in view of the disarray in which all Pauline materials have come down to us.

The seventh chapter is itself highly complex. In it appear many diverse strands. It is probable that materials dealing with the questions of marriage and sexual relations accumulated, being classed together because they dealt with the same problem rather than because they exhibited the same point of view. Verses 17-24 deal with entirely different matters.

If we have in this chapter Paul's own point of view in regard to marriage it would seem to be that first set forth. While it were better for all to remain single, for a man not to touch a woman, this might not be possible, because lust or sexual instinct and desire were so deeply rooted that Christians might be carried away into impurity. It were better to marry than to engage in a losing struggle with sexual passions. So let each have her own husband, his own wife. Those who are married should be faithful to the obligations of the married state which entail that they should live in sexual relations, each satisfying each other's need and desire, abstaining from sexual intercourse only upon special occasions by mutual consent for deeper cultivation of the religious life, after which sexual relations should be resumed. (vii: 1-5.) This would seem to exclude the possibility of maintaining virginity within the marriage relation, which is contemplated in verses 36-38.

But while it is preferable that all, if possible, should remain unmarried, it were better to marry than to be tormented with sexual desire. And if married, they should remain true to the marriage vow. If married to one not a Christian, the Christian should not leave the non-Christian partner, first, for the sake of peace, and second, because it might be that the non-Christian partner might be won to the Lord. (vii: 6-15.)

In the fourteenth verse we find the interpolation of an entirely alien point of view. Marriage relations have been viewed as upon a lower plane than celibacy; it is not a matter, however, of right and wrong, but merely of that which is better, and that which is less good. Absolutely no distinction has been made between Christians, and non-Christians. It is merely a matter of sexual relations between a man as such, and a woman, as a woman. Religious faith has not figured in the discussion. But here the viewpoint seems, strangely, to be that sexual relations between Christians are holy, while such relations between non-Christians are impure. In the case of a mixed marriage it is a question whether the purity of Christian sexual life or the impurity of non-Christian sexual life would dominate the relationship and the children which resulted therefrom. The comforting assurance is given that the unbeliever is sanctified in the believer, and that the children are holy. From this is necessarily to be drawn the corollary that all the children of non-Christians were unclean. This consideration is entirely unnecessary because no point has been made as to the distinction between Christians and non-Christians in their sexual relations.

The conclusion of the discussion is to be found in verse 17a, "Only as the Lord has distributed to each man, as God has called each, so let him walk."

But in 17b, or in 18-24 we meet with one of the generalizations so common to the later use of the epistles in the guidance of the church. The injunction that each continue to walk in the state in which he has been called is taken out of its setting, the question of the marriage relation, and applied to other questions that had become insistent in the life of the community, those of race, and of servitude. Should those who were Jews, set aside by the mark of circumcision, repudiate their race and nationality, and seek to become as though uncircumcized? By no means! Should those who were gentiles seek to become members of the Holy Nation, taking upon themselves the fleshly mark of the People of God? Certainly not! Neither circumcision nor uncircumcision was anything; all that mattered was the keeping of God's commandments. It were better to become free if possible, rather than to remain a slave; but even this was not essential, for all were slaves of Christ. The conception "ye were bought with a price" is entirely apposite here. The church is to be guided by the principle that so long as our relation to the Lord is right, no outer or earthly relationship is of any great importance.

The question of the genuineness of 17b may be left open. It is quite possible that Paul sought to secure a uniformity among his churches by appealing to his prescriptions for other groups. It seems more probable, however, that he dealt with each case on its own merits, and that all of these appeals to the common practice of the church come from the age when the church as a whole is becoming conscious of its unity, and certain views or practices had acquired the sanction of custom.

In verse 25 the discussion reverts to the question of marriage and sexual relations, showing that the preceding paragraph is at best a digression. In the remainder of the chapter three separate points of view are clearly discernible. The basis of authority seems quite strange for Paul. "I give my judgment, as one that has obtained mercy of the Lord to be trustworthy," (vs. 25) and "I think I also have the Spirit of God," (vs. 40). This is in stark contrast to Paul's usually confident assertion of authority as one who has been commissioned by God and by the Lord Jesus Christ.

Verses 26-31 are apparently devoted to the consideration of marriage from the apocalyptic point of view. The fashion of this world is passing away; the time of distress is upon us; those in the flesh shall have great tribulation. It is passing strange, however, to read that the effect of the imminence of the end of this world is the negation of all values. Henceforth those who have wives are to be as though they had none, those who rejoice as though they rejoiced not, those that weep as though they wept not. The only sensible conclusion to draw from this state of affairs is that marriage and celibacy are matters of indifference. The conclusion, "Don't marry, because marriage is indifferent!" is an exhibition of stupid incompetence.

It must be pointed out that the apocalyptic point of view has not governed the discussion of marriage with which the chapter began. There the long pull is clearly before the mind of Paul. It is simply silly to think that he feels it necessary to lay down principles for the governance of life throughout the years because he is dominated by the apocalyptic point of view, and is convinced that by about day after tomorrow everything will have given way to the age that is to come. But here, forsooth, Paul has suddenly waked up to the realization that it is all a matter of indifference because the time is so short; and because it is a matter of indifference, it were better if no one were married.

Neither are verses 32-35 written in the expectation of the imminence of the end. Here an entirely new reason is advanced for remaining single. The married state makes one careful for the things which one's partner desires, so that it is not possible to serve the Lord without distraction. One who is single, however, may give all his thought and energy to the religious life. It is as true of other cares and entanglements, as it is of marriage, that they distract from whole-hearted and exclusive devotion to the religious life. This paragraph would seem to come from one who is already walking in the way that leads to monasticism.

Verses 39 and 40 also seem to fall without the sphere of any apocalyptic conception. Marriage is to endure only during the lifetime of the husband; if the husband die, a consideration that need not come in for any attention if the end is already upon us, the widow may marry again, but only in the Lord, whatever that may mean. In any event this is a counsel for the years.

In verses 36-38 we encounter the strange question of preserving virginity within wedlock. This meaning is entirely obscured in the English versions by supplying the word "daughter." This problem did arise in the later life of the church. But if it pressed upon Paul, it seems impossible that after having elaborated so fully the duty of married persons to fulfill the sexual desires of their partners he should have thus commended the preservation of virginity in the marriage relation, looking upon sexual relations only as a concession to those who could not achieve the higher way of life. This seems a wandering bit of stray material written from a later point of view which has found a resting place in the collection of "Pauline" materials. It has some affinity with the immediately preceding paragraph in that it is dominated by the same self denying, other-worldly point of view which ultimately leads to asceticism and monasticism. It is Catholic, rather than Pauline.

The problem of what the Christian should do in regard to things sacrificed to idols was one which caused grave concern both to the apostle and to his Corinthian converts. This problem might arise either through the sale in the market of those parts of the animal sacrifice that were not consumed, or through the use by one's host of such meat. Should one buy for his own use the meat offered for public sale if that meat had been consecrated to an idol? Or should one partake of such meat if he were invited to dinner in a house where it was served? Must the Christian always inquire into this question before making any purchase, or before accepting any hospitality? Since the Christians in Corinth were few, and the pagans were many, it might be that most, if not all, of the meat that was available would be that which had been offered to idols. The question is discussed in chapters eight and ten.

We note first the interruption of the discussion in chapter eight, and its resumption, from a slightly different point of view in chapter ten. There appears to be no reason for the disarrangement of materials. It seems to be either fortuitous, or due to some cause we cannot discover.

Paul's fundamental attitude toward the question of things sacrificed to idols is very clear, and is held consistently. To him an idol is nothing (vs. 4); it follows that things sacrificed to idols have not been contaminated. No possible harm can come from their use. The Christian is, then, to buy freely things that are offered in the market (x: 25), raising no question as to the possibility that they have been sacrificed to an idol. He is likewise to go freely to those houses into which he may be invited, and is to eat what is provided; he is under no obligation first to inquire whether the meat has been sacrificed (x: 27). viii: 10 even seems to contemplate that the Christian may without wrongdoing sit at meat in the very temple of the idol.

There is but one circumstance that may modify this practice of full liberty in the matter. There may be some who do not know, as does the wise Christian, that idols are nothing. To him they are real divinities; things consecrated to them acquire in his eyes a real sanctity growing out of the supposedly real divinity of the idol to whom they have been sacrificed. In this case the "wise" Christian is not to insist upon his right to be governed by his superior wisdom; the weaker Christian may feel that if he partake of things sacrificed to the idol, whose real divinity he recognizes, he is honoring another god. The old associations may prove too strong; he may be drawn back into the maelstrom of his former life. His faith, never any too strong, may be lost. The brother for whom Christ died may perish, not because he has done anything in itself wrong, but because eating meat sacrificed to an idol has led to his separation from Christ, and his going back into his old belief, and his old way of life. (viii: 9-12; x: 28-32.)

Paul is clear and consistent throughout. He cannot admit the reality of the idol, nor the actuality of any supposed consecration. There has been no contamination of meats, and the Christian may at all times and under all circumstances partake of them, without the slightest harm. His liberty may be abridged only by his respect for the scruples of a weaker brother, which scruples are mistaken and due to ignorance of the real nature both of the idol, and of the effect of any consecration to it. However we may explain the separation of viii: 1-13, and x: 23—xi: 1, it is imperative that we see that both paragraphs are dominated by the same basic point of view.

This question of things sacrificed to idols seems to have been debated at length in the Christian church. It occurs both in Revelation (ii: 14, 20), and in the famous decrees of the Council in Jerusalem, as reported in Acts (xv: 29; xxi: 25). The church was not broad enough to accept Paul's sensible point of view. The upshot of the long debate seems to have been the recognition of the reality of the idol; it is made a demon rather than a god; the use of things sacrificed to idols seems to have been forbidden because they are really contaminated, and will necessarily defile or destroy everyone who partakes of them.

This later attitude comes to clear expression in x: 14-22. Here some Christian leader vehemently denounces the use by Christians of things that have been sacrificed to idols. He writes from a sacramentarian point of view, which holds to the Real Presence of Christ in the bread and the wine, and the Real Presence of the demon to whom it has been sacrificed in anything sacrificed to an idol.

It should, of course, be crystal clear that in this paragraph we have conceptions which are diametrically opposed to every point which Paul has made in his discussion. He has said that an idol is nothing; this annotator says that an idol is a demon. The question in x: 19, "What say I then? that a thing sacrificed to an idol is anything, or that an idol is anything?" seems to contemplate an answer "No!" In that case the question might be thought to be written from the Pauline point of view. The annotator, however, is determined that no one shall blunder into that mistaken idea. If the question be his, he expects the answer "YES!" For he proceeds immediately to say that idols are demons, and that anyone partaking of things sacrificed to idols has communion with demons. It may be that the insertion of the question is the skillful attempt upon the part of an editor to create the illusion that the materials are in essential agreement with Paul's standpoint.

There is the same diametrical disagreement concerning the effect upon the meat of sacrificing it to the idol. There is not the slightest hint in the Pauline materials that the thing sacrificed to the idol has been at all contaminated. It is to be partaken of without raising any question. But for this annotator there is a quasi-physical oneness set up between the thing sacrificed, and the demon to whom it had been offered. His theory of sacrifice is that it sets up a real bond between the worshipper and God. It had been so in Old Testament times; those who ate the sacrifices had communion with God. It is astonishing that any scholar should miss the reverential substitution of the altar for God, and think this passage mean that the worshipper communed with the altar itself! It is so in the Eucharist. In the bread we are partaking of the body of Christ; in the cup we are partaking of his blood. Even so, one partaking of that which has been sacrificed to an idol is partaking of the idol himself. The sacramentarian point of view is unmistakable; it is applied with equal rigor to the Old Testament sacrifice, to the Christian Eucharist, and to the sacrifice to idols. He who would depend upon this passage to substantiate any theory of the sacramentarianism of Paul is leaning upon a bruised reed.

The diametrical contradiction persists if we raise the question as to when and under what circumstances a Christian may partake of things sacrificed to idols. Paul has been specific in saying that a Christian may eat anything sacrificed to an idol anywhere and under any circumstances, provided only that any offense to a weaker brother which might lead to the loss of his Christian faith be avoided. Even then the Christian is free; he merely foregoes his liberty because the welfare of the group must take precedence over any right he may have. But this annotator says that no Christian may at any time or under any circumstances partake of anything sacrificed to an idol because of the essential character of that sacrifice which has actually contaminated the offering so that it must automatically and necessarily defile the one eating of it. We cannot drink the cup of the Lord and the cup of demons; we cannot partake of the table of the Lord, and of the table of demons. To do so is to recognize another god beside him; it is to provoke his jealousy; it will array all of his might against us; are we stronger than he?

There is no point at which the modification of Pauline materials may be more clearly perceived, and more definitely established than in regard to this question of things sacrificed to idols. We see the intrusion of a diametrically opposite set of ideas, whose development seems to have left its record in other New Testament documents. It cannot increase our confidence in "Luke" as a historian, especially in the Pauline field, to observe his agreement, in his report of the council in Jerusalem, with the spurious, rather than the genuine Pauline viewpoint, especially since Paul himself testifies that this council laid no requirement upon him, or upon his churches. (Gal. ii: 10.)

It is unimportant to decide whether the doxology in viii: 6b is original or secondary. Such an interruption of the thought is more natural in the reading of materials in worship than in writing a letter. The addition of "one Lord Jesus Christ" may be from one who feared that the insistence upon rigid monotheism which functioned well in Paul's argument might weaken confidence in the belief in the divinity of Christ.

The situation lying back of the ninth chapter is easily recreated, though it is by no means certain that all of its materials are genuine. It would seem that Paul's apostle-ship, and the rights perquisite thereto, have been questioned. His enemies were saying, "He is no apostle; he is himself aware of his lack of authority, for he does not demand that you support him." Paul's reply is that he is an apostle; he has seen the Lord; he has every right an apostle has. It is interesting to note that the rights specified are to eat and drink (evidently what he wished), to lead about a wife as did the rest of the apostles, the brethren of the Lord, and Cephas. Those in the early church who did not accept celibacy were evidently in illustrious company.

In particular, the right to forbear working, and to be supported by those to whom he ministered, evidently because this was the right most questioned, is supported at length by instances of the soldier, the husbandman, the shepherd, the ox treading out the corn, and the ministers of the temple. The prescription of the Lord himself is cited. The right existed; it was his. He was an apostle. He had seen the Lord.

But although this right was his he was willing to forego it, not because of any doubt as to his right to insist upon it, but because the insistence upon it might interfere with the success of his ministry. He would not glory in any rights he possessed, but in the fact that he had made the gospel available freely to all. He does all things for the gospel's sake, that he might be a joint partaker thereof. It is enough for him to share in the gospel which he proclaims.

Upon this clear and consistent argument (ix: 1-18), two alien lines of thought seem to have been imposed. Paul had been speaking of the giving up of rights lest his insistence upon them interfere with the success of his ministry. In verses 19-22 there is again raised the old question of the Jew and the gentile, of observance of the law, and freedom from it. Instead of the giving up of personal rights to avoid interference with the success of the gospel, the question is raised whether one might not conform to the law, or live in complete freedom from it, according as he is in a Jewish or a gentile situation.

This interpolation, for such it is judged to be, is just close enough to the Pauline point of view to be troublesome. It is safe to assume that Paul's irenic spirit would lead him to conform to any situation he met so far as his conscience and his basic understanding of the Christian life would allow. But his stand in essentially similar circumstances is clear in Galatians, where he insisted that there could be only one gospel. His opponents have suggested that observance of the law be added to faith in Christ, only to provoke the answer that such a course would be unthinkable; it must be

Christ OR circumcision. (Gal. v: 2-4.) If Paul could ever have admitted the contention of this passage it would have lost for him his whole Galatian battle. Perhaps his Galatian adversaries would only have said, "In dealing with the Jews, it is right that you should adopt their viewpoint of conformity to the law." This would seem to be the pronouncement of one living at a later time, when the fires of Jewish-gentile controversy had died down, and his more catholic spirit could see no harm in conformity.

It is true that certain passages in the book of Acts represent Paul as being actuated by this point of view. It is surprising how uniformly "Luke" agrees with later and spurious passages in the Epistles. If it had been possible to point out to the Galatians that Paul had himself taken a vow, or paid the expenses of those fulfilling a vow, what havoc would have been wrought in that church!

Verses 24-27 seem to have missed the entire point of being "a joint partaker" of the gospel. Here we have a little sermon, not on the genuine Pauline theme of how to live so that as many as possible might share with you in the gospel, but on how to run so that you may get the prize. Many run, but only one wins! Be sure that you do not fail. Undergo all the rigors of training; run the race itself with all the concentration of which you are capable, so that you yourself may be saved. This exhortation would be of the greatest value in dealing with Christians dismayed by the difficulties of the Christian life, and grown lax in its living. It is entirely beside the point of Paul's argument.

The theme of the danger of missing salvation, and the exhortation to make sure of it, are continued in the first thirteen verses of chapter ten. The basic problem of the genuineness of Paul's apostolic authority, especially as this is affected by his failure to demand support from his converts, which is supposed to be the subject of discussion, is completely lost sight of it. The abrupt change in style should at once arouse our suspicions. Had this paragraph been found adrift upon the stream of Christian literature it would perhaps without hesitation have been referred to Hebrews. It has the same interest in typology. It plays with words in much the same fashion. Its exhortations are repetitive and wearisome. Its teaching is clear. As there are many more runners than there are winners, we must remember that not even all the Israelites were saved, although all of them passed through the marvelous experience of the wilderness. But there is no need to fall short as they did, for with every temptation there is a way of escape. So run that you may win! There is a distinct tendency to allegory; the author sees in the cloud and the sea the counterpart to baptism; he is probably thinking of the Eucharist in the allusion to the spiritual food and the spiritual drink; in the account of the water from the rock he sees a reference to Christ. The affinities of this material with Hebrews should be clear. If this be one of the supports for thinking that Paul was Rabbinical in his methods, it is apparent how insecurely this theory is based.

This passage has all the earmarks of later, non-Pauline material. There is the same homiletic generalization; it does not apply to any specific situation, but to the generalized circumstance of "any temptation." Its argument is labored, quite in contrast to the vivid, rapid movement of Pauline thought. Its fundamental conception of the Christian life seems to be the endurance of temptation, in which no place is given to the power of God in spiritual oneness with Christ. A further detail is that the passage is mildly apocalyptic in its statement that the ends of the ages are come upon us. This apocalypticism, however, does not seem to impart any sense of urgency to the situation. It does furnish just one more instance in which the idea of the apocalypticism of Paul is found to be derived from secondary, rather than primary materials.

The section dealing with the veiling of women xi: 2-16 is one of the most obscure and difficult ones we have. Very little is known of the circumstances out of which it grew. We search the Pauline literature in vain for any parallel. Paul does not seem to have had to deal with this question in any other church. This is, however, by no means a definite indication that the passage is spurious. But there are many arguments to be urged against its Pauline character.

There is first the appeal to tradition. This must mean something received and handed down, because the case is finally rested upon the custom that prevails in all the churches. In the days of Paul, the churches were new; he was a pioneer dealing with new and strange situations, having no body of precedent and custom to fall back upon. The appeal to tradition and custom is the mark of a later day after doctrines and practices had had time to become crystallized, and the churches could become acquainted with what was going on in Christendom.

The recognition of women as intrinsically inferior to men is also un-Pauline. And even in this passage the viewpoint does not seem to be maintained, for in verse 11 their real equality seems to be recognized. This must either be a countervailing gloss, or represent utter incapacity upon the part of this thinker. But the rest of the passage is clear in asserting the glorious supremacy of man; he is the image of God; the woman was made of him, and through him. There is the naïve assumption that the growing of long hair would dishonor the man, and would honor the woman. This is "natural."

There is very little sense in the whole of the passage. One would think that the reason for insisting that women have their heads covered would be found in the social situation; if women were forward, it might bring calumny upon the infant church. But this reason seems to have occurred only to commentators upon the passage, not to its author. Or it would seem that the woman ought to have her head covered as a sign of her intrinsic inferiority to man. This is the foundation which the author painstakingly builds, only to fail to erect his superstructure upon it. They are to have a sign of authority upon their heads because of the angels. All of his premises are ignored in his reaching of his conclusion. It might be well to remark in passing that in chapter xiv: 33b-36 there is another passage dealing with the activity of women in the church, which also rests its final appeal upon the custom of the churches. But in that passage women are not to be veiled when praying or prophesying; they are not to pray or prophesy in public at all. Let them be silent in the churches! An attempt might be made to reconcile the two passages by maintaining that xi: 2-16 refers to praying at home; but the women would scarcely prophesy at home. The latter detail seems to be conclusive that the passage is dealing with public worship. By accepting as genuine all passages in the present Pauline epistles, we get a picture of Paul as utterly confused upon a great many problems, only one of which is that of the real worth of women, and their place and function in the church.

In the discussion of the Lord's Supper in xi: 17-34, the earlier and the later materials should be easily discernible. Two definite situations are contemplated, each with its own problem, and for these two different problems, two differing solutions are proposed. There is first the material found in verses 17-22, 33, and 34. Here we are given the picture of the early practice of eating a common meal which is often boisterous to the extent of drunkenness. The problem seems to be caused by the irreverence for the house of God manifested in such rowdy feasting and drinking, and the social divisions between the rich and the poor, because of which some gorge themselves, and get drunk, while others do not have enough. This seems to the Corinthians to be eminently proper, for unless there were divisions among them, how would anyone know who's who? The remedy for this situation lies near at hand. They must reverence the house of God. It is not the place for gluttony and drunkenness. And the distinction between the Christians who have, and those who have not, is not proper; the common meal must be a common meal, in which each one waits for his fellow. The rest Paul will set in order when he comes.

In verses 23-32 we face an entirely different situation. There is a new problem for which an entirely different remedy is proposed. The early boisterous common meal in which there might be gluttony and drunkenness has given way to the stately ritual of the symbols of the broken body and shed blood. The ceremony has become traditional; both its content and its form are developed and prescribed. But through long familiarity some Christians are heedless as they partake of the sacred symbols. They fail to realize that they are partaking of the broken body and shed blood of the Savior. The result is that these sacred elements exercise a magic potency; they inflict sickness or even death upon the irreverent worshipper. The remedy is to "Discern the body." It may seem strange that the body thus receives more stress than the blood. This is perhaps a testimony to the fact that the Eucharist was first a breaking of the bread, the cup being a later addition.

It would seem impossible that any church trained in the stately ritual of the developed Eucharist could have allowed the Lord's supper to degenerate into the rowdy meal contemplated in 17-22, 33, 34. The two passages seem to be entirely independent of each other, and each develops its thought without any reference to either the situation existing in the other one, or the remedy proposed for it. There is the possible exception of the words in verse 34, "that your coming together be not for judgment." This may, however, be a ligature designed to give some coherence to discordant materials.

The style of the two passages is as different as their contents. In the first we see the simplicity and vividness of Paul's customary style, while verses 23-27 in their lofty phrasing and their balanced periods unmistakably betray the influence of a long liturgical development.

Verses 31 and 32 are a characteristic generalizing homiletic gloss. In it the basic situation is entirely lost to view. It is no longer a question of a contrast between those reverent worshippers who discern the body, and those who do not, but between the church and the world. The Christian should examine himself, so that he may not come under the condemnation of those in the world, whose fault is certainly not that they have failed to discern the body. But if we are judged, we are merely chastened of the Lord. This overlooks the fact that such chastening often led to death. This is the basis of a little sermon vaguely connected with its context through a play upon the various meanings that may be assigned to the words, "discern," "examine," "judge," and "condemn." This examination, and its resulting judgment, or lack of it, has nothing whatever to do with the Lord's Supper, but with the whole of one's life. The primary situation has been completely forgotten.

Two points of importance for the understanding of Paul emerge from this study. The first is that of his relationship with the early church. This passage is but one of many which try to counteract his independence of the early church, and his difference from it, by representing him as one who had nothing but what he received, and who did but faithfully hand on to his converts that which had been handed to him. In this case, it is true, he is represented as receiving this from the Lord. But it has appeared that this traditional interpretation of the Lord's Supper is alien to the idea of the supper as a common meal, by no means restricted to the bread and wine, which underlies the earlier and undoubtedly genuine materials. Paul was no traditionalist, in spite of the many attempts to make him such.

The second point emerging from this study has to do with the supposed sacramentarianism of Paul. The sacramentarian character of some of the materials is evident. The worshipper is actually partaking of the body and the blood of the Lord. There is a Real Presence, by virtue of which the elements are endowed with a magic potency through which they inflict sickness and death upon the unworthy. The passage is closely akin, both in its fundamental sacramentarianism, and in its harsh spirit, with the materials found in chapter x: 14-22. But neither of these passages belongs to Paul. They cannot be taken as evidence of his sacramentarianism.

If we are to judge from the bulk occupied in the epistle, and the elaborateness with which it is argued, the question of spiritual gifts was one which was causing very great trouble in the Corinthian church. It was not an independent question, but was closely integrated with the divisions among the brethren rooting in pride which grew out of the conceit of superior knowledge. The point of greatest stress seems to have been the gift of speaking with tongues. While this proves to have been an unintelligible babbling, which must be interpreted before it made any sense, it may have been thought to be the embodiment of an esoteric knowledge, greater than any that could be put into words. At any rate, the ability to speak with tongues seems to have been greatly prized, and the gift seems to have been exercised in so unbridled a manner as to interfere seriously with that edification of the group which Paul held to be the chief purpose of their meetings.

Most of the materials in chapters 12-14, which are given over to the discussion of this problem, are genuine. They exhibit the characteristics of Paul's style in writing, and of his method of dealing with the problems that arose in his churches. The whole discussion grows so directly out of the concrete situation faced in the church, and sticks so closely to the issues involved, that there is not the slightest difficulty in reconstructing fully the circumstances which have called for treatment. This is epistolary material; this is the type of letter Paul wrote. In it there are no glosses setting forth countervailing points of view; in it there are no doxologies; there are no little sermons generalizing the principles enunciated. The whole is written clearly, and from a consistent point of view. (Only xii: 2, 3, 13 and xiv: 33b-36 seem suspicious.)

Paul's viewpoint is this. All gifts are by the enduement of the one and self-same Spirit. But although they all have the same basis of spiritual power, there is a difference of function. All functions are necessary to the well rounded development of the whole body. They are to be estimated, not by what they appear to be in themselves, but by what they can contribute to the upbuilding of the whole group. As the human body is one, yet has need of seeing, of hearing, of smelling, and of all other natural functions, which are to be estimated solely by their necessity for the well being of the entire body, so the church is one body of Christ, having need of the different functions vouchsafed to individuals by the ministry of the Spirit. However ordinary and humble any function may seem it is not so if the body need it. (xii: 1, 4-12; 14-30.)

The Corinthians prized the more spectacular gifts, those which would call attention to the individual exercising them, above all the gift of tongues. But Paul points out that speaking with tongues is of relatively little importance in the up-building of the church. It should be restricted; it ought not to be exercised unless there be one present who by a like gift of the Spirit can interpret the meaning of the incoherent outburst. Much greater than the gift of tongues, whose effect would be to set aside the one who had it as superior to his brethren, intensifying the tendency to division and pride so characteristic of the Corinthian church, is the gift of prophecy, which is evidently the impartation of some spiritual insight to enlighten and quicken the spiritual life of the hearer. It is better than the gift of tongues because it contributes more to the welfare of the whole body, the edification of the church. (xiv.)

But there is one gift of the Spirit which is supreme. Tongues, knowledge, and prophecy, all shall vanish away, but love shall never fail. While all should humbly seek any gift of the Spirit which God is pleased to give, love is the greatest of all. Love unites, where other gifts divide. It makes one humble, self forgetful, thoughtful of others, patient, and kind. One who loves will truly build up the body of Christ. (xiii.)

Few questions press as to the genuineness of materials in these three chapters. Those which do occur are easy of solution, because of the very closeness with which the structure of the whole discussion is knit together.

We must set aside xii: 2, 3. There is not a single point at which these verses are germane to the discussion. Paul is discussing the different functions of Christians, all of whom have the Spirit of God. But in these verses the two parties contrasted are not groups of Christians, but Christians and the idolaters outside the church. The contrast is not between the different functions of those who have the Spirit, but between those who have the Spirit, and those who do not. The result of having the Spirit is not a ministry to the church, but an attitude toward Jesus. The fundamental contrast underlying these verses affects nowhere the course of the following discussion. It should be clear that every element comprising the universe of discourse is entirely different. This seems to be an interpolation from the hand of one intent upon separating the sheep from the goats. It coheres closely with those passages which exalt "confession" as one of the greatest of the Christian virtues.

Again in xii: 13 we seem to be confronted with an interpolation or a gloss. The primary distinction between different groups of Christians, who have different functions, although they are endued with the same Spirit, is here lost sight of. The distinction encountered is that between racial groups, Jews and Greeks, between those of different social status, slaves and free men. The vocabulary itself strongly indicates the different cloth of which this verse is made up. Here alone is baptism mentioned. In the words, "we were all made to drink of one Spirit" we have a link with the spurious materials in x: 1-5.

It has often been thought that in chapter xiii we find an independent Stoic-Cynic hymn, which has been incorporated into the epistle, whether by Paul, or by some subsequent writer. This seems to be unlikely. It is so vitally integrated with the context that it appears to be an original part of the discussion. Its style is perhaps somewhat more elevated and polished than is usual with Paul, but, polished as it is, it manifests strikingly his simplicity of style, and his directness in dealing with concrete situations. Its two foci are the partiality and temporary value of all "spiritual gifts," and the very evident concern over the divisions and strife in the Corinthian church which root in pride. Love is not thought of abstractly, but against the background of complacent pride.

That which would give versimilitude to the contention that this was originally an independent hymn is the place that is given to knowledge, especially the idea that knowledge will ultimately come to fulness and completion. But this material dealing with knowledge is much more closely integrated with the Corinthian situation than might appear. For we must always bear in mind that the first difficulty Paul had to face in this letter to the Corinthian church, as it now lies before us, was that occasioned by pride which grew out of the conceit of knowledge. His thought seems to be that all spiritual ministries are partial, in need of being supplemented by others, and of coming to fuller development. This is especially true of knowledge, which is always partial, and of prophecy, which Paul exalts over knowledge. But we may look forward to a time of fuller development when all partialities shall vanish into completion, even as childhood yields to maturity. But faith, hope, and love, always remain, being in need neither of supplement, nor development. It must be freely admitted that the turn given to the close, which in a context deprecating knowledge, still almost allows the argument to reach its climax in the idea that the time will come when knowledge shall be full and true, indicates that there may be here the quotation of materials, which though used with admirable skill, were still sufficiently intractable to tinge the conclusion with a color slightly different than that intended in the whole. But this is immediately counteracted by the climactic summary which leaves knowledge completely out of account; only faith, hope, and love, "abide."

The little paragraph in xiv: 33b-36 so evidently interrupts the context, verses 37-40 following so closely upon verse 33a, and so evidently introduces a question utterly alien to the discussion of spiritual gifts, that it must unhesitatingly be set aside. It is based upon the fundamental idea of the intrinsic inferiority of women, which Paul has expressly repudiated, (Gal. iii: 28). Its appeal is not to the authority which Paul so consciously exercised, but to the custom which prevailed in the churches.

There is very little in the fifteenth chapter which we would attribute to Paul. Perhaps here and there we find the remnants of some genuine passage, greatly worked over. But even these are few and dubious.

We are first struck with the evident purpose to force Paul into conformity with the doctrine of the early church. He who in Galatians so vehemently maintained that his gospel was the only possible one, and that it was entirely independent of any influence from the leaders of the Jerusalem group, is here made to say that he did but preach the common orthodox gospel, which he had received from others, (xv: 1-4). It was that Christ died for our sins according to the Scriptures. It is true that in Acts Paul is made to argue elaborately from the Scriptures, but that can hardly counteract the impression gained from all his extant writings that he did not base his gospel primarily upon them.

It is precisely in the matter of Christ's death and resurrection that the non-Pauline character of this chapter is most clearly to be perceived. In it the dying-rising of Christ is expounded in terms entirely apart from the true Pauline conception of the oneness of the faithful man with Christ in that crucial experience, and the meaning it had for his daily living. Nothing is said of our crucifixion of the flesh with him; nor of our sharing with him in a newness of spiritual life in which the flesh has been done away, and the power of that risen life is manifested in the attainment of righteousness.

This chapter is dominated by the conception of the resurrection, to the exclusion of the cross, in spite of its starting from the orthodox gospel that Christ died for our sins. Christ's resurrection has no immediate meaning for our present lives. It merely establishes the certainty of immortality. Because he lived again; so shall we. And because we shall live beyond the grave, this life becomes worthwhile, especially the work of the Lord, in which we should abound. For

Paul this life was worthwhile, because in it we are able in the power of the indwelling Spirit of God to attain the righteousness which is well pleasing to him; we can fill it with goodness, love, joy, peace, and all other things that are lovely and of good report. Apart from immortality it is still worthwhile. We are more than conquerors. But for the author of this chapter this life is one to be borne in the hope that the best of it may endure into another and better existence.

The possibility of the resurrection, and its meaning for us, are argued in "the persuasive words of wisdom" which Paul has so definitely eschewed. With the exception of a few verses there is closeknit logical argumentation, and the materials move with a stateliness which has not only won them a place in the ritual of the church today, but which also indicates strongly that they had undergone the shaping of liturgical use in the ancient church. In verses 20-28 the movement of thought is much like certain passages in Hebrews. It would seem to make the effects of the resurrection of Christ universal, entirely without raising the question of the need of faith upon the part of the believer. The use of materials drawing a parallel between Adam and Christ seems peculiarly liable to this universalizing fallacy.

In verses 35-58 we have a majestic vindication of the possibility of immortality, and a confident assertion of the reality of our resurrection. Its sustained march of closely knit argumentation is quite unlike the rapier play of Paul's mind.

Coming between two passages which move in stately periods, verses 29-34 immediately impress one with their difference in style. They are much simpler in construction and diction; they refer to a concrete situation in which the author, presumably Paul, is said to have fought with beasts in Ephesus. But they are not free from difficulties. They refer to the custom of baptism for the dead, of which we otherwise know nothing in the Pauline church. The conclusion found in verses 33 and 34 does not seem to be especially appropriate. The movement is quick enough for Paul; at least three topics are introduced in the brief paragraph. But it lacks entirely the vividness and power of his writing. If Pauline, this material is at best out of its proper connection. It can only most doubtfully be ascribed to him.

Again in verses 56 and 57 we find a comment which seems definitely irrelevant and anti-climactic. The argument is, "We shall be changed; corruption shall put on incorruption." This must refer to the resurrection of the body. The corruption in question simply cannot refer to sin, for it is impossible that sin shall put on immortal glory. How much better it would have been to pass immediately from the triumphant statement that death is swallowed up in victory to the concluding exhortation to abound always in the work of the Lord! The introduction of sin and the law, which introduce an element of moral failure entirely alien to the question of the resurrection of the body, must be regarded as a modification of original material. It may be either a homiletic gloss, jotted in the margin by one who wished to preach, not on the topic of the resurrection of the body which has dominated the discussion, but upon the utterly different sequence of ideas, the law bringing sin, and sin leading to judgment, or it may be the deliberate attempt of an editor, familiar with Romans, to give a Pauline color to these materials which he has recognized as alien to genuine Pauline thought.

There remains only the question of the Pauline character of verses 8-10. One can hardly read them without realizing their vividness, and their basic idea of the enabling grace of God. One would, therefore, gladly recognize their Pauline color. But this should not lead us into the error of thinking that the entire paragraph 1-11 is equally Pauline. We may not be able to determine the exact extent of the genuine materials in this passage. It may well be that Paul has recorded the evidences for the resurrection. But two alien elements unquestionably remain, the effort to force Paul to acknowledge the agreement of his gospel with the orthodox creed of the church which is redemptionist rather than mystic, and the idea that success in Christian living, if, indeed, we do not prefer the term "salvation," is to be obtained by holding fast to certain traditions which have been received.

In chapter xvi we are again dealing with genuine epistolary materials, with their feet on the ground in concrete situations. Paul turns to the question of the collection, gives directions as to methods to be used in gathering it, speaks of his plans to tarry at Ephesus till Pentecost, after which he hopes to come to them. He commends Timothy, speaks of his desire that Apollos come to them, (the danger of partisanship has happily subsided, or Paul is confident that his dealing with it in chapters i-iv will be effective); he urges them to be in subjection to all who are helping in the work. There is evidently no recognized leadership with an official status. In spite of his definite acquaintance with many there are no individual salutations. He concludes simply with an autograph signature, and the parting benediction. The "Amen" which occurs in some late MSS. may be the result of the use of the epistle in worship.

But even into this genuinely epistolary material there seems to be obtruded one alien verse. "If any man loveth not the Lord, let him be anathema, Maranatha." (verse 22.) Why it should have occurred to Paul to have added in the conclusion to his epistle, this malediction, so out of keeping not only with his own Christian spirit, but also with the definite charge that everything the Corinthians do is to be done in love, and the commendation of his love to them all in Christ Jesus, passes comprehension. Surely it is best to see this as coming from another hand, in a totally different situation. The allowing of alien matter to slip into either the introduction or the conclusion of a letter would seem almost conclusive proof that such alien matter had found its way into the text when the document in question was no longer thought of as a letter, but rather as material to be used in religious education and exhortation. It will seem unfortunate to some that this verse with its "Maranatha," which might be used as evidence both of the survival of Aramaic in the early church, and particularly in Paul, and of the apocalyptic expectation of the Lord's coming, must be denied to the apostle. Far better to give up both the Aramaism and the apocalypticism of the early church, and of Paul, than the sweetness of Paul's Christian spirit. Every consideration must speak against the genuineness of this verse.

Chapter VI

THE SECOND EPISTLE TO THE CORINTHIANS

THE importance for our understanding of Paul of a thorough analysis of Second Corinthians can hardly be overestimated. For in this epistle we encounter in their most pronounced form some of the phenomena which characterize the entire Pauline corpus. It is quite easy to point out the severe disarrangement of its materials. In ii: 12 we find Paul much troubled because he had not found Titus in Troas. In spite of a great opportunity he pressed on into Macedonia. He evidently found Titus there with a good report, but our letter has, for no apparent reason, broken off at ii: 14, and does not resume the matter of the trip into Macedonia until vii: 5, where the thread is again taken up with no apparent explanation, and where there is not the slightest continuity with the context.

This is only one illustration of the disarray into which the materials in our epistle have fallen, or into which they have been forced. We are many times faced with like displacements of materials, or incoherence of thought. In fact, the epistle as it lies before us is thought by many scholars to be made up of at least parts of two or three separate letters which Paul had written to Corinth, and which have been combined into one, either haphazardly, or for the purpose of taking the edge off a severe and threatening letter by the expedient of placing it at the end of a letter of comfort and commendation. The complexity thus envisaged has been complicated by the insertion of the pharagraph vi: 14—vii: 1 which is entirely independent of its context. One must choose between the composite character of the Pauline corpus, and the irresponsible tendency upon the part of Paul to go off on a tangent at any moment. These aberrations might be explained and overlooked if they were indeed true tangents. Too often, however, the intruded materials are not even tangential to the discussion, but move in an entirely different orbit.

The epistle begins (i: 1, 2) with a characteristic Pauline salutation in which Paul, asserting his apostleship through the will of God, associates Timothy with himself, and addresses the church, and possibly all the saints in Achaia, concluding with the usual formula of greeting, "Grace to you and peace from God our Father and the Lord Jesus Christ." Paul did know how to begin a letter. The only detail which calls for comment is the inclusion of "all the saints in the whole of Achaia." This may witness to the stage in the use of the letter in the instruction of all the church when its reference was extended from Corinth to the whole of the province. Or it may witness to the fact that the ministry of Paul in the provincial centers was not restricted to the city itself, but reached out into the surrounding territory.

The immediately following paragraph (i: 3-11), at once raises some questions. It does not conform to the general Pauline practice of turning immediately from the salutation to thanksgiving for some trait or some achievement in his church which he could commend. This would not constitute a fatal objection to the genuineness of the material, for it must be granted that a man may once in a while vary from his habit in the construction of a letter.

But we are at once struck with the similarity of the formula, "Blessed be the God, and Father of our Lord Jesus Christ," with that found in Ephesians i: 3, and in I Peter i: 3. This may have little significance. It may be entirely fortuitous; it may be that the later writers, (assuming these epistles to be later than Paul), have conformed to a Pauline formula; but it may be that there is here the occurrence of a formula developed in liturgical usage, whose presence bears witness to the lateness of this passage.

The content of the passage is confused, and there follows hard upon it a complete break in the line of thought. The passage lacks so greatly the vividness and clearcut movement of thought usually characteristic of Paul that it must be analyzed closely to determine its content. It would seem that there is confused the idea of the comfort which comes to one in the patient bearing of affliction with the idea of deliverance from the affliction, or from the danger of a threatened affliction, in which case there would be cause for rejoicing, but not for comfort. The basis of the passage is undoubtedly that of comfort in an affliction that is manfully borne. Christ was not delivered from his sufferings; he bore them, and thus is able to comfort us in like afflictions. The Corinthians likewise have to bear the same sufferings which the apostle is supposed to have borne; they are exhorted to bear them patiently; they are assured of comfort in them. The confusion comes from the allusion to the great danger which had threatened the apostle; he had the sentence of death within himself; he could only trust in one whose power was not to be manifested in this life, but who could raise the dead. From this death he was delivered. It is true that some sort of a reconciliation between these different points of view may be achieved by assuming that the apostle underwent an affliction, perhaps an illness actually suffered, perhaps some persecution such as a severe beating or even a stoning, which he thought would prove fatal. But that does not alter the case that there has been introduced into a passage dealing with comfort in affliction the alien idea of deliverance from it, or from danger. This is at best tangential to the main course of the passage. Comfort has been displaced by deliverance. It must be admitted, that this, too, cannot be urged as a fatal objection to the passage. But this difference in color, slight as some may judge it to be, must be taken into consideration in reaching our conclusion, not alone in regard to this passage, but in regard to the epistle as a whole.

The abrupt break in the line of thought at verse 12 is unmistakable. This, too, must be taken into consideration in estimating the genuineness of verses 3-11. It may be that the current theory that a letter of commendation and comfort was prefixed to the "sorrowful letter" found in chapters x-xiii may be modified to hold that merely this paragraph, (vss. 3-11), assembled out of surviving Pauline fragments, has been inserted here to modify the tone of the entire collection which has come down to us as our second epistle. No certain judgment can be recorded.

In verse 12 the discussion certainly turns from comfort to troubles. (i: 12-18.) For Paul here seems to be under the necessity of meeting charges which have been brought against him. He has been accused of insincerity, of unholiness, or of preaching in words of fleshly wisdom. He replies that he has behaved only as actuated by the grace of God. They can glory in him, as he glories in them. The postponement of this glorying to the day of Jesus Christ robs the argument of most of its cogency, (vs. 14). It seems a futuristic gloss. Verse 13 seems to imply that not only Paul's conduct when with them was in question, but even certain letters which he is supposed to have written to them. It is not certain that other letters are referred to, although this is a most natural meaning of the verse. If pseudo-Pauline letters were in existence, this fact must modify our estimate of some of the surviving materials ascribed to Paul. No great weight can be given to this implication of the verse.

The charge of insincerity seems to focus (vs. 17) in the fact that Paul had changed his mind in his plan to visit them. But he points out he had not come, because his visit must have caused them grief. The Greek is by no means clear as to whether he had come once in controversy, and did not wish to make a second painful visit, or whether he had refrained from coming, and had written to them instead, because he was aware of the crucial situation that would have arisen had he come. That the visit was actually made appears likely from xii: 19—xiii: 2.

He did write to them, with anguish and affliction of heart and many tears, (ii: 1-11.) The letter evidently had a salutary effect. The Corinthians had returned to their allegiance to Paul; they seem to have inflicted some punishment upon some individual, who must have been the ringleader in the opposition to Paul. Paul has to urge them to temper their wrath against him, and to forgive him, as the apostle had already done. It should be evident that this does not refer to the incestuous person of I Cor. v. The individual here in question has seemed to have offended primarily against Paul, who would not have been personally injured by a flagrant case of incest.

If we can count upon the continuity of our materials, (a most dubious assumption), this tearful letter was written before Paul had come to Troas, (ii: 12, 13); here he expected to find Titus with some report from the Corinthian Church. Not finding him, he continued to Macedonia. Here the materials break off with a most extraordinary ascription of thanks to God, and it is not until the fifth verse of the seventh chapter that we learn that Titus had come to Paul in

Macedonia when the latter was overwhelmed with anxiety over the Corinthian situation. This should make it evident how out of place is the outburst of thankfulness in ii: 14-17. It fits badly into a situation in which Paul could find no relief for his spirit. Titus had reported (vii: 6, 7) that the Corinthians had sorrowfully, yet zealously, done everything they could to clear themselves of any charge of estrangement from Paul, or of rebellion against him. With the danger removed Paul could afford to be generous toward his opponent, whom the Corinthians had repudiated. It is here, rather than in their present context, that ii: 5-11 should be placed.

Having made the elisions and rearrangements that seem to be called for, we may with some certainty recover the situation out of which at least one of the letters to the Corinthian church arose. Paul had been intending to visit the church when there arose some circumstance in which some leader among the Corinthians had organized a rebellion against him. He had been charged with depending upon fleshly wisdom, (a strange charge it seems to us after perusing the first four chapters of First Corinthians), with being insincere, and even with failing to be holy in his life. The charge of insincerity had been made biting by the fact that Paul had not carried out his purpose to visit them.

In the materials surviving to us in our Second Corinthians we may learn that Paul had denied their charges. In answer to the most specious of them, that his failure to visit them as he had announced showed his insincerity, he goes at length into the situation which has called forth his letter. His failure to come had been due to the gravity of the controversy that had arisen in Corinth. He had feared that his coming might have resulted in an open and irretrievable break between him and the church. He thought it much better to write to them in the attempt to bring them back to their senses. It was a painful letter, written in anguish of heart, with many tears, perhaps with threats, certainly with passionate pleading. A portion of such a letter could with much plausibility be found in I Cor. iv: 14-21, whose inappropriateness to its present situation has already been pointed out.

This letter had probably been dispatched at the hand of Titus. So greatly is Paul exercised over the situation in his beloved church that he hastens to Troas, where he must have planned to meet Titus. Whether that be the original plan, or whether Paul simply could not wait for Titus to return to the place where the letter had been written, for whose identification we are dependent upon our uncertain framework of the life of Paul derived from Acts, we have no means of ascertaining. It is certain that when Paul did not find Titus in Troas, which might indicate that his mission had not been going as speedily and as happily as it might, his anxiety overwhelmed him, and impelled him to abandon the door that had been opened to him in Troas, and hasten on into Macedonia. This abandoning of an open door is the measure of the almost inconceivable load of anxiety under which the apostle was living.

In Macedonia he did find Titus with the unspeakable relief of his report that the Corinthians had reacted to Paul's letter with an intensity at least equal to their rebellion against him. They had done everything possible to clear themselves, inflicting upon Paul's opponent a punishment which was so severe that Paul had to plead his cause, pointing out that the only thing that mattered was the relationship of the Corinthians to Paul, their "earnest care" for him. Now that has been established, both Paul and the church could afford to forgive him who had caused the trouble.

Whether Paul could take time in such an epistle for the long drawn out treatment of the question of the collection for the saints in Judea, or whether its location, following immediately the materials growing out of the poignant struggle just detailed, is due to the nature of our Second Epistle, a miscellany of fragments of Pauline literature, with some non-Pauline additions, which had grown up in the Corinthian church, one must judge for himself. The evident disarray of the materials which we have been discussing, which must surely not be attributed to any inability of Paul to hold a situation clearly in mind or to keep to the point of his discussion, together with the presence of extraneous and alien materials, make a negative answer almost inescapable.

Verses 19-22 of chapter i interrupt Paul's assertion that his failure to come to them was not due to fickleness, but that his word to them was as dependable as the faithfulness of God, whom he calls as a witness upon his soul. This paragraph is another illustration of early homiletics, which inevitably grew out of the use of the epistles in the edification of the church. Paul's calling upon God to witness the sincerity of his purpose to come to them as he had said would furnish but meagre opportunity for sermonizing. But the faithfulness of God could be made applicable to a much wider range than that of Paul's sincerity. What is the place of the faithfulness of God in the "plan of salvation"? especially as that plan was interpreted in the redemptionist sense of later orthodoxy? The meaning of the phrase must be not only generalized, but also Christianized. Hence the turn from Paul's statement that God is faithful to "the Son of God" is faithful. Looked at from the broader point of view of the later preacher, the faithfulness of God does not function to guarantee the sincerity of Paul's purpose, but to ensure the fulfillment of every promise made in the Old Dispensation. It further functions as establishing the Christians in Christ, as anointing them, as sealing them, and as giving them the earnest of the Spirit in their hearts. An examination of the details in this list is most revealing. It betrays a Jewish and futuristic outlook upon religion. Jewish is the item of the fulfillment of the promises; probably also the detail of the anointing of Christians, which betrays a sacerdotal outlook. The futurism appears in the idea that we are sealed, and that the Spirit is merely a foretoken of something that is to come. The result is a sermon of very wide applicability in the preaching mission, and of very great value for those who looked into the future for the realization of the purposes of God in human lives. Among these Paul was certainly not to be found. We should not need to be reminded that the question at issue, the sincerity of Paul's purpose to visit them, as guaranteed by the faithfulness of God, has dropped completely out of sight.

As has been previously indicated, the outburst of thanksgiving in ii: 14-17 is entirely out of place in Paul's account of his journey into Macedonia, during which he was utterly overwhelmed by his anxiety for his relations with the Corinthian church. The content of the paragraph is not in the remotest degree connected with the question of the relations existing between Paul and his converts. Upon examination, it appears to be a reflection upon the fate of Christian ministers, and upon the results of their preaching. Two figures underlie its teaching. "Being led in triumph in Christ," may rest upon the triumphal procession, in which the captives are led to the glory of the conqueror. The minister cannot expect reward or prominence; enough that he contribute to the glory of Christ.

Nor can he expect success in his work. Turning to the sacrifice, our author finds the ministers to be a sweet savor of Christ unto God. The odor of the sacrifice, spreading to all, is the basis for the understanding of the results of Christian preaching. Some are saved; others perish. It cannot be said that our author is at all happy in the choice of his figure. It is easy to see how to some it can be a savor of life unto life. It originates in life, and it gives life to those to whom it comes. But the contrary gives no sense. It is the savor of the knowledge of Christ, the sweet savor of Christ; but this becomes the savor of death unto death. Has our author been caught in the meaningless play of words which so often characterizes homiletics? Has he been intent upon carrying out the parallelism "life unto life" through the addition of "death unto death" utterly oblivious of the fact that his figure has made the gospel of the living and life giving Christ a mass of putrefaction, from which issue the lethal stenches of the plague? It is true that the gospel does not save all of those who hear it, but how much better it is to understand this tragic fact from the standpoint of Jesus' admonition, "He that hath ears to hear, let him hear," than from any position of arbitrary predestination, or as here, from any conception of the gospel, or Christ himself, as dead and leading to death! The most charitable judgment possible upon the application made of the figure of the sacrifice is that it is nonsense.

It might be thought that 16b, 17 are worthy of Paul, setting forth his feeling of insufficiency, and attesting his sincerity. Quite often genuine materials are found to be mingled with those from later times. But here two details would seem to indicate that the section in question is indeed late. It contemplates the many as preaching; this may indicate a well established church, with large numbers of preachers. The reference to the basis of their ministry as "the word of God" may indicate the time when preaching was Scriptural, although of course this is not to be pressed. But the indication found in the word translated "corrupting" lends color to the assumption of the lateness of the passage. The primary significance of the expression is "We are not as the many who make a trade of the word of God." We may envisage the age of professionalism in the ministry. The derived meaning of "corrupting" the word of God is the result of the ethics which grows up around professionalism, whether in the adulteration of commodities, and the falsification of weights and measures upon the part of the petty tradesman, or in the carelessness, or in the special pleading of the professional minister.

While some of the indications just pointed out are stronger than others, the impression based upon all of them seems to be inescapable that we are here (vss. 14-17) dealing not with the mind of Paul, but with the homiletic practice of the later church.

In chapters three through six we find a tangled skein in which the genuinely Pauline portions need to be separated from the spurious, and to be placed in some setting to which they are germane. While this is a difficult task, it does not appear at all hopeless; we can keep ever before us the question of the relations between Paul and his Corinthian church, and we can see which materials relate to this situation, and which are so generalized that they have no relevance to it.

In iii: 1-6 Paul is again commending himself to the church. This paragraph will find its proper place in some epistle sent to the church when there was danger of misunderstanding or rebellion against his leadership. He points out that he needs no commendation to them; they are his epistle of recommendation. The results of his ministry speak for themselves. God had made him the minister of a new covenant, not to be thought of in terms of the literalism of Jewish legalism, which made much of the fact that the law had been written upon tables of stone by the very finger of God, but of a covenant which they had realized in the power of the Spirit of God in their own hearts in a life-giving experience. Here is the basic Pauline conception that the gospel of Christ comes to men in a spiritual experience which imparts to them an actual righteousness, so that, in this case, all may see from the lives of Paul's converts the genuineness of his ministry.

The rest of the third chapter (iii: 7-18) is given over to a meditation upon the contrast between the Christian gospel and the law of Moses, suggested by the figure of the old covenant and the new. This is not only conceived from a non-Pauline point of view, but is utterly unsuited to any situation of desperate tension in which Paul had had to struggle for the loyalty and obedience of his Corinthian converts. This annotator does not feel any urgency of conflict; he is not pressed for time, but can with full leisure give himself over to an allegorical exposition of the relations between the old and the new. The movement of thought and the exploitation of the significance of detail remind us strongly of the viewpoint and method of the Epistle to the Hebrews.

While the argument is by no means clear, what the author is trying to say is that the new is much more glorious than the old; yet even the old had so much glory that Moses had to veil his face before the children of Israel. This circumstance is seized upon to explain and to excuse the failure of the law; those who heard the law had not had any chance to understand it, or to respond to it. A veil lay upon their hearts and minds. The old familiar doctrine of predestination reappears, their minds were hardened. It had not been revealed to them that the veil was done away in Christ. But there would be a turning to the Lord, and the veil would be taken away. The basic viewpoint of this annotator is pro-Jewish. That which is to be hoped for is not the turning away from Moses to Christ, but the taking away of a veil which has prevented Moses from being understood and appreciated. Here is another passage which looks toward the solution of the Jewish-Christian problem in the direction taken by Ephesians; all are at last to be gathered into the commonwealth of Israel. There are many such annotations which attempt to modify Paul's radical Hellenism toward the recognition of the ultimate value of Judaism and the ultimate interpretation of Christianity in Jewish terms.

This passage seems also to have a slight gnostic coloring. It is the mind that is darkened. Salvation is the result of clear vision of the glory of the Lord; by gazing directly upon that glory we are transformed into its image. This is salvation through contemplation of the divine. This is characteristic of a type of religion often called "mysticism," but it is utterly different from the true mysticism of Paul.

Did they not appear in this context, verses 1 and 2 of chapter four might well be taken to be Pauline. Bits of genuine materials may rest undisturbed in annotated passages. The "manifestation of the truth" as opposed to the "handling of the word of God deceitfully" might be taken to contemplate an intellectualistic basis of religion, and thus be considered non-Pauline. But we at once remark that the truth is manifested to the conscience; it is moral, and not intellectual.

The contrast is with wickedness and the hidden things of shame. But verses three to six revert to the viewpoint of the spurious materials in chapter three. There is the same idea of the veiling of the gospel, even as the glory of the law of Moses was veiled. This is due to the agency of the god of this world, not to any fault of those who beheld. The basic figure is the gnostic conception of light and darkness, of vision and blindness. The essence of religious experience is illumination. Light shall shine in our hearts; this will give us knowledge of the glory of God. It is the light of the gospel of the glory of Christ, who is the image of God, that is to dawn upon us. Not only is this passage in the line of development toward the Christology of Colossians; it is basically much closer to John than to Paul. It is only the failure to separate these spurious passages from the genuine that has allowed scholars to form the judgment that the Johannine ideas are the development of Pauline; they are not; they rather exhibit the final form of these forces which have been playing upon the genuine Pauline materials.

The paragraph iv: 7-11 resumes the thread of the Pauline argument which was broken off by the introduction of the allegorical and gnostic interpolation iii: 7—iv: 6, (with the possible exception of iv: 1, 2). Paul had not been commending himself, only pointing out the genuineness of his ministry as evidenced by the power of their spiritual experience. He himself is worthy of no esteem, being but as an earthen vessel, containing a precious treasure. He is subject to all sorts of limitations and oppressions, which stop short only of ultimate destruction. But these are but manifestations of the sufferings of Jesus. He shares in the dying-rising of his Lord. He bears about in his own body the dying of Jesus, that the life of Jesus may be manifested in his mortal flesh.

The meaning of this sharing in the dying-rising of the Lord may be known not only from Paul's usual and fundamental usage of the concept, but from the resumption of his thought in v: 11, 12, 16, 17. It is not himself he commends, but only the power of a gospel which can make every man a new creature in Christ. It is through the death of Christ that the old things in a human life can pass away, and all things become new. iv: 12 may be genuine, and express the climax of this portion of the argument. We are nothing; we are delivered to death for Jesus' sake; death worketh in us. But there has come to you an experience of spiritual renewal through the life giving Spirit of God, imparting a new life of righteousness; life worketh in you.

It is characteristic of the modification of the Pauline materials that Paul's basically mystical conception of the gospel as a participation in the dying-rising of the Lord is so frequently set aside by some perversion which attempts to limit the meaning of the resurrection of Christ to the assurance of immortality. And this accrues to us not through any soul testing experience of conformity in our lives and desires to the dying of the Lord upon the cross, but by some such superficial process as believing and confessing or professing our faith in God. This is what has happened in iv: 13 ff. We believe that God raised Jesus from the dead; we confess our belief; therefore we shall be raised up with him. In another context verse 15 might well be Pauline, but here the concept of "grace" has been perverted from its proper Pauline meaning of enabling spiritual power, to this boon of immortality bestowed upon us in virtue of our faith and confession. The contrast between the outer and inner man (verses 16-18) is conceived in terms congenial to I Cor. xv. It is the contrast between this body and this life, and the body and the life beyond the grave. Our light affliction is but temporary; it is more than overbalanced by an eternal weight of glory that shall be ours. Our attention is, therefore, fastened, not upon the things of the body and of this life, which we can see, and which are but temporary, but upon the glory of that other life, which we cannot see, but which is forever.

The first ten verses of chapter v proceed consistently in this strain. This life is but a tabernacle in which we groan, presumably looking for release; it will be dissolved; but we shall not be left naked, we shall rather be clothed upon much more gloriously; this earthly tabernacle will be replaced by one not made with hands, eternal in the heavens. That which is mortal shall be swallowed up of life. This is the goal alike of life and of religion. This is the very thing for which God created us. And as a token of what is to happen, God has given us the earnest of the Spirit. While in this life we are absent from the Lord, but we can be of good cheer, knowing that if we die, we do but go to be with him. Meanwhile we must see to it that we do those things that are well pleasing unto him, knowing that at last we shall be made manifest before him, and shall receive the consequences of the things done in the body, whether good or bad.

All of this is in stark contrast to Paul's usual thought in regard to these matters. We are now present with the Lord; he lives in us, and we in him. It is this life, with the moral victory which comes through the crucifixion of the flesh and the resurrection to newness and righteousness of life, not some awaited consummation in the life beyond the grave, which Paul sees as the essence of Christian experience. His emphasis is ever upon the gift of the Spirit, not as an earnest of what God is graciously going to do for us in the dim, long to be awaited future, but as the enabling power which brings forth in our life the fruits of beauty, sweetness and goodness which make us more than conquerors through him who loved us. The idea that we live through this life with our eye upon the final reckoning in the day of judgment is thoroughly Jewish.

As evidence that we are dealing with an interpolation, it is to be noted that in verse 11 the topic of Paul's discussion is resumed. Paul does not need to commend himself to his church. He is acting according to the dictates of his conscience in the sight of God, and he trusts that his sincerity will be manifest in their conscience, as it is in his. Verses 14 and 15 are an obvious interpolation. 14a "For the love of Christ constraineth us" fits in well with Paul's contention that all that he does is either to please God or to serve them. He is driven to his ministry by the love Christ has manifested toward all, or by the love which he has for Christ. But 14b and 15 have no place in the discussion. They are an attempt to impose the universal-depravity-substitutionary-redemption complex upon the Pauline point of view. Perhaps the genuine Pauline teaching lay near at hand; it is stated that Christ for their sake died and rose again. But the resurrection is stripped of all real meaning for this life. It drops out of sight. It is the death of Christ which is emphasized. He died for us, not that we might die with him, but that we might be obligated to live with reference to him. We have been bought with a price; we are not our own; we must live to please our master. It is the servant-master relationship, rather than mystic identification, which dominates the interpretation of the Christian life.

The relevancy of verses 16 and 17 to the discussion is not as clear as might be wished. It may be that with the interpolation of 14b and 15 there was also some elision. But the fundamental congruity of this passage both with the basic Pauline point of view, and with the tenor of Paul's present discussion, is unmistakable. It is a clear and compelling statement of the Pauline gospel. The old things are passed away (through the crucifixion of the flesh with him); they are become new, the man in Christ is a new creature (new because he who died with Christ has been raised with him to a new life). It also dovetails exactly into Paul's contention that the only commendation to them which he needs is for them to reflect upon the genuineness and power of the spiritual experience which had come to them as the result of his ministry. A link with the immediate context appears in the thought in verse 12 that there are some who glory in appearance, and not in heart. To these it must be said that no fleshly distinctions matter, only that one be new and different in heart and all his conversation.

The remainder of the chapter, verses 18-21, have flown completely out of the orbit of the discussion. Paul's ministry is looked at not from the viewpoint of one who has brought the gospel of our identification with our dying-rising Lord in the crucifixion of the flesh and the resurrection to a newness of life which has made everything new, but from the viewpoint of one commissioned to bring the utterly different message that God will not reckon to us our trespasses, and that we are therefore to become reconciled to him. This is built upon the gift theory of salvation. God will forgive, and all we have to do is to accept. There is no need for the transforming experience of spiritual death and resurrection.

Verse 21 appears to be a scholion added by someone who cannot accept the idea that God can forgive, or overlook, our trespasses unless there be some satisfaction for sins. He finds this satisfaction in the statement that God made Christ to be sin on our behalf. This is substitution driven to its limit, or even beyond it. Not that our sins are laid upon him, but that he becomes sin. How that could be done, or what good it would do, we are not told. Nor are we informed how we might become the righteousness of God in him. The idea that we do become righteous is close to Paul's thought, but Paul's characteristic conception of the way in which God's purpose is accomplished is conspicuously absent. Our identification with Christ is reversed. Instead of our becoming one with him in a spiritual experience in which we crucify the flesh, he becomes one with us in our sins, or rather he becomes the very sin which mars our life, and which is so hateful to God. The conception that we become the righteousness of God in him is far superior religiously to the idea of the context that God is pleading with us to be reconciled with him, because he is willing to overlook our trespasses. But that which does not appear is that we become righteous by identifying ourselves with Christ in an experience of spiritual power which issues in the new, the resurrected life. That which cannot be allowed is Paul's basic concept of our spiritual identification with our dying-rising Lord in an experience which corresponds to his death and resurrection. In other words, Paul is hereby in this passage also, purged of the "mystery taint" in his basic theology.

After we shall have set aside those passages therein which are inappropriate to their context, we may find that vi: 1—vii: 4 continue the line of thought found in the genuine materials. Paul's exhortation that they do not receive the grace of God in vain, which means that they are to become new creatures in Christ, is perverted by a quotation introduced by the formula "he saith," characteristic of Hebrews, which reverts to the appeal in the interpolation (v: 18-20) that we be reconciled to God. Now is the time to respond, now is the day of salvation. The inappositeness of these verses is indicated in our English version by their being inclosed in parentheses.

Paul continues with a moving appeal to them to regard in him no marks of the flesh which the world would recognize; he commends himself rather by the power of his spiritual experience, by the purity and righteousness of his life, and by the labors, privations, and hardships which mark his ministry. This section concludes with the appeal (vi: 11-13; vii: 2-4) that they enlarge and open their hearts to him, as his heart is enlarged and opened toward them.

With vii: 5 there is a resumption of the materials interrupted after ii: 13. Their basic situation is not Paul's commendation of himself to them by the results of his ministry in their lives, but the threatened rebellion of the Corinthians under the leadership of some offender; the rebellion had not materialized, because they had repented, and returned to their devotion to the apostle. It is not certain what relationship the two groups of materials which have been recognized as genuine have to each other. It may well be that those in iii: 1—vii: 4 were part of the letter which Paul sent by the hand of Titus, and that they were influential in winning the Corinthians back to their allegiance. The chaotic disarray of the materials in the first seven chapters should be very evident, no matter what theory of their relationship to each other may be adopted.

vii: 10 seems to be a characteristic homiletic gloss. Its inappositeness may be realized by an attempt to integrate it with the historical situation. The sorrow in the genuine material is one which the Corinthians felt because of their rebellion against Paul; here it is sorrow presumably for "sin." The repentance thought of in the genuine passage is their returning to their allegiance; here it is a repentance which leads to "salvation." A worldly sorrow would have led the Corinthians to persist in their rebellion; here it causes them to fail of salvation, and leads to death. This is clearly a text for a sermon on the later theological thesis, redemptionist in character, that we can avoid death and achieve salvation only by repentance. It has no applicability whatever to the Corinthian situation.

There has been much discussion of the paragraph now found in vi: 14—vii: 1. It has been thought to be the survival of the letter, or of part of it, which Paul says in I Cor. v: 9 he wrote to them telling them to have no company with impure persons. But the content of the paragraph does not at all agree with at least the explanation which Paul there proceeds to give of his letter. There is here no direct reference to fornication. It can only be inferred from the use of the expression that we are a temple of the living God, which concept has occurred in connection with fornication in I Cor. vi: 12-20. Here the whole stress is upon the yoking together of believers and unbelievers. It is not a question of fornication and purity, but of righteousness and iniquity, of light and darkness, of Christ and Belial, of the temple of God and idols. It does not appear that we have sufficient data upon which to pronounce a judgment, but if we are forced to do so, it would seem that we have here either the question of the marriage of believers with unbelievers, in which the annotator responsible for this paragraph categorically sets aside Paul's sensible prescription (I Cor. vii: 12-16) that mixed marriages are not to be broken up on the initiative of the Christian partner, or we may even be confronted with the ascetic viewpoint that the church must withdraw from the world in order that it perfect its own holiness. This latter point of view explicitly contradicts Paul's teaching in I Cor. v: 9-13.

There is further evidence of the spuriousness of this paragraph in its conception that we are constituted the temple of God by the fact that he has promised to dwell within his people, not by reason of the fact that the Spirit has taken up his abode in us. This passage is based squarely upon Jewish presuppositions, the holy people, the promises of God, his dwelling in us, cleansing from defilement, and the perfecting of holiness. This defilement may be of the flesh, as well as of the spirit; it might seem to come from the very sojourning among unclean people, and from touching unclean things. This passage should take its place among all those which seek to modify Paul's teachings in favor of Jewish valuations in religion.

Chapters eight and nine are given over entirely to matters in connection with the great collection which Paul was taking in all of his churches for the relief of the poor among the Christians in Judea. It may well be doubted whether such matters could come at all into epistles taken up with such crucial personal relationships as those under discussion in the first seven chapters. There is no reason to question any extended passages; with the exception of a possible gloss or two, everything in these chapters fits in well into the situation contemplated.

Here we find all the criteria by which materials should be judged to be genuinely epistolary. They tie in so well with the current situation that it may be recreated in detail. We can see Paul's great interest in the collection, the zeal with which the mercurial Corinthians had undertaken the project, the lag which had come over their enthusiasm, the exhortations with which Paul sought to rekindle their ardor, his practical directions as to the method which would ensure regular and substantial offerings, his fear of any accusation being brought against his integrity in administering the funds, and his wise precautions in associating with him brethren whom all the churches could trust.

There can be no doubt of the genuineness of the materials. But it almost passes belief that they could have been included in any letter which fell within the period of storm and stress in the personal relations between the apostle and the Corinthian church. He seems to be under no strain, but can take his time to deal leisurely with what is at best a minor problem. Nor is there any question of the allegiance of the church to him, nor any doubt as to their obedience. From viii: 7 we learn that in this period the Corinthians were abounding in their love for the apostle, as well as in faith, utterance, knowledge and earnestness.

Not even this passage, dealing with such a practical matter as a collection, has escaped from homiletic glosses. viii: 9 has all the earmarks of such an addition. It makes no contribution to the discussion; Paul is not under the necessity of laying a foundation upon which he could appeal to them for liberality; they had undertaken the project a year ago; they are abounding in earnestness. It is quite possible that such a consideration as that contained in this verse might have had to be urged upon them had they been insensible or reluctant, but such does not seem now to be the case. The elimination of the verse does not at all disturb the continuity of the resulting context. This seems to be the inevitable generalizing and theologizing of a concrete situation which had no longer any significance for the purposes of the preacher. It has nothing to do with the duty of the Corinthians to give;

it deals rather with their having in Christ obtained great riches. Sermons on getting are much easier to preach than sermons on giving; they have a much greater popular appeal.

In ix: 15 there seems to be another gloss. It may not be for the purpose of generalizing and spiritualizing a situation to provide a text for a sermon. It may be merely the spontaneous outburst of one at a later time meditating upon the matter of giving. One might even here see the often postulated disorderliness of Paul's habits of thinking, if his study of the Pauline materials could bear out such a theory, and attribute the verse to Paul himself.

It has often been thought that in chapters ten to thirteen we have the "painful" letter which Paul wrote to the Corinthians when there was the threat that they would rebel against his authority. A careful analysis of the contents of these chapters, and of the background out of which they grew, does not seem to support this conception. For the situation does not seem to be unitary. Two definite sets of circumstances may be envisaged. The first of these introduces an entirely new element, the presence of other leaders, who, much after the fashion of Paul's opponents in Galatians, seem to raise the question of his inferiority to the real apostles, and who not only asserted that they were real apostles themselves, but insisted upon exercising all the rights and privileges of that exalted status. Only chapters ten through twelve, verse eighteen, seem to deal with this problem. Beginning with xii: 19, the remainder of the epistle seems to contemplate a situation in which there were divisions, strife, and unrepentant wrongdoing in the church. In these passages Paul does not fear a rival leadership, but only the continuance of his converts in wrong-doing, and the repudiation of his authority.

The first difficulty with which Paul is faced, (x: 1—xii:

18) has to do with these false apostles. They had exalted themselves, asserting an authority which rested upon fleshly marks, such as their lineage, their official status as apostles, their haughty demeanor, lording it over their converts, and especially their demand that the Corinthians support them.

This forces Paul to point out the basis upon which his real authority as a minister of Christ rested. He would not glory in the things of the flesh, although he was as much a Hebrew, and a son of Abraham as any, (xi: 22). He was a real minister of Christ. He had a real authority which the Lord had given him. This also rested upon the fact that it was he who had brought the gospel to them. (x: 15, 16.) They were his province; he was not working in the field of another. His opponents derided him, saying that he was unassuming and weak when among them, not comporting himself as an apostle with full authority should; he only became bold when he was absent; his letters were weighty enough. Paul replies that if he is forced to do so, he will exercise that authority among them, and that they shall find out that his action is as strong as the threats in his letters. (x: 8-10.)

But that upon which his real authority rests is to be found in no outward and fleshly marks. He will speak rather of his labors, of his hardships, of his sufferings, of his perils, and of the anxiety that presses daily upon him in regard to his churches. He is so one with them that he shares every one of their weaknesses, and burns with each one of their temptations. (xi: 23-30.)

Let his opponents boast. Paul ought to have no need of commending himself to the Corinthians; they ought rather to have sung his praises to all. But if necessary, he, too, will boast. Although it is foolish, their very conceit of their own wisdom will make them patient with him in this weakness and folly. For there had come to him revelations from the Lord, in which, rapt out of the body, he had been caught up into Paradise and had heard things it was not lawful to utter. (xii: 1-6.)

To counterbalance the exquisiteness and magnitude of this spiritual experience there was given to him a thorn in the flesh, so that he might be kept ever mindful of his own weakness. From it he could secure no relief; he did but learn that with every demand which life could make there could be found a sufficient supply of grace. He would, then, glory not in strength and achievement, but in the weakness which would impel him to seek that grace, so that the strength and sufficiency of Christ should be manifested in his weakness. (xii: 7-10.)

The point which seems to have been the source of the acutest trouble had to do with the demand for support. The false apostles evidently demanded that the Corinthians support them, and pointed to the confidence with which they enforced this demand as evidence of the reality of their apostolic authority. Paul had not demanded support, they said. He would have done so had he been confident of his apostolic status. But the apostle answers that the failure to demand support did not grow out of any doubt as to his right to demand it. That right is elaborately argued in I Cor. ix: 1-19. But it was given up in order that it might not interfere with the success of his ministry. No one could deprive him of his glorying, not in that he had demanded support, but that he had made the gospel available to all without charge. (xi: 5-15.)

Paul's sincerity, as well as his authority, seems to have been attacked. They said his refraining from taking any money from them was but a crafty trick to gain their confidence, and to pave the way for greater exactions to which they would later be subjected, at the hands of either Paul himself, or of his subordinates. But had Titus, or the brother Paul had sent with him, taken any advantage of them? (xii: 17-18.) Paul further states that it was not because he loved them any less, nor that he had made them inferior to any other church, that he had failed to demand support from them. (xii: 13.)

The material in xii: 19—xiii: 10 does not seem to have any reference whatever to this controversy between Paul and the false apostles. It has to do with his immediate relations with his converts. He fears that when he comes there may be found an unsatisfactory situation, in which he and the Corinthians may be disappointed in each other; that there may be factions, and strife; that those who had been impure and unclean had not repented of their wrong-doing; and that in his failure to enforce discipline among them, God would humble him before them. But he will come, and he will not spare. He will be strong in the power of God. He appeals to them to prove themselves, doubtless by the test of the purity and righteousness of their living, to see that they be not reprobate. He hopes that they will not find him reprobate! The sarcasm should be apparent. His whole concern is not for himself, but for their upbuilding and perfecting.

He refers to a second visit to them, which had evidently been unsatisfactory; he is writing as he does so that when he comes again the third time, as he plans shortly to do, he may not have to deal sharply. He does not wish to cast anyone down.

Even in these so evidently genuine epistolary materials we find passages which may be strongly suspected as interpolations or modifications. x: 3-6 immediately arouses our suspicion. The radically different connotation of "walking according to the flesh" should be at once apparent. In the genuine materials the question is the reality of Paul's authority, and the marks which constitute the criteria of such a status. His opponents "walked according to the flesh," that is they depended upon their lineage, their supposed relation with the Jerusalem church, their haughty ways, their demand for support. Paul appealed rather to his spiritual experience and the marks of a successful ministry. But here the contrast is not between fleshly distinctions and spiritual experience but between human systems, especially those which are gnostic in character, as is evidenced by the strongholds, and the high things that are exalted against the knowledge of God, and casting down imaginations bringing every thought into captivity to the obedience of Christ, and the true Christian gospel. The annotator has at least become enough of a gnostic himself to recognize some reality in these strongholds and things exalted against the knowledge of God. But he is confident that there is in the Christian gospel some occult power which can invade these celestial ramparts and maintain the "truth" against all rival philosophies. Apart from its entire dissociation from the situation to the fore in Paul's relations with the Corinthian church, this passage reeks of a gnostic occultism entirely foreign to the apostle's mind, all the passages which deal with the "Colossian heresy" and related materials to the contrary notwithstanding.

The sixth verse may be an awkward attempt to link this annotation to the context. It is apparent that there is no relevance to the Corinthian situation. Very well, it may be supplied by evolving from the conception of obedience to Christ the threat that Paul will avenge all their disobedience as soon as their obedience has been reëstablished. But this link is gained not only at the expense of a total alteration of the connotation of "bringing every thought into captivity to the obedience of Christ," but also at the cost of introducing a drastic threat into the midst of a very tense situation. One hardly seeks to win obedience by threatening the dire things he is going to do as soon as that obedience is established!

In xi: 2-4 we again find material which calls for examination. The whole paragraph might seem a slight digression from the main tenor of the discussion; or it might be held within the main channel of thought by being considered the reason Paul has given for his foolishness of boasting about the things which constitute him a real apostle. The crux of the passage is found in the fourth verse, in which it seems to be categorically stated that they would do well to bear with other preachers, even though they be preaching another Jesus, a different gospel, or a different Spirit. This is a diametrical denial of Paul's contention in Galatians which he consistently maintains throughout his ministry, that there could be no other gospel than that which he proclaimed. (Gal. i: 6-9.) The passage can be allowed to stand only if it agree with this contention. It may very easily be made to do so. There is the simple question of the force of the expression "ye do well." This is a literal translation, although it is by no means certain that it is idiomatic. Two senses may be found which would allow the passage to stand as genuine. The first is that it is sarcastic. This force would be brought out by the translation "A pretty kettle of fish, the way you receive these alien preachers!" The other sense to be given these words is to receive them as a plain statement of fact. They do afford these preachers a beautiful reception; how much more, then, ought they to receive Paul, who alone brings them the genuine gospel! He fears that they will be beguiled because they give these false apostles such a hearty reception. With this caution the passage may be allowed to stand.

Another difficulty is encountered in xi: 29-33. In our treatment of the passage we have taken 29 as an illustration of the anxiety which presses upon Paul in his care of the churches. The contiguity of verse 30, however, must speak against this interpretation. For Paul has expressly said in verse 21 that he had not been weak; the catalog of labors, and perils, and hardships, is an assertion of his strength rather than his weakness. Perhaps 29 and 30 are genuine verses displaced from a more appropriate context, such as that of xii: 7-10.

Verses 31-33 do not seem to be very happy in their present location. The assertion that before God he is not lying must weaken any such moving passage as the impressive catalog of his perils and sufferings for Christ. And the episode in Damascus is distinctly anticlimactic. It may be an annotation by someone familiar with Acts, who wishes to bring about a closer connection between "Luke" and Paul. It must be noted that all of the incidents in Paul's catalog are general; no indication is given of the circumstances under which any detail took place. Here the account is full and circumstantial. It must also be noted that an external danger is listed after Paul has specifically said that he is turning from those things that are without to those that are within. This account of Paul's narrow escape from Aretas, if genuine, must be regarded as displaced from its true context.

The concluding paragraph of our epistle (xiii: 11-14), sounds very much like a genuine conclusion. The benediction in verse fourteen is one of the most used and best beloved phrases of our modern liturgy. It seems to rest upon a definite Trinitarian foundation, which in all probability was much later than the days of Paul in coming to full development and conscious recognition. It must be noted, however, that this Trinitarianism is implicit, rather than explicit, and may be read into the passage, rather than deduced from it. But while Paul has made no attempt to work out a theology, certainly no Trinitarianism, each detail in the benediction is truly and characteristically his, the grace of Christ, the love of God, and certainly "participation" in the Holy Spirit. Although we must not rule out the possibility that this is a later summarization of basic Pauline ideas, gathered into one by the process of liturgy, we must recognize it as a particularly happy one.

Chapter VII

THE FIRST EPISTLE TO THE THESSALONIANS

I T MIGHT be well for our understanding of Paul's work and message if we were to recognize I Thessalonians as one of his typical epistles. There is in it very little that we are given cause to suspect. Perhaps this is because it contained very little doctrinal matter, and it was thus not so necessary that it be modified to bring it into line with the developed teaching of the church. It does give us a rather clear picture of the type of work carried on by the apostle, of the relations he maintained with his churches, and of some of the conditions obtaining in a Pauline community.

The first verse of chapter one is a very simple and wholly appropriate salutation. No doctrinal matter has been introduced into it.

There follows immediately (i: 2-9), Paul's customary praise for those things in his converts to which he could give his approval. His gospel had come to them not in word alone, but also in power. Paul's gospel in Thessalonica, as everywhere else, had been a dynamic gospel, preached not in the excellence of human wisdom, but in power and demonstration of the Holy Spirit. They had received it in much affliction, but with great joy in the Holy Spirit. It had produced in them a real and a present righteousness; they had turned to God from idols, and had patiently and hopefully produced works of faith, brought forth in love. This had made them imitators of the evangelists, and they had become examples throughout the Pauline field (the expression, "in every place," (vs. 8) need not here be given any wider connotation).

One has but to keep the details of this commendation in

mind to see how utterly different is the basic viewpoint of verse 10. Paul has not even alluded to the redemptionist idea of religion, that it is to provide a future salvation which is to consist in the deliverance from coming wrath. He has been speaking, in a manner characteristic of him, of the effect of their reception of the gospel being their embarkation upon a present life of righteousness, without even a hint that is a temporary and provisional experience, merely preliminary and preparatory to that which alone can be thought of as real, the life that should be theirs when Jesus should come. Apocalyptic this verse may be; it certainly testifies that someone looked forward to the coming of Jesus as the time of salvation, which is to be construed in terms of deliverance from wrath. But it is in basic contrast to the conception of Christianity which Paul has expressed in the context, and to which he characteristically adheres. The verse seems to exhibit the modification of true Pauline teaching by apocalyptic and redemptionist forces.

In chapter two we have a defense, not so much of the contents of the Pauline gospel, as of its motives. Knowing as we do the close connection between the genuine Pauline epistolary materials, and the situation out of which they grew, it is easy for us to see that certain accusations had probably been levelled at the apostle. Opposition may have arisen in the group itself; there is no specific allusion to false leaders coming in from outside to disturb the church. It has been charged that Paul had been unholy, unclean, sly, time-serving, flattering, covetous. He replies that he had come to them from an experience of persecution and suffering, and had spoken to them in great anxiety. He was unassuming, surrendering his rights, gentle, affectionate, industrious, holy, and blameless, dealing with them as a father with his children. His only desire had been that they walk worthily of God. It is a matter of unceasing thankfulness that they had received the word as true and that it worked in them. Paul's gospel was ever one that produced real results in the present, not one that promised benefits in the future. (ii: 1-13.)

The chapter concludes (vss. 17-20), with the expression of Paul's longing over them in his absence from them, and of his thwarted desires to visit them. They were his hope, his joy, his crown of glory, in the presence of the Lord Jesus. This is a present rejoicing because of a present triumphant attainment upon the part of his converts. This is obscured by the translation, "before our Lord Jesus at his coming." While some may think that the Greek demands this translation, it.is true, rather, that it seems to exclude it.

The word translated "coming" is the one which has come over into theology as "Parousia," with the meaning of the Second Coming of Jesus. It is unquestionable that it held this meaning among wide circles in the early church, and that in many passages it should properly be thus translated. But it is equally unquestionable that the primary meaning of the term is "presence" rather than coming. And that this meaning should be applied here necessarily follows, not only from all that Paul has said as to the result of his gospel in the present attainment of his converts, but even more from the fact that while the future tense was available for Paul's use if he had been thinking in future terms, he repeatedly uses the present. What is, not will be, our hope? Ye are, not will be, our glory and our joy. The ambiguity of the word for "presence" is unfortunate, but its connotation is made abundantly clear by the context. The alternative possibility must not be overlooked that the words, "at his coming" might have been slipped in because they could have a

futuristic interpretation, in order to reinforce the futuristic
modification which seems to have been made in i: 10, and are
thus a modification of the original. But if genuine, the word
in question must be given here its primary meaning of "presence," not its secondary meaning of "coming."

There is severe question as to the appositeness of ii: 14-16.
There is a drastic change in the external situation contemplated. Paul has referred to them (i:6) as having become
imitators of himself, or of himself and any others who might
have been associated with him in his preaching. But here
they are said to have become imitators of the churches in Judea. In Paul's thought they had been imitators in that they
had manifested a righteousness which had made them a con-
spicuous example throughout the Pauline field. But here
they are imitators in the endurance of a persecution like
that which the Jewish Christians had undergone. This
change in situation is not conclusive of a modification of
genuine materials, but it must be noted and estimated.

There are other details which are much more questionable.
The passage is marked by the hardening of the attitude
toward the Jews into settled and vindictive enmity which reflects a later stage in the Jewish-Christian controversy, and
which does not accord with Paul's own brokenhearted grief
over the obstinacy of Israel. How the author of this passage
hates the Jews! They killed the Lord Jesus and the prophets;
their sins are filled up! And most important of all, the wrath
has come upon them to the uttermost. It seems merely specious to argue that this does not refer to the destruction of
Jerusalem. That for Christians was the final manifestation
of God's just anger against his unfaithful people. Of course,
it is quite easy to argue that this cannot refer to the destruction of Jerusalem, for that did not take place until after the

death of Paul. It must be admitted that he could not have referred to the destruction of Jerusalem as an accomplished fact. Granted, therefore, either that this does not refer to the destruction of Jerusalem, or that Paul did not write it. The disjunction is inescapable.

But every factor in the equation points to the non-genuineness of the paragraph. The complete change in the outer circumstances alluded to must cast some weight, however slight, into the scales against the genuineness of the materials. We have already pointed out how incompatible with Paul's love for Israel and his grief over their rejection is the venomous hatred for the Jews expressed here. The idea that they are contrary to all men is the echo of the Roman attitude toward this troublesome folk. The statement that they drove Paul out, presumably from Judea, is a drastic modification of our conception that Paul had not been in Jerusalem, Acts to the contrary notwithstanding, except incidentally, for many years after his conversion. We know that the Jewish Christians were indifferent to the Gentile mission, if not actually hostile to it, but it is here alone that we learn that the Jews tried to hinder the carrying of the gospel to the gentiles. It is easy to see that the Jews in Hellenistic communities might realize that the success of the church would be at least partly at the expense of the synagogue, and might do all they could to undermine it.

The historical circumstances seem to be most inadequately conceived. Every consideration marks this paragraph as a leaf out of the developed Jewish-Christian controversy. It is therefore best to see in the coming of the wrath to the uttermost upon the Jews its natural meaning of the destruction of Jerusalem, and to recognize the secondary, non-Pauline character of these verses. They may, of course, be separated, and 14 be considered genuine, and 15 and 16 be recognized as later, but this is most improbable.

In the third chapter we learn that Paul had anticipated that the Thessalonians would be subject to persecution or affliction, and had told them so. He had been apprehensive lest this cause them to give up their Christian profession. He resorted to what appears to be his usual practice of sending one of his helpers, in this case Timothy, to see how they were getting along, and to do what he could to strengthen them in their allegiance to Christ and to Paul. Timothy's return with the news that they were well disposed toward the apostle, and were steadfast in their faith and love brought him unspeakable relief and joy. (iii: 1-10.) Verses 11-13 form an altogether fitting conclusion not only to this incident of Timothy's visit and return, but to a letter dealing with the situation. His prayer is that their love may increase and abound, and that their hearts may be established unblamable in holiness before God in the presence of our Lord Jesus Christ and all his saints. He longs and prays that their present life be characterized by holiness and love.

There is in verse 13 the same ambiguous word usually rendered "coming" which here necessarily means rather "presence." Paul is not worrying about the fate of his converts in some future day of judgment, when Christ shall come again; he has been concerned lest now they fall away from their faith and their love. He wishes that they be kept holy here and now in the presence of Christ with all his saints.

It is queer to encounter such a word as "finally" at the beginning of the fourth chapter. Paul's letter has seemed to reach its conclusion in iii: 11-13. It is strange to find a new topic treated after the letter has seemed to close. Nor is the first topic of this fourth chapter the last one discussed in our present epistle. The use in this place of such a word as finally does not seem to have any justification.

But apart from this one word the first eight verses of this chapter may be recognized as typically Pauline. A genuinely Christian life requires a walk well pleasing unto God. Among other demands, this calls for a mastery of sexual passion, especially the respect of other men's rights in this matter, in other words, avoidance of adultery with other men's wives. It is typically Pauline to approach the matter of sexual purity, not from the basis of some commandment which has been given us, but from the fundamentally mystical standpoint of our relationship with God, especially the gift of the Holy Spirit to dwell within us, which makes us a temple of God.

In verses 9-12, which are also genuinely Pauline, we encounter a topic very commonly misunderstood, the problem of idleness and disorderliness in the Thessalonian church. It is commonly assumed that this was an effect of intense apocalyptic expectation, and that some of the brethren had concluded that it was not worth while to work, because Christ was immediately to come. A careful reading of our materials must show how baseless any such assumption is. Paul associates their being quiet and working with their hands rather with their relations with each other and with the outside world. They do love each other; they are exhorted to abound more and more in this love, one manifestation of which is to be found in their orderliness and industry. And the reason that they are to be orderly and industrious is not the one that the interpreters of this passage have given it, because the Lord is not coming so soon after all, which Paul could very easily have stated here had it been in his mind, but rather because the apostle is anxious that they do not acquire the reputation of being shiftless busybodies. It is an amazing illustration of the ingenuity of exegesis that this problem of idleness in the Thessalonian church is so dextrously dissected out of the tissues in which Paul has embedded it, their love for the brethren and their reputation in the community, and grafted on to an assumed ferment over the second coming of Jesus.

The only possible connection of this idleness with apocalyptic preoccupation is in the fortuitous juxtaposition of the next paragraph, iv: 13-18. But having learned of the great present disarray of our Pauline materials, we should not place too great stress upon mere sequence of passages. iv: 13—v: 10 must in any case be looked upon with the gravest of suspicion.

If the treatment of this problem of idleness in II Thess., (iii: 7-12), be thought to throw any light whatever upon the problem of its connection with apocalyptic thinking in the Thessalonian church, we must note that there, too, we cannot find the slightest connection between idleness and the supposed imminence of the Second Coming. For this material appeals to the example set them by the apostle; they should imitate him in labor for self support, that they be not a burden upon any. The disorderly and busybodies are not instructed in the fallacious nature of any supposed expectation of the immediate coming of Jesus. They are merely told to be quiet and to eat their own bread; otherwise they are not to be supported. Any supposed expectation of the imminent end of the world must be assumed; any other explanation of their conduct may with equal right be postulated. It is certain that Paul himself nowhere gives this as the reason for their conduct; we are not justified in ignoring the reasons he does give for his exhortation to them, in favor of one which we must ourselves supply.

The paragraph iv: 13-18 is one of the strangest ones in our epistle. It may fairly be questioned whether in the brief interval which we must assume to have intervened between the founding of the church and the writing of the epistle the problem caused by the death of their brethren could have caused an acute question in the church. It would seem rather to grow out of a situation in which many have died, and there has been time to reflect upon this condition. In no respect is this passage congruous with Paul's thinking, or worthy of him. It is definitely apocalyptic. The coming of Christ is expected within the present generation; many of us shall still be alive. Our belief in the death and resurrection of Christ is shorn of any idea of mystic participation; it is made the ground for hope of immortality. The clear contrast between the functions of the death and resurrection of Christ has become blurred. He died and rose so that we may rise with him.

It is the content of the passage which is utterly unworthy of such a teacher as Paul. To supply comfort in this situation, he has been given a special revelation from the Lord. It is this: the Lord is coming, while many of us are still alive, with full apocalyptic trumpery; he will descend from heaven with a shout, with the voice of an archangel, with the trump of God. And the particular comfort for the Thessalonian church is supposed to be, not that their dead shall live again, but that they shall be raised first, so that they shall not miss a minute of eternity. After they are raised, then they and we together with them shall be caught up into the clouds.

We are here dealing with a very primitive mentality. The author musters all the trappings of celestial pageantry; the

{ 241 }

coming of the Lord is dramatized so as to appeal to the most illiterate and unthoughtful. And the climax of the passage is that the beloved dead shall not miss a minute of eternity. No objection could be raised to deducing from this passage the extremely low level upon which the gospel was preached in some circles of the early church. But to attribute such puerility to Paul must severely modify our idea of his understanding of the gospel, while to think that this is a real revelation of the mind of God in regard to this problem is to reduce the mentality of God to the level of the childishness of the passage.

The impression made upon us by the materials in v: 1-11, if we do not conclude the paragraph with the tenth verse, is distinctly that they are sub-Pauline rather than Pauline. The passage deals with the day of the Lord, whose coming is thought of in terms, not of imminence, but uncertainty. It will come suddenly, not soon, and unexpectedly; when everything seems quiet and safe, then it will burst upon us. This attitude is utterly inconsistent with any expectation of the certainty of the immediacy of the coming of the Lord. For if we were sure it would be soon, it could not come unexpectedly upon us. To say that that which is ardently expected is to come unexpectedly is sheer nonsense. It was only because the Lord tarried that his attendants could slumber. Their carelessness could grow only out of their conviction that he was not coming soon.

The contrast involved in the passage is that between darkness and light, between sleeping and waking, between sobriety and drunkenness. We must stay awake, and be sober, because we are children of light. This contrast between light and darkness is more gnostic and Johannine than Pauline.

If it stood alone, this consideration ought not to be urged strongly against it. It must, however, be estimated in connection with all the passages in our Pauline corpus which show Johannine coloring.

We shall look in vain in this passage for the characteristic Pauline gospel. Its fundamental conception is not the radical transformation of our natures, but the putting on of armor. Salvation is not present, but future, our helmet is the hope of salvation. The opposite of salvation is not failure in the struggle for righteousness, but suffering the wrath of God. The death of Christ is separated from his resurrection. He died for us, that whether we wake or sleep, we should live together with him. In this passage, the connotation of living together with him is our immortality. In Paul's thought, our new life is associated with the resurrection, rather than with the death of Christ, and connotes righteousness, rather than immortality.

Verse 11 is a transitional one which might with equal right be considered either the conclusion of the previous paragraph, or the opening of a new topic. The remainder of the letter (11 or 12-28), is typical of the way Paul often wound up a letter. He has the conditions prevailing in the church before his mind, and deals with them in summary fashion. It is a typical Pauline church. The brethren must be exhorted to peace, orderliness, courage, patience, forbearance, and forgiveness. The functioning of the Spirit in ecstatic behavior is to be seen in the admonition that the Spirit is not to be quenched, prophesyings are not to be despised. Paul beseeches them to recognize the worth of those that labor among them, and are over them in the Lord, for their works' sake. This is an informal leadership, resting upon no official status and recognized authority, but upon the sufferance of the brethren and their recognition of the value of their leaders' efforts. While this is genuine material it may not belong to the letter in which Paul is so happy over the report of the abounding of their mutual love for each other.

Paul's prayer for them is that the God of peace may sanctify them wholly in the presence of the Lord Jesus. God is faithful, who has called them to lead holy lives, he will accomplish this in them. The epistle concludes with Paul's request for their prayers; with the injunctions to salute all the brethren, and to see that the epistle is read to all. This may be the germ out of which grew the practice of the reading of Paul's letters in church meetings. The formal conclusion is "The grace of our Lord Jesus Christ be with you all." The absence of "Amen" here is some indication that where it occurs, it may be a liturgical addition.

Chapter VIII

THE EPISTLE TO THE PHILIPPIANS

THE complexity of the Epistle to the Philippians has been recognized by many scholars, although there is by no means as large an agreement as in the case of II Corinthians. There is evidence of the miscellaneous character of its materials, and there is frequent indication of more or less serious modification. There is, however, no sufficient indication that our present epistle grew up simply by the combination of two separate letters to the church.

In the first two verses (i: 1, 2) we have a very simple and fitting salutation. No doctrinal matter has been added. But it is most surprising that Paul should have included among those sending the letter, or more naturally interpreted, among the recipients, the bishops and deacons with whom we are so familiar in the later church, but for whom we seek in vain in the Pauline organization. This is a later modification, arising not from developed doctrine, but from developed organization.

There follows at once, as is characteristic of Paul, the combined thanksgiving and prayer for his converts, (i: 3-11). This appears to be glossed, (6, 7a, 10c), in such a way as to obscure his meaning. Omitting these indicated phrases, or verses, we recover a simple continuous passage in which he thanks God for their participation with him in the furtherance of the gospel from the beginning to the present day, and prays that they may abound more and more in knowledge and all discernment, so that they may be sincere and void of offense, being filled with the fruits of righteousness, which come through Jesus Christ unto the glory and praise of God.

Two comments seem to be called for as we try to understand the fundamental position from which this passage is composed. The first is an inquiry into the meaning of the terms "knowledge" and "discernment." These may be taken to have an intellectual connotation, and to lend some support to the contention that the thought of Paul has a more or less "gnostic" tinge. But we have only to read on to see that Paul is here using these terms in his characteristic fashion. They are to approve the things that are excellent, and to put them into practice in their living. Their connotation is moral, not intellectual.

The other comment which seems to be called for is that Paul is, as is also characteristic of him, thinking of their past and of their present attainment. They have coöperated with him in the furtherance of the gospel; they have shared with him in the grace of God; he is concerned that they be filled with the fruits of righteousness. His emphasis in understanding the Christian life is always upon the real attainment of a present righteousness.

This will explain why 6, 7a, 10c have been challenged. For by them Paul's characteristic conception of the present attainment of moral victory is obscured by the conception, equally characteristic of a later theology, that the only real work of grace is to be awaited in the future. Here and now there can be only a beginning, a foreshadowing, an "earnest" of that which is to come. All that grace can do is to give us a hope that something may be done for us "in the day of (Jesus) Christ." This futurism is definitely sub-Pauline. The alien character of this intruded material is further evident from the looseness of the syntactical structure, and the extreme awkwardness with which our attention is suddenly switched to the future, only to be as abruptly switched back to the contemplation of the present. Any presumption of the dominance of apocalyptic conceptions in the thinking of Paul is, of course, ruled out by the recognition of the spuriousness of these additions.

In the remainder of the chapter we find genuine epistolary material growing out of the immediate situation. Paul is in prison, but he rejoices to tell them that even his misfortune has resulted in the furtherance of the gospel. His imprisonment and its cause have become known throughout the pretorian guard, and in much wider circles. One result is that the brethren have been encouraged, perhaps by the example of his courage, to proclaim the gospel without fear. (i: 12-14.) In verse 19 he says that he knows that something (in the immediate context it seems the insincere and factional preaching of the gospel), shall through their prayers, and the supply of the Spirit turn out for his salvation; but in any event he shall not be put to shame, for Christ shall always be magnified in his body, whether he live or die. (i: 19, 20.)

He is hard put to it to choose whether he would live or die. Should he die he thinks of going to be with Christ in an experience of communion even more intimate than had been possible to him in this Christ-filled life. (i: 21-23.) There is here no mention of an intervening period, of a future judgment, or of a resurrection day. But this conception of the immediate attainment through death of a more intimate fellowship with Christ is quite congruous with Paul's fundamental ideas as to the flesh and the Spirit. He who is dominated by the flesh is the servant of sin. It is the flesh that thwarts our desires, and makes it impossible for us to attain to fulness of life. Morally the handicap of the flesh may be done away by sharing in the death-resurrection of the dying-rising Lord. We may crucify the flesh, and rise to newness of righteous living. By this means we come as close to pure spirituality as is possible to those still in the flesh. From this basic standpoint it is entirely intelligible that Paul should think that the actual putting off of the flesh would enable one to enter more fully into an experience of spiritual living. To live now is to have Christ live within one's self; but if we die, we, too, will live entirely within that spiritual realm wherein he dwells.

But while thus it would be better for him to go to be with Christ in all the fulness of actual spiritual presence, it were better for them that he remain in the flesh, so that he might be with them, and minister to their upbuilding. Hence he is confident that their prayers for him, added to his own prayers for his greatest usefulness, will be granted, and that he will remain in the flesh and see them again. (i: 23-26.)

But in any case let their manner of life be worthy of the gospel so that he may know they are standing fast in Christian unity, and that they are boldly meeting any adversaries that may arise, knowing that they are sharing both in the sufferings of Christ, and in the same conflict in which Paul is taking a part. (i: 27-29.)

It will have been noted that this exposition has disregarded not only verse 28b, but also verses 15-18a. 28b seems to be a not particularly intelligent gloss. Its excision restores the very evident continuity between 28a and 29. It is a drastic modification of Paul's argument that they are not to be frightened by adversaries, because it is their privilege to share in the suffering of Christ and the struggle of the apostle himself. It intrudes the quite different idea that the very antagonism which the adversaries manifest toward them will result in the destruction of the enemies, and in their own salvation. This is a far cry from joyful participation with Paul and Christ in struggle and suffering.

Verses 15-18a raise a severe problem. To understand how some could preach Christ out of enmity toward Paul, thinking to raise up affliction for him in his bonds, we must speculate upon what the situation could be in which this would obtain. The simplest explanation would be that Paul had been arrested because the authorities considered the preaching of the gospel a disturbance, and these opponents of his were anxious that the situation should not quiet down; they took up Paul's ministry so that the agitation would continue, and the authorities would be the more exasperated. If one could think such a situation possible, and could feel that any such preaching would be accompanied by so great an increase of the church as to provoke the authorities, he might see how this preaching of Christ would raise up affliction for Paul in his bonds. But in that case it would not appear how any could see that he was set for the defense of the gospel, and preach Christ out of love. It is most difficult to envisage any situation which would impel friend and foe alike to preach because of their attitude toward Paul.

It may seem simpler to some to explain the situation in terms of the content of the gospel preached by friend and foe, in spite of the fact that our record speaks exclusively of the motives which prompted them to preach. In this case those who preached the same gospel which Paul proclaimed would do it out of love for him, while those who were preaching a different gospel would be increasing his affliction. This explanation is ruled out alike by the fact that the context deals with motives, and not content, and by Paul's vehement assertion that there could be but one gospel. (Gal. i: 6-9.)

Since we have to exercise our speculative fancy in the understanding of the passage, it seems much better to assume that the material is spurious, and from a later time, than it is to assume that it is genuine and speculate upon its meaning. It is easy to see how in the later church when the ministry had become a trade, and when labels had been attached to different groups, one could realize that not all Christian preaching was properly motivated. Theology had become complex and generalized, and someone in that more Catholic period could rejoice in the fact that "Christ was proclaimed." Since his own theology was generalized he did not worry unduly over the content of the message. Any proclamation of Christ might win his approval. In that case the allusions to the defense of the gospel, and to the increase of Paul's affliction would be attempts to give verisimilitude to the passage.

To regard the passage as secondary materially reduces the difficulties in connection with it. It seems impossible to reconcile rejoicing in the insincere and factional preaching of the gospel with Paul's well known attitude that the church should be one, and that the gospel was also one, no matter by whom proclaimed. Then, too, the elimination of the verses in question enables us to understand Paul's expression, "This shall turn out for my salvation." It is easy to see how he hoped that the spread of the knowledge of his imprisonment through all the pretorian guard and beyond, and the resulting boldness of those who, scorning their personal safety, gave themselves without fear to the proclamation of the gospel, might, together with the prayers of the Philippians, result in his safety. But how the insincere and factional preaching of Christ could thus result, is exceedingly difficult to imagine.

The second chapter begins (verses 1-5), with an exhortation based on all that was most real in Christian experience, and most tender in human relations, that the Philippians live in a unity which grew out of a real humility, like the mind that was in Christ, which manifested itself in a lowliness of disposition which made self of no importance, but in utter self-forgetfulness esteemed one's fellow more highly than oneself, and found its only concern in the things that made for the welfare of the brethren. It was this utter unconcern for self which was the mind that was in Christ.

This reference to the mind that was in Christ is made the basis for a remarkable speculation upon the supposed incarnation of Christ, and its glorious outcome, (verses 6-11). It is only because we habitually read this passage for what it is, a generalized theological treatise upon a phase of Christology, completely dissociated from the situation in the Philippian church which is supposed to have called it forth, and to which it is supposed to apply, that we ever fail to see its utter inapplicability.

A comparison of these verses with those which immediately precede them and those which follow will at once show how completely different they are. Paul has just been exhorting them, in a passage made up of simple words, and without elaborate syntactical structure, to live in a humble simplicity of mind which shall issue in a loving accord. In the next paragraph (verses 12-18), there is the same concern with the affairs of life, the same simplicity of diction and lack of elaborate syntactical structure. But in these verses we are translated immediately into a discourse built up in balanced phrases, impregnated with a technical philosophical vocabulary.

An analysis of the contents of the passage will show how amazing it is in its context. The mind which was in Christ Jesus proves to be a disposition to go through a show of that which had no reality, with the result that after a period of humiliation, which was at best only simulated and approximated, he was restored to the overwhelming glory which had been his all the time. The passage is written by one who could not accept the reality of a genuine incarnation. Christ merely took the "form" of a servant; he was made in the "likeness" of men; he was found "in fashion" as a man. This writer just could not bring himself to the point that Christ became man. And the whole emphasis of the passage is not humiliation, but exaltation. God has given him the name that is above every name, that at his name every knee should bow, in heaven, on earth, and under the earth.

The non-Pauline character of the passage should appear from an assessment of the meaning given to the death of Christ. It was merely an act of obedience; it was something else to which the lordly being who was approximating incarnation stooped; it was merely a valley lying across the way which had to be crossed en route to the heights of glory.

If we should try to give serious attention to the function of this passage in an exhortation to a faction-riven church, whose divisions evidently grew out of an overweening self-esteem, we can see how stupid it would have been of Paul to have employed it, even though, as is sometimes thought, he merely quoted it from some available source. The effect it would have must be to make each proud self-glorifying Christian think, "I will be like Christ; I will ever be conscious of my true dignity; I will stoop to a temporary subjection of myself to my fellow in the hope that God will see the merit of my self-abnegation, and exalt me far over this fellow to whom I temporarily submit myself." It could but accentuate the divisions and the rivalries, although it suggested the method of humility as the goal to the realization of the superiority each one thought himself to possess. Such an as-

sumption of humility as a means to self-exaltation is utterly
contemptible.

It is best to interpret the passage for what it is, a meditation upon the humiliation of Christ written by someone at
a later time when the emphasis had been shifted more and
more to his divinity, so that anything which resembled humanity had been reduced to mere seeming and shadow. The
Philippian situation is not even remotely in the mind of its
author.

The remainder of the chapter is made up of materials closely associated with conditions obtaining in the church and in
Paul's relations with it. In 12-18 Paul is urging that they
make their salvation a reality; this is to be accomplished by
obedience, and by their effort to work out God's good pleasure, not in their own strength but by the power of God working within them. Here again we are in touch with Paul's
fundamental conception of a gospel which is the power of
God resulting in the achievement of a real and present righteousness. Here we encounter the "day of Christ" to which
Paul is looking forward; but it is to be noted carefully that
it is merely the day upon which his work shall be assessed
at its true value, by virtue of its revelation whether the
Philippians have shone as lights in their generation by reason
of their righteous obedience. It is not looked forward to as
the time at which the real work of grace will be wrought in
the lives of Christians.

In verses 19-30 we learn that Paul is sending to them Timothy whom alone he could trust to deal sincerely with the
Philippians; he himself hopes to comes shortly. He had already sent Epaphroditus who had come to him as the mes-
senger of the Philippian church to minister to the apostle's
need. He had fallen sick, and they are urged to receive him,

and to honor him as one deserved who had risked his life for the gospel.

Many difficulties have been recognized in connection with the third chapter. It seems to introduce very abruptly a ferocious attack upon opponents such as we encountered in other Pauline churches, notably in Galatia, who are often called "Judaizers." It is often thought that materials from another letter are encountered here. It is true that the expression "finally" is too often used. It seems to be merely transitional without any sense of finality. But if our present epistles be more or less miscellanies of surviving materials, it may be that "finally" was final in its original connection. It would seem that we have here evidence of at least disarrangement of materials. If Paul were so greatly concerned over the situation caused by these Judaizers that he must denounce them so harshly as he apparently does, it is unlikely that it would be introduced so casually into a context in which he has been dealing with the mission of Epaphroditus and Timothy to the church to inquire as to how they were getting along. In the circumstances contemplated in the beginning of the third chapter he presumably knows how they are getting along; they are in an evil state. The only trouble we find in this chapter is in the second verse, and in materials following verse 18. The second verse repels us by its harshness; it may be a gloss by some more vindictive spirit. Or we may accept it as genuine and see an indication that Paul was at times so deeply stirred as to cause him to break out in terms which seem to us unduly harsh.

But whatever may be our judgment upon certain of its details, the chapter as a whole is a priceless statement of the fundamental Pauline gospel. Paul speaks of writing to them the "same" things. These do not seem to be things which he has just been writing. It will appear that the things which are so safe for them, and so congenial to him, are just the things which he has preached and written over and over.

The discussion seems to have reverted to one of the most familiar of Pauline themes. The legitimacy of gentile, or Hellenistic, as contrasted with Jewish, interpretations of the gospel is squarely in the center of interest. It is a question of race, and circumcision, as over against the knowledge of Jesus interpreted in out and out Hellenistic or mystery terms.

The Christians are the true Israel; they are the real circumcision. Whatever advantages race might give, or the institutions of a race might bestow, Paul had in abundance. Whatever confidence anyone might have in the flesh, he had yet more. He was of the stock of Israel, of the tribe of Benjamin, a Hebrew of the Hebrews. He had been circumcised the eighth day and had exemplified the utmost zeal for the law. His sober pronouncement that he was found blameless in regard to the righteousness as found in the law must go far toward causing us to doubt whether the seventh chapter of Romans is autobiographical. Whatever advantages Israel had were his. (iii: 1-6.)

But there had come to him the knowledge of a more excellent way, an experience of deeper spiritual power. These things which the Jews prized so greatly and which he had himself evidently set great store upon, he came to regard as mere refuse, unhesitatingly to be discarded in favor of what he had learned to be the true way of life. (iii: 7, 8.)

This righteousness which was of self, of the flesh, in conformity with commands of the law, was given up for a more real and greater righteousness which came through faith in Christ. This faith in Christ enabled him to know his Lord

{ 255 }

in spiritual experience. And this knowledge is expounded
in unambiguous "mystery" terms of identification with Christ
in his suffering, his death, and his rising again. (iii: 9-11.)

It should be impossible to miss the fact that we are here
exploring the deep things of the human spirit. There is no
connection whatever with the ideas of physical death and
immortality. Paul is expounding a righteousness which is
of God and comes through faith in Christ. It is in the power
of a mystic experience that we come to know Christ as we
participate in his sufferings, and achieve in ourselves that
which corresponds to his death upon the cross. But this is
only for the purpose of knowing him in the power of his
resurrection, which alone, in the thought of Paul can take us
out of the sphere of the flesh into the sphere of the spirit
where we can be dominated by the Spirit of God and bring
forth the fruits of that righteousness which is of God through
faith in Jesus Christ. The only sufficient commentary upon
this passage, if the details of its context do not make its
meaning sufficiently clear, is to be found in the opening verses
of the sixth chapter of Romans, where we learn that we are
to be conformed to the likeness of his death, which is defined
as the crucifixion of the flesh, and the putting off the old
man of unrighteousness, and also to the likeness of his resurrection, which means that we are to be raised to newness
and righteousness of life.

Paul thinks of himself as exerting every energy of his
being to reach a goal clearly set before him, to lay hold of
the prize of a high calling which he has received. That goal,
that calling, is simply to attain to this mystic knowledge of
Christ through identification with him in his dying-rising
again. To interpret it in terms of physical, rather than spiritual death, and of immortality, is sheer stupidity. "I count

not myself yet to have obtained"; this is silly if immortality is in question. Anyone could see that Paul was not yet dead, much less risen from the dead.

All who are fully initiated are to strive to make their own this experience for which Paul strove with all the desperation of his being. It is often objected that this mystic ideal of the Christian life, this dying to sin in the crucifixion of the flesh, and the achievement of righteousness through rising to newness of life, is impracticable. It is good in theory, but impossible in practice. The answer is clear and inescapable. However doubtful we may be of our ability of reaching it, the goal lies before us. It will never be reached by the runner who is so sure he cannot reach it that he gives up the race. But toward it we are to stretch every nerve in the confidence that with every step we take we are coming nearer and nearer to the realization of our efforts. It is the glorious reality of Christian experience that he who through faith in Christ makes the conscious effort to identify himself with his Lord in something which corresponds to the crucifixion of the flesh, and to the resurrection to new and righteous living, finds the gospel to be the power of God which works in him toward the realization of the goal he has set before him, and which will abound more and more in its approximation in his life of that for which he has been laid hold on by Jesus Christ. And so we are to be thus minded, stretching every nerve toward the realization of our ideal, walking every day in that manner. (iii: 12-16 or 17.)

It is uncertain how far the genuine materials extend. It is quite possible that verse 17 is a continuation of Paul's exhortation. But that has seemed to reach its adequate climax in verse 16. Verses 18 and 19 might be thought to be Pauline; but they lack much of his usual vivacity and vividness of thought and expression. 19 seems especially bunglesome.

But in verses 20 and 21 we are entirely out of the Pauline orbit. This can be seen clearly by comparing its basic positions with the glorious exposition of Paul's mystic gospel in verses 7-11. For Paul the Christian life was an earnest struggle to attain to a present righteousness which should be pleasing unto God. But for this annotator the present had only a provisional value. We are only pilgrims here below; our citizenship is in heaven whence we await the coming of a Savior. His saving work is to consist, through a power which can subdue everything unto himself, in the fashioning anew the body of our humiliation, making it conformable to the body of his glory. What poverty of spiritual thinking to confine all the working of divine power to the transformation of the body! This is as crass a materialization of spiritual experience as to insist upon the reality of the streets paved with gold, upon the long white robes and the starry crowns. It is a much easier and cheaper gospel than Paul's consistent demand that the flesh be crucified with Christ. Otherworldly this passage is; it looks forward to the coming of the Savior from heaven; it prostitutes the benefits of religion by reducing them to the transformation of our physical bodies; it may be thought apocalyptic, although it seems to have lost the urgency of expecting Christ to come at any time in the immediate future. But it has no coherence with the context, nor any characteristic which would lead one to think it to be Pauline.

Although there is no sufficient reason to suppose that in the fourth chapter we are dealing with any spurious materials, it does appear that they are poorly arranged. They seem to be a miscellany that has grown up without any principle of organization.

Verses 10-19 seem to be closely connected with ii: 19-30; they resume the topic of the mission of Epaphroditus with material assistance for the apostle, and his gratitude for this manifestation of the love of the Philippians for him. The twentieth verse has every appearance of an intruded doxology, probably occurring at the close of one section in a lectionary. There seems to be no especial reason for its occurrence here if the original context has been preserved.

In verse 8 the expression "finally" again occurs without any sense of finality. The section itself (vss. 8 and 9), may be genuine. The style and diction may be thought a little strange, especially the repetition of similar adjectives in verse 8 and of similar verbs in verse 9. Only a superficial objection could be urged against the expression "think" upon these things, for the context immediately translates thoughts into actions, "these things do." It would be equally superficial to find in verse 9 a reference to a traditional type of theology, for the things which they received are not things to be believed, but things to be done. If this passage should be thought to be from another hand, which seems most unlikely, it is very close to Paul's fundamental position. The Christian life consists in putting into practice in our daily living everything true, beautiful, and good. How far this is from any conception of waiting for something which we hope will happen to us in the future, and from any thought of a verdict of "not guilty" through any process of imputation!

The first seven verses would seem to be the conclusion of a letter. They do not conclude with the closing formula, "The grace of the Lord Jesus Christ be with your spirit," such as we find in verse 23, but the seventh verse is in itself a fitting word of conclusion, although not the one Paul habitually used.

Two features of genuine Pauline thought and practice appear clearly in these verses. There is the unmistakable witness to the part which women played in the ministry of the Pauline church. "Help these women, for they labored with me in the gospel." There are other indications that women did take part in the work of the Pauline church, but even though it stood alone, this one declaration ought forever to set at rest all contentions that Paul assigned to women an inactive or inferior status in the work of his church, and to demonstrate the spuriousness of all contrary passages.

The other feature of Pauline thought is found in verse 5 in the expression rendered, "The Lord is at hand." The only reason for commenting on this expression is that it may be given an apocalyptic connotation, as though it meant, "The Lord is soon coming." The Greek reads, The Lord is "near." The expression is used of both spatial and temporal nearness, and in absence of any definite indication in the context, neither is to be preferred over the other. There is certainly not the least indication in the context that Paul is expecting the imminent coming of the Lord. They are to stand fast in the Lord; the women are exhorted to agreement; the Philippians are urged to rejoice always, to manifest forbearance, to offer supplications and thanksgivings; the peace of God is to guard them. Everything here speaks of the long pull; not of the imminent conclusion of all things. If we should look away from the immediate context to our knowledge of Paul's basic thinking, it would seem that his continued insistence that we live daily in the presence and power of the indwelling Christ would make it quite natural to understand his meaning here in the simplest possible terms. The Lord is near, we live with him, he lives in us; why worry, and fret, why not live in joy and peace in the presence of the Lord? Any apocalyptic significance that may be given to the expression must be imported into it.

The miscellaneous character of the materials in the Philippian letter may be indicated by the fact that we have in this chapter no indication that the Apostle is still in prison; the implication to be drawn from their sending to him supplies at the hand of Epaphroditus is rather that he is upon his own resources.

Chapter IX

THE SECOND EPISTLE TO THE THESSALONIANS

THE Second Epistle to the Thessalonians is one which must always occasion the most diverse estimates if it must be taken as a whole, but which yields most readily to an approach through the recognition of the complex nature of the materials in our Pauline Corpus, and the attempt to separate by analysis the genuine from the spurious passages. The interpolated sections appear in two large blocks, i: 5-10, and the entire second chapter. Apart from these we have materials which are direct, simple, clear, and which manifest genuine Pauline characteristics.

The letter begins with a simple salutation, i: 1, 2, which attempts nothing beyond its proper function, to salute the recipients of the letter, and to introduce to them its writers, Paul, and his present associates Sylvanus and Timothy.

There follows at once, as is customary with Paul, a paragraph i: 3, 4, 11, 12, in which he combines an expression of thanksgiving for their present attainment with a prayer for their continuation in the Christian life. These four verses constitute a homogeneous unit, and are thoroughly Pauline. He must give thanks for them because of the growth of their faith, and their mutual love, even in their endurance of persecution and affliction. He prays that God may count them worthy of their calling (to this life of growing faith and love in the midst of affliction), and that he may powerfully fulfill every approval of goodness and every work of faith, so that the name of the Lord Jesus may be glorified in them, according to the grace of God and the Lord Jesus Christ.

The student of Paul will find himself thoroughly at home

in this paragraph. He is face to face with the dynamic conception of the Christian life, lived in that power of God which is manifested in his grace. The entire emphasis is placed upon the present attainment of the Christians in faith, in patience, in love, and every type of goodness. The glorification of the name of Jesus is entirely secondary to this attainment in Christian virtue; it results from the observation by others of the goodness and love which characterize the life of the saints.

Any attempt to understand the basic presuppositions of verses 5-10 will show how radically every value in the genuine Pauline portion has been altered. There is no interest whatever in the attainment of Christians of a real and present goodness in the power of the grace of God. The whole emphasis is upon what is going to happen in the future, when the Lord Jesus shall be revealed in all the trappings of apocalyptic fancy. In Paul's thought affliction must be patiently endured in the strength given us by the grace of God. But for this annotator, there is no meaning or value in this experience of endurance through the grace of God. Its end is that we be counted worthy of that kingdom of God which is to come. In accord with the modification in Phil. i: 28b, where attention is turned from the value of the experience of sharing in the suffering of Christ to the idea that God will destroy the adversaries, but save the Christians, the whole interest in this passage is in looking forward to the day when the righteous judgment of God will give rest to his afflicted saints, and mete out to their adversaries the direst of punishment.

The glory of Christ has completely supplanted the development of the Christians in faith, in love, and in goodness. He is the cynosure of all eyes; he is to be glorified in his saints, he is to be marveled at in all of those who believe. Instead of contributing to the glory of Christ by the exhibition of virtues wrought in us by the power of his grace, so that all must look upon us to see his glory, we are to be merely spectators of a glory which is seen by looking at him; spectators, apart from whose admiring and adoring presence it might not be thought worth while to stage the celestial exhibition.

This is truly an apocalyptic passage. It is centered altogether in the future, in the glory of Christ, and in the terror and vindictiveness which he is thought to be about to inflict upon the enemies of his church in that day when he shall come with his angels and flaming fire. Fortunately for our understanding of Paul, and our estimate of him, it completely reverses every value to be found in the genuine verses still surviving in the first chapter.

Although the annotator makes use of the transparent device of supposedly reminding them of something which he has already taught them, the second chapter proves upon examination to be an attempt to convey to them a little apocalypse which is utterly sporadic, not only in Pauline literature, but in the entire New Testament. It passes even the greatest capacity for credulity to believe that if Paul had held to as clearcut and definite a schedule of future events as is set forth in this chapter, and had taught it, whether in Thessalonica, or in his churches at large, there would have survived to us no other echoes of it in his writings, or that he would have found it necessary to reiterate it in such detail in this letter to the Thessalonian church.

Some very interesting indications should be noted at the outset. The idea of the imminent onset of the kingdom seems to be troubling at least some of the Christians. Why the consummation should ever occasion anything but the very intensest of joy to an apocalypticist is very hard to understand. The trouble seems to have been occasioned by ecstatic prophecy, or by word, whether from the apostle or from others, or by a supposedly Pauline epistle, to the effect that the day of the Lord is immediately at hand. The connection between ecstatic prophecy, and an extravagant apocalypticism which needed to be restrained, is interesting, if not, indeed, important. Paul had found it necessary in I Corinthians to devote much argument to the control of an abuse of ecstatic enduements. It is perhaps worthy of remark that he nowhere in Corinthians finds it necessary to restrain an extravagance of apocalyptic teaching. His own proclivity for speaking with tongues, together with the coupling of apocalyptic teaching with ecstatic prophecy, would lead us to expect an acute disturbance in Corinth in connection with the approaching consummation, granted only that Paul was as dominantly and consistently apocalyptic as many suppose him to be. No trace of this, however, occurs in his treatment of the abuses of ecstatic gifts in Corinth. But in II Thessalonians they are shaken in their mind as though by a "spirit." Apocalyptic extravagance may be one of the later developments of ecstatic prophecy.

Another most interesting indication is that at the time when our annotator wrote there might be raised the question of the spurious character of supposedly Pauline epistles. A mistaken apocalyptic teaching is referred to as contained in an "epistle as from us." Such a reference is pointless unless there should be in circulation epistles supposedly from the pen of Paul which could be attacked as spurious. This ought to throw a flood of light upon the existence of such materials as are to be found in the Pastorals, Ephesians, Colossians, and even in the second chapter of II Thessalonians.

The apocalypse which our annotator is conveying to us tells us that there can be no mistake as to the coming of the day of the Lord. There are certain recognizable signs which should make it clear to all just when it is to appear. Unless and until these signs shall have become manifest, no one should for a moment be disturbed as though there was danger that the end of all things were at hand. There must be first an apostasy of the faithful; this will be followed by the appearance of The Man of Sin, who will come when a certain, presumably well known factor, now restraining him shall no longer exist. But he will no more than manifest himself than the Lord Jesus will come, slaying him by the breath of his mouth, and bringing him to nought by the manifestation of his presence. (ii: 1-8.)

Here the apocalypse should find its logical close, but our annotator is theologian as well as apocalypticist. He is lured into a continuation by his desire to explain not only the origin and power of the Man of Sin, but also the sin and damnation of unbelievers. Both are elucidated upon the intellectualistic basis of the hardened orthodoxy of the later church. Both the content and the spirit of the passage are thoroughly congruous with the viewpoint of the Pastoral epistles. The effectiveness of the Man of Sin is the working of Satan with power and signs and lying wonders to deceive them that perish, because they received not the love of the truth. The ultimate explanation of his pernicious success is that God had sent into the hearts of men a spirit of error, so that they might not believe the truth, and hence might come into judgment. (ii: 9-12.)

It is to be granted freely that we encounter the expression

"unrighteousness," and that we shall in verse 13 find the phrase, "in sanctification of the Spirit," but whatever moral significance these terms may be thought to convey is overwhelmed by the fundamental and repeated insistence upon intellectualistic values. Satan deceives through lying wonders, through the deceit of unrighteousness. Salvation is determined, not by moral victory or failure, but by whether men believe the truth or a lie. The parting exhortation is to hold fast the traditions they have been taught, whether by word, or by a Pauline epistle. The combination of a rigorous predestinarianism with this conception of the intellectualistic foundation of the Christian life, (it is God who sent the spirit of error into the heart of man), is alike unworthy of Christianity and alien to Paul. Should one by the most strenuous of exegetical endeavor attempt to save this passage for Paul, he would then be confronted with the infinitely greater task of having to attempt to save Paul for religion. The affinity of this material with the Pastorals in its intellectualistic interpretation of the Christian life is sufficient to demonstrate that it belongs to the period of the hardened orthodoxy of the later church, and not to Paul.

The benediction found in ii: 16, 17 may indicate that this originally closed the document in which the interpolated apocalypse was found. Its interpretation of grace is diametrically opposed to that customarily found in Paul. Its function is to give us eternal comfort and good hope. The only Pauline note is in the wish that God may establish their hearts in every good word and work.

In the third chapter we revert to materials such as we expect in Pauline letters. They connect naturally with the genuine passage which we recognized in i: 3, 4, 11, 12. Paul asks them to pray that the word of the Lord may be as successful in the field in which he is working as it has been in the lives of the Thessalonians, and that all opposition may be overcome before him. As to them, he is confident that they will continue to obey him, and to experience the love of God, and the patience of Christ. (iii: 1-5.)

The only specific thing which he feels at this point that it is necessary to urge upon them is that they be orderly and industrious. He himself had not been an idle parasite while he was among them; even so must all labor with their own hands so that they be not dependent upon their brethren. Should any refuse to obey this command, the Christians are to have no company with such; still they are to maintain an attitude of brotherly love even toward those whom they feel compelled to discipline. (iii: 6-15.)

It is of the utmost importance to note that there is in this third chapter not the least hint of apocalypticism, either in direct expression, or in the basic presuppositions from which it is written. Indeed, the only apocalyptic coloring in the entire epistle is in the two passages which are so easily recognized as extraneous, i: 5-10, and chapter two. It is especially important to observe that the question of idleness and disorderliness is not in the remotest fashion associated with apocalyptic speculation. Paul appeals exclusively to the example he had set while he was in their midst. It is wholly a matter of the peace of the church, which would of course have no great significance if the Lord were to be on the very verge of coming. The whole chapter implicitly contemplates the long continued life and development of the church.

In our study of I Thess. we pointed out that there was in that epistle no actual association between the problem of idleness and any apocalyptic speculation. The Thessalonians were exhorted to work merely so that they would have no need, and so that they would give no offense to outsiders. The connection with apocalypticism is in I Thessalonians entirely fortuitous; it has arisen through the juxtaposition, in the present arrangement of the materials composing our canonical document, of the paragraph dealing with the problem occasioned by those who had fallen asleep before the coming of the Lord.

In such an epistle as II Thessalonians, it would be unwise to lay too much stress upon iii: 17. After the reference to epistles whose genuineness may be questioned, and especially in connection with the too patent endeavor to commend spurious matter by the device of a supposed reminder that he had already taught them all of this in detail, this may be another attempt to authenticate materials which the arranger knows may be open to serious question.

Chapter X

THE EPISTLE TO THE COLOSSIANS

THE case for the modification of the Pauline epistles might, if necessary, be rested entirely upon the study of the Epistle to the Colossians. This is by no means necessary, for the examination of any one of the longer letters coming to us under the name of Paul will yield many evidences of disarrangement and modification of its materials. But nowhere is the evidence of an underlying Pauline original more convincing than in Colossians; nowhere are the indications of the drastic modification of this underlying original more definite.

The study of Colossians has long ago led scholars to two very obvious conclusions. These are the great similarity between Colossians and Ephesians on the one hand, and the very great difference between them, and any other letter Paul has written. The difference is at once apparent even to casual readers. Paul's style is vivid and trenchant. His sentences are short; his constructions uninvolved. But the style of Colossians, and more markedly of Ephesians is slow, turgid, fulsome. The sentences are long; the periods balanced. The vocabulary of Colossians is quite different from Paul's usual diction. This is often explained by the fact that Paul is here dealing with a new subject, and it is even maintained that many of the strange words are taken from the philosophical speculations of the heretics he is opposing. But there is a difference even in such a word as that for "comfort." Nowhere is the difference between Colossians and the genuine Pauline writings greater than in the field of Christology, where Colossians is much closer to John than to Paul. All of these criteria taken together ought to be more than enough

{ 270 }

to convince literary critics of divergence of authorship; the persistence of the ascription of Colossians to Paul, (Ephesians is happily more and more being recognized as spurious), is a commentary upon the persistence of traditional views in literary as well as in doctrinal questions.

The salutation, i: 1, 2, is a simple Pauline introduction of a letter, associating Timothy with himself in greeting the Colossian church, concluding with the formal, "Grace and peace to you from God our Father." Paul usually includes Jesus Christ. But there is no attempt to introduce doctrinal matter into what should be, and is, the formal opening of a letter.

The usual Pauline pattern is maintained in adding at once a thanksgiving for the continuance of the Colossians in faith and love (vss. 3, 4), and praying that they may be filled with the knowledge of God's will, and strengthened with all of God's power to walk worthily of him, to bear fruit in every good work, and to manifest all patience and long-suffering with joy, (9-11). Here again we may read of Paul's intense interest in the daily walk of his converts, and his conception that they may, and should, manifest a righteousness made possible through the supply of the grace and power of God. There is no gnosticism here, for even though the terms "knowledge," "wisdom," and "understanding" are used, the context gives to them an unalterable moral and spiritual, rather than an intellectual connotation. They convey the meaning of a knowledge of God and his will, which is to lead to a worthy, fruitful, patient life. The only futurism to be detected is that which realizes that one day follows another, and which envisages the living of the Christian life day by day.

This simple, genuine Pauline exhortation is modified by the intrusion of verses 5 and 6 which do not at all look upon life in the terms of present moral conduct, but rather in terms of intellectualism, and futurism. Their present life is of no value in itself, but grows out of the hope laid up for them in the heavens. It was the heavenly hope of which they had heard, not the life of fruitful, patient godliness. And the gospel is "true"; they have known the grace of God, not in power, but in "truth."

It is not certain just how far the genuine materials continue; the most plausible break is to be found in verse 12, where by use of a participial expression, which is as slight a grammatical connection between parts of a sentence as syntax knows, the topic of thanksgiving is seemingly resumed, although Paul has turned from thanksgiving to prayer. Such a resumption is not unthinkable, but the device seems to be used so that by beginning with the phrase, "giving thanks unto the Father," the annotator may introduce a long theological discussion, verses 12-23. This little theological treatise is highly complex, and is marked by many conceptions foreign to Paul. It reflects so faithfully the attitudes of verses 5, and 6, that it is possible that they were introduced to set the stage for this longer discussion.

There is first the futuristic conception of salvation. The worthy, fruitful, patient walk before God is put aside for the idea that we have been made partakers of an inheritance which shall some day be ours. We have been delivered out of the power of darkness, and translated into the kingdom of the Son of his love; but it is not intimated that that kingdom consists in moral values. In fact, the theory of salvation seems to be redemptionist. This is not a gospel of power, issuing in achievement, but of forgiveness. (i: 12-14.)

The discussion of salvation is interrupted to set forth an exalted Christology, in which Christ is related to God, as being his very image, the embodiment of all the fulness of his glory; to creation, as the agent through whom all things were made, and in whom they all consist; to the church as its head. (i: 15-19.)

Resuming the theme of salvation (i: 20-23), our annotator makes it universal; Christ died to reconcile to God all things in earth and heaven. It is the blood of the cross that is effective. The student of Paul must judge whether this gospel of forgiveness, and of reconciliation through the blood of the cross is the same as the gospel that we are identified with Christ in the crucifixion of the flesh, and rise with him to newness of life, or whether it is a different gospel, and hence, in the eyes of Paul, anathema, even though preached by himself, or by an angel from heaven. (See Gal. i: 6-10.)

It would seem that in verses 21 and 22 we are somewhat near Paul's fundamental idea, so different, from the terms in which our annotator has been expounding our salvation, that we are in Christ transformed from those who work evil, to holy and righteous persons. But we must notice that although the effective means seems to be the body of his flesh through death, (the Pauline idea of the death of the flesh may be thought to be in mind), it is still a reconciliation, rather than a transformation which is contemplated; this may be in the future, rather than in the present, for we are to be presented unreprovable before him; our alienation and enmity were in our mind, rather than in our actions. To clinch matters the futurism with which our theological treatise opened is superimposed upon whatever Pauline color may be detected by insistence that our fate will be determined by our continuance in the "hope" of the gospel.

Thus every value in the passage proves upon examination to be un-Pauline, and to rest squarely upon the later theology of the church which was futuristic, intellectualistic, and redemptionist in its basic attitudes. The section has at least a tinge of gnosticism. This is seen in its use of darkness to represent evil, and in its preoccupation with speculative philosophical conceptions, among which are prominent the things in the heavens, especially thrones, dominions, principalities and powers. All of this is alien to Paul. The concluding words of our passage, "whereof I Paul was made a minister," may be intended to function as a device to remind the reader that far as we have fared from the Pauline field, we are, after all, supposed to be dealing with Pauline materials.

Verses 24-29 are at best a reworking of Pauline matter. There is the note of sharing in the sufferings of Christ, but the non-Pauline values are very apparent. A "mystery" cannot be allowed to refer to a spiritual experience of identification with Christ in his dying-rising; it is given the later interpretation of an esoteric truth, long hidden, but now revealed. The indwelling of Christ is not explained as the basis of a holy life, but as a "hope of glory." Paul's teaching is referred to as in all "wisdom," to present every man "perfect" in Christ. These terms may be given a connotation congruous with Paul's basic ideas, but that is unlikely in this context. In addition to the semi-gnostic tinge of the passage, its involved style speaks strongly against its genuineness.

In chapters ii and iii there is the strangest conglomeration of Pauline and non-Pauline elements. The reworking of genuine materials is transparently evident. In the first seven verses of chapter ii, although there is much to resemble i: 24-29, such as a reference to Christ as the mystery of God, and the use of the terms "understanding," "wisdom," and "knowledge," the interest is centered in the genuine Pauline concern for their walk in Christ, their comfort, their unity in love, their order, and their steadfastness. The danger with which they are threatened certainly does not appear to be the adoption of a heretical philosophical point of view.

In ii: 8—iii: 17 we have materials from which an unequivocal statement of Paul's fundamental Hellenistic mystical gospel is recoverable, but in which it has been shamefully mutilated by the imposition upon it of Jewish and redemptionist values. The underlying Pauline material shines brilliantly through the debris under which it has been all too successfully buried. In ii: 11 we read of the putting off of the body of the flesh, in 12 of having been buried with him in baptism, and also of being raised with him, in 13 of those dead in their trespasses being made alive together with him, in 20 "if ye died with Christ," in iii: 1, "if ye were raised with Christ." iii: 5-15 proceed to argue in true Pauline fashion, on the basis of the genuine Pauline idea that the basis of the Christian life is our identification with him in his dying-rising, through the crucifixion of the flesh, and the resurrection to the new life of righteousness, that we must put to death all of our members upon the earth, uncleanness, passion, evil desire, anger, malice, shameful speaking, lying. These are moral, not philsophical values. We must put on the new man, where there can be no differences of race, circumcision, or bondage, but Christ is all and in all. The Colossian gospel is the Galatian gospel.

The mutilation of this glorious statement of the Pauline gospel is apparent in the substitution of the Jewish value of circumcision for the Hellenistic mystical value of identification with Christ in his death. This involves the annotator in difficulties which would be ludicrous if the modification of Paul's thinking were not so tragic. The circumcision of Christ is substituted for the death of Christ; the circumcision of the believer for his crucifixion of the flesh. But it is apparent that death, rather than circumcision, stood in the original, for there is not only the associated value of putting off the body of the flesh, so reasonable from Paul's idea of sharing in the death of Christ through the crucifixion of the flesh, so utterly unrelated to the meaning of circumcision, but the annotator has allowed the sequence of ideas to proceed to the logical consequence of death, that is, burial and resurrection. To see these as the sequence of circumcision is either tragic, or ludicrous. It is very difficult to see how anyone in his senses could have so naïvely allowed the true Pauline consequences of death to stand as the consequences of circumcision. But it is infinitely better to see this as the clumsy work of an annotator, resolved at all costs to substitute more orthodox Jewish values for Paul's Hellenistic gospel, than to see it as the stupidity of Paul himself.

In the original Pauline materials the dying with Christ (which is amazingly allowed to stand in ii: 20, although the annotator has done his best to supplant death with circumcision), is in characteristic Pauline fashion equated with putting off the body of the flesh. But in ii: 20 it is equated with dying to the rudiments of the world. Far from the Pauline idea of putting off unclean, unworthy, and unlovely things is this idea that we are set free from the observance of ordinances and the doctrines of men.

The significance of our resurrection with Christ is likewise perverted. Although the genuine Pauline meaning of putting on the new man, in a life of kindness, meekness, and love still stands in iii: 12 ff., our being made alive with him is in ii: 13b-15 interpreted as the forgiveness of our trespasses, the nailing to the cross of the bond that was contrary to us, and the despoiling of all the dread powers of evil. The nailing of the bond to the cross is germane to the idea of forgiveness, but the further interpretation of the work of Christ as stripping the powers of evil of all their defenses, preparatory to driving a death-stroke home, is something which seems, however fascinating and important it may be to the annotator, to have no relation either to the forgiveness of sins, or to making us alive through Christ.

A further perversion of the Pauline meaning of our resurrection with Christ is found in iii: 1b-3. It is not the putting on the new man of righteousness in daily living; it is the setting of our mind upon the things that are above, where Christ is, and whence he shall in due time be manifested, whereupon we, too, will be glorified. An otherworldly spiritual mindedness, especially if it be given no content, but is allowed to look to the future for its realization, is infinitely easier than sharing in the resurrection of Christ in an experience which makes us kind, meek, lowly, and loving.

Much study has been given to what is called the "Colossian Heresy." The modification of Pauline materials, and the more or less miscellaneous character of our surviving epistles, must raise an insistent question whether we have sufficiently unitary sources to enable us to judge what this heresy was, if any there were. The genuine materials still surviving in Colossians show that Paul's interest here was, as everywhere, much more in the practice of his converts than in their opinions. But if we must compose a picture of this Colossian heresy we must take notice of the large space given to the discussion of Christology, in which Christ's practical equality with God is stressed; the allusion to the "rudiments of the world," which we met also in Galatians; the reference to subjection to ordinances, such as holy days, and dietary regulations; and hints as to worshipping angels.

In iii: 18—iv: 1 we have a list of ethical precepts governing domestic relations, so similar to other lists in Ephesians and I Peter, that many scholars have thought all of them rest upon lists of domestic duties current in the Graeco-Roman world. The occurrence of such materials in other later documents must argue much more strongly for the lateness of this passage in Colossians than for the early date which must be assigned to these "Haustafeln" if Paul were making use of them. This little paragraph is entirely unrelated to anything in its context.

The remainder of the epistle iv: 2-18 is made up, apart from the tidings that Tychicus and Onesimus would tell them how he was getting along, and greetings to the Colossians as a whole from those who surrounded the apostle, (Archippus alone is mentioned by name among the Colossians, and that because he is to be given a charge to be faithful in his ministry), with exhortations which, in characteristic Pauline fashion, are related to the problems arising in the lives of his converts. These exhortations have to do with moral struggle, not with philosophical aberration.

An analysis of our canonical epistle to the Colossians thus makes it most probable that basic to it is a characteristic Pauline writing, in which Paul unequivocally presented his customary Hellenistic mystical gospel of identification with our dying-rising Lord, dealing at length with conduct values in the present life of his converts, and that upon it have been imposed modifications which attempt to wrest it toward Jewish and redemptionist interpretations, and to deal with some philosophical and ritualistic aberrations which seem to have been fairly widespread in the later church.

Chapter XI

THE EPISTLE TO THE EPHESIANS

THE acceptance of the Epistle to the Ephesians as a genuine letter from the hand of Paul will immeasurably complicate the problem of understanding Paul and the Pauline church. Fortunately the number of scholars who recognize its spuriousness is rapidly increasing, while even those inclined to accept it as genuine are feeling themselves more and more upon the defensive.

In it we do not seem to be confronted, as in Colossians, with the reworking of an original Pauline writing. On the contrary, the impression it makes upon us is that we are dealing with the work of one who has endeavored here and there to introduce some Pauline touches into his composition in order to give it a Pauline appearance. It is a pseudo-Pauline fabrication.

The author has made use of the entire apparatus of a genuine Pauline letter. He has begun with a salutation from Paul alone, to the saints in Ephesus, and to the faithful in Christ Jesus, wishing them grace and peace from God the Father and the Lord Jesus Christ. (i: 1, 2.) This man knew his Pauline salutations; the only question is whether his introduction of the phrase "and to the faithful in Christ Jesus," does not imply a wider reference than to the Ephesians alone, and hence whether this salutation does not reflect a knowledge of Pauline salutations after the epistles had begun to be used for the church as a whole, and had accordingly been modified by the addition of such phrases as these to give them wider applicability.

As in the Pauline manner, our author utilizes also the device of a combined thanksgiving for his converts, and prayer for their further development. (i: 15 ff.) He has, however, allowed it to be displaced from its true Pauline position, immediately after the salutation, by a long paragraph, vss. 3-14. This opens with the phrase, "Blessed be the God and Father of our Lord Jesus Christ," which we find also in II Cor. i: 3, and in I Peter i: 3. It would seem that this had become a standardized phrase in established liturgy.

The paragraph seems to be a devotional meditation upon salvation, which partakes of the nature of a theological treatise. In it we find most of the characteristics of the modifications which the rest of the Pauline letters seem to have undergone.

There is first the almost unbelievable complexity of the style. It is discursive, repetitious, bunglesome. Then we note its interest in theological definition. All of its definitions are from the standpoint of later orthodoxy, rather than Pauline. Predestination is made very clear, and repeated again and again. We were chosen before the foundation of the world; we are foreordained unto adoption; things are according to the good pleasure of his will which he purposed unto a dispensation of the fulness of the times, according to the purpose of him who worketh all things after the counsel of his will. One may read the paragraph carefully without receiving any full understanding of its contents; he cannot escape the impression of predestination.

Salvation is defined as redemption. An oversight in Colossians, that of not making it clear enough that we are redeemed through his blood, is corrected, (vs. 7). Redemption is through his blood; it consists in the forgiveness of sins; we are made a heritage in Christ; we are foreordained unto adoption as sons, though it is not stated when this will take place. This salvation is evidently futuristic, for the Holy

Spirit is specifically made a Spirit of promise, an earnest of the inheritance which shall someday be ours. In all of this we are passive recipients of that which God is pleased to bestow upon us through his grace, which here means "undeserved favor."

The slight intellectualistic tinge of the passage should be noticed. The gospel of salvation is the word of truth; his grace is made to abound to us in all wisdom and prudence; he has made known to us the mystery of his will, here his purpose to sum up in Christ both things upon earth, and the cosmic forces, "in the heavens," in which gnostic speculation was so deeply interested.

This intellectualistic, quasi-gnostic idea of religion is clarified and emphasized in i: 17-23, in which it is prayed that God may give us a spirit of wisdom and revelation in the knowledge of Christ, our eyes being enlightened to know the hope to which he has called us, and the glory of his inheritance in the saints. The passage speaks of the greatness of his power toward us who believe, but nothing is made of the value of that power for our life; its working is thought of in terms of what it has done for Christ, his resurrection, his session at the right hand of God, and the subjection of all things under his feet. The gnostic tinge is indicated in the list of things subjected to Christ, rule, authority, power, dominion, and every name that is named in this world and the next. It was perhaps inevitable that a church developing amid the gnosticism of the Graeco-Roman world would have to address itself to these problems inherent in the question of the relationship of Christ to these dread imagined powers. It is important to note the pronounced gnostic coloring of such a document as Ephesians, to whose genuineness so many objections must be raised.

In the second chapter our author makes use of an underlying Pauline figure of death and resurrection. He has, however, grasped neither the simplicity of Pauline style, nor Paul's basic understanding of death and resurrection in the Christian life. Here death has no reference to the death of Christ, nor to the process by which we crucify the flesh. It is used merely to describe the state in which we were as sinners. We were dead through our trespasses and sins. Gnostic coloring appears in the conceit that sin is due to the prince of the powers of the air. The process is not through death to life, but from death to life. We are raised with Christ, but this is not a resurrection to a newness and righteousness of life, but to a sitting with Christ in the heavenly places. The influence of Colossians is evident. The contrast with Pauline teaching further appears when we reflect that with Paul we become new creatures in Christ through the effort of our faith by which we make ourselves one with him in his death and resurrection. But here salvation is passively received; it is the gift of God; our holiness is a manifestation of the workmanship of God, who created us that we might walk in good works. (ii: 1-10.)

In ii: 11—iii: 12 our author has taken up anew the vexed question of the relationship between Jews and gentiles, Judaism and Christianity. He has resolved this by maintaining Jewish values so strenuously that he has in effect made the death of Christ to consist in the taking away the wall of partition between the Jews and the gentiles, not that the Jews might abandon their narrow arrogance in thinking themselves the People of God, but so that the gentiles might obtain a share of their benefits by becoming members of the commonwealth of Israel. How strongly these Jewish values are main-

tained against the breadth of the true Pauline position may
be seen in the remarkable assertion that this is the mystery of
God, so long hidden, but now revealed, not only to the world,
but to the dread powers which are the figments of gnostic
imagination, that the gentiles have become fellow heirs with
the Jews. (iii: 3-6.) This is the dispensation of the gospel
that has been committed to Paul to preach, the gentiles may
become Jews. This is the exact opposite of Paul's own idea
that the Jews would at last abandon their arrogant self conceit, and turn to Christ in that faith that would make them
one with their dying-rising Lord. The student of Paul can
never forget that he has said that the gentiles are the first-
fruits, which shall leaven the lump, the root which shall sanctify the branches. (Rom. xi: 16.) The same force which
modified Romans by immediately in the ensuing verses re-
versing the connotation of root to signify Israel instead of
the gentiles has come to its fullest and most determined expression in Ephesians. The inclusion of the gentiles in the
fellowship of Israel has been made not only the burden of
Paul's ministry, but the purpose for which Christ died!

The third chapter concludes, (vss. 14-21), with a prayer
whose profundity and beauty often blind our eyes to its fundamental gnostic coloration. It seems to the superficial
reader to have the Pauline conceptions of our being strengthened through the power of the Spirit in the inner man, and
having Christ dwell within our hearts. These are true sub-
Pauline touches, in which the Pauline ideas are allowed to
remain, but are shorn of all of their genuine connotation. It
is overlooked, or suppressed, that Christ dwells within our
hearts, for Paul, solely by reason of our mystic identification
with him; and that the power of the Divine Spirit strengthens
us in order that we may bring forth in our lives the fruits of

righteous and holy living. But here we find no trace of mystic identification; and the end of the mighty strengthening of our inner man is that we may have knowledge, even though it passes knowledge, of the love of Christ, and that we be filled with the fulness of God. This interpretation at least veers toward the gnostic ideal of our being merged with God through the means of a knowledge that transcends the capacity of our senses. This is often called mysticism, but is totally different from the mysticism of Paul. The beauty and adequacy of the doxology in verses 20 and 21, for us, is in an interpretation we impose upon it by taking it out of its context, overlooking that its immediate precedent is a quasi-pantheistic incarnation of divinity within us through supersensible knowledge, while just before that the topic under consideration had been that both the ministry of Paul and the death of Christ had been to bring the gentiles back into the Jewish fold!

The fourth chapter comes back more nearly into the Pauline orbit. It begins with the exhortation that those addressed walk worthily of their calling, manifesting the moral qualities of meekness, forbearance, and above all unity in the one Spirit, (vss. 1-3). 4b, 5 and 6 are probably a gloss. There follows the reflection of the Pauline figure of the one body, and the enduement of individual Christians with differing spiritual gifts, all for the edification of the body of Christ.

The association of ideas brings in, in connection with these "gifts," a quotation from Ps. lxviii: 18, in which he who ascended on high gave gifts unto men, (vs. 8). It is doubtful whether the quotation itself be not interpolated; but the interpretation which is added, (vss. 9-10), to incorporate the "descensus ad infernos" is a remarkable modification of early

Christian writing by the influence of one phase of the myth of the mystery religions, in which the god is said to have "descended into hell." A clear illustration is found in the myth of the rape of Proserpine. This phase of the mysteries does not seem to have influenced Paul.

The familiar Pauline strain continues as we read that we are no longer to walk as the gentiles walk, (verse 17), but to put away (22 ff), the old man, and to put on the new. This has been modified by making the lusts that corrupt "deceitful," and by stipulating that we be renewed in the spirit of our mind, and making holiness and righteousness to be "of truth." This is another semi-gnostic modification. In iv: 25 —v: 5 we are in the field of the familiar Pauline interest in the daily walk of his converts in the moral qualities that characterize the true Christian life. v: 15-21 are also near to the Pauline spirit. It is doubtful whether any more genuine materials may be recovered from the epistle. It is, in fact doubtful whether these materials we have been discussing be true Pauline passages. If so, they are merely drifting survivals which have been utilized by our author in his exhortation.

It is apparent that in vi: 18-22 we have the completion of the utilization of the apparatus of a Pauline letter, by attempting to bring our attention back to the supposed condition of the apostle, who is in chains for the gospel, and who is sending Tychicus to inform the Ephesians of the state in which he is. These verses concerning Tychicus, (21, 22), seem to be taken almost verbatim from Colossians.

Not even the benediction is genuinely Pauline. It departs markedly from the usual Pauline formula; it extends the reference of the letter to the whole church, to all those who love the Lord Jesus "with a love incorruptible."

But even these passages which may be recognized as close to the Pauline orbit have been repeatedly and extensively modified. iv: 13-16, which speaks so nobly of our development into a full maturity, "unto the measure of the stature of Christ," approaches the Christian life from the basis of the orthodoxy and the developed ecclesiology of the later church. Paul's figure of the body, finding a unity in the complementary functioning of different capabilities has become rather the figure of the close dependence of each member upon the head, while the danger to development is that we may be deceived by the crafty wiles of those who preach heretical doctrines; genuine Christianity is after all a matter of "truth" or "error."

iv: 17b-19 (it may be questioned whether 20, and 21 be not an editorial device to afford a transition to 22 ff), are absolutely at one, both in spirit and content, with the interpolated materials in Romans i: 18-28. Man's alienation from God is to be understood primarily in intellectual terms; it is due to the vanity of the mind, the darkening of the understanding, the ignorance that is in him. Its predestinarianism is somewhat milder than that in Romans, where "God gave them up to a reprobate mind"; here men "give themselves up"; but it is nonetheless due to the hardening of their hearts. And the result is the same revolting lascivious uncleanness.

In iv: 30 there is an interpolation which has no relation to its context, in which the Holy Spirit is made a seal "unto the day of redemption." This not only gives to the work of the Holy Spirit an interpretation quite alien to Paul, but in the midst of a passage dealing with our present daily walk inserts a futuristic and redemptionistic interpretation of religion.

In v: 6-14 we have a somewhat generalized exhortation, at

least slightly gnostic in its tinge, that we are not to be deceived by empty words, but, shunning the works of darkness, which are given no specific content, are to walk as children of light in those equally undefined things that are well pleasing unto God. The only meaning which the quotation in verse 14 has in its context is that there is light in Christ.

The "Haustafeln" again appear, in much more extended treatment than in Colossians, in v. 22—vi: 9. Their connection with the context is of the slightest. In verse 21 Christians have been exhorted to subject themselves to each other in the fear of Christ. This ought to mean that husbands subject themselves to their wives, as well as that wives subject themselves to their husbands. But there was no idea of reciprocal subjection either in the "Haustafeln," or in the minds of certain anti-feminists in the early church. "The husband is the head of the wife." This cuts directly across Paul's fundamental position, as well as across the plain meaning of the preceding verse.

The beautiful figure of putting on the whole armor of God (vi: 10 to an indeterminate point) is squarely superimposed upon the quasi-gnostic background of wrestling with the superhuman and supersensible specters which find their only reality in the pseudo-philosophical imaginings of gnostic speculation.

One must arise from a study of Ephesians with the realization of its immeasurable distance from genuine Pauline writings in style, in spirit, and in content. It would seem as though one who still made use of a few Pauline phrases, but with entire disapproval of their Pauline connotation, and who perhaps may have utilized some fragments of genuine Pauline materials still surviving in the stream of Christian literature, has written a letter in which most of the Pauline values are distorted or denied. It is addressed to the church with which Paul was most closely associated, but has no word of personal greeting, and but the scantiest of connection with any concrete situation. It has embodied all of the modifications which have been found in the spurious materials in our canonical epistles, with the apparent sole exception of apocalypticism. It rests squarely upon the assertion of Jewish values in religion; it makes salvation to consist in a redemption which is the forgiveness of sins; it stresses orthodoxy, a knowledge of God and of the truth; it deprecates error; its head swims with gnostic speculations; it lays heavy stress upon predestination. In short, if one should undertake to gather up all the forces which have modified the genuine Pauline writings and to give them definite expression, he could improve upon our Ephesians only by including one or two good apocalyptic passages. But our author is too near the Johannine position to make use of apocalyptic. Ephesians is essentially the product of the forces which have modified the genuine materials in the Pauline epistles.

AN ANALYSIS OF THE PAULINE EPISTLES

Passages enclosed in parenthesis are considered of doubtful authenticity, or are thought genuine materials which have been displaced.

PHILEMON. All is thought genuine, with the possible exception of (9b, 25b).

GALATIANS. Genuine: i: 1-3, 6-24; ii: 1-21; iii: 1-9, (10-12, displaced), 14-16a, 17, 18, (21a), 23-29; iv: (6, 7), (11-20, displaced), v: 1-4, 6-26; vi: 1-5, 11-18, (18b "Amen").

Rejected: i: 4, 5; iii: 13, 16b, 19-22; iv: 1-5, 8-10, 21-31; v: 5; vi: 6-10.

ROMANS. Genuine: i: 1, 5-17; ii: 1, 11-15, 17-29; iii: 1-8, 19a, 20-22, 27-31; iv: 1-3, 9-14, 16, 23-25; v: 1, 2a; vi: 1-14; vii: (1-4), 5-24, (25 displaced); viii: 1-10, (11), 12-14, (15, 16), (26, 27), 31-34a, 35-37; ix: 1-5a, (5b), 6-9, 24-26, 30-33; x: 1-3, (4), 5, 6a, b, 7a, 8a, (11-13), 19-21; xi: 1, (2a), 11-16, (33-36); xii: (1, 2), (3-21); xiii: (1-7), (8-10); xiv: (1-8), (10-22); xv: 14-33a, (33b "Amen").

Rejected: i: 2-4, 18-32; ii: 2-10, 16; iii: 9-18, 19b, 23-26; iv: 4-8, 15, 17-22; v: 2b-21; vi: 15-23; viii: 17-25, 28-30, 34b, 38, 39; ix: 10-23, 27-29; x: 6c, 7b, 8b-10, 14-18; xi: 2b-10, 17-32; xiii: 11-14; xiv: 9, 23; xv: 1-13; xvi: 1-27.

FIRST CORINTHIANS. Genuine: i: 1-7a, 9-29, 31; ii: 1-6a, 10-16; iii: 1-9b, (9c), (16, 17 displaced), 18-23; iv: 1-4, 6-13, (14-21 displaced); v: 1, 2, (3, 4), 6, 7a, 9-13; vi: (1-9a), 12, 13, 15-19a, 20b; vii: 1-13, 15, 16; viii: 1-6a, (6b), 7-13; ix: 1-18, 23; x: 23-33; xi: 1, 17-22, 33, 34; xii: 1, 4-12, 14-31; xiii: 1-13; xiv: 1-33a, 37-40; xv: (29-34); xvi: 1-21, 23, 24, (24b "Amen").

Rejected: i: 7b, 8, 30; ii: 6b-9 (some fragments of 6b-9 may be genuine); iii: 10-15; iv: 5; v: 5, 7b, 8; vi: 9b-11, 14, 19b, 20a; vii: 14, 17-40; ix: 19-22, 24-27; x: 1-22; xi: 2-16, 23-32; xii: 2, 3, 13; xiv: 33b-36; xv: 1-28, 35-58; xvi: 22.

SECOND CORINTHIANS. Genuine: i: 1, 2, (3-11), 12-18, 23, 24; ii: 1-13; iii: 1-6; iv: 7-11, (12); v: 11-13, 16, 17; vi: 1, 3-13; vii: 2-9, 11-16; viii: 1-8, (9), 10-24; ix: 1-14, (15); x: 1, 2, 7-18; xi: 1, (2-4), 5-28, (29-33); xii: 1-21; xiii: 1-13, (14).

Rejected: i: 19-22; ii: 14-17; iii: 7-18; iv: 1-6, 13-18; v: 1-10, 14, 15, 18-21; vi: 2, 14-18; vii: 1, 10; x: 3-6.

FIRST THESSALONIANS. Genuine: i: 1-9; ii: 1-13, 17-20; iii: 1-13; iv: 1-8, 9-12; v: (11), 12-28.

Rejected: i: 10; ii: 14-16; iv: 13-18; v: 1-10.

PHILIPPIANS. Genuine: i: 1-5, 7b-10b, 11-14, 18b-28a, 29, 30; ii: 1-5, 12-30; iii: 1, (2), 3-16, (17-19); iv: 1-7, (8, 9), 10-19, (20), 21-23.

Rejected: i: 6, 7a, 10c, 15-18a, 28b; ii: 6-11; iii: 20, 21.

SECOND THESSALONIANS. Genuine: i: 1-4, 11, 12; iii: 1-16, (17), 18.

Rejected: i: 5-10; ii: 1-17.

COLOSSIANS. Genuine: i: 1-4, 7-11; ii: 1-7, 11b, 12a, b, 13a, 13c, 20a; iii: 1a, 5, 7-10a, 11-17; iv: 2-18.

Rejected: i: 5, 6, 12-29; ii: 8—iii: 17 is a reworking of genuine materials, only fragments remaining, which have been indicated in the passages listed above; even these are doubtful. iii: 18—iv: 1.

EPHESIANS. No materials may be recognized with any certainty as genuine.